Women and Leadership
in Canadian Education

Edited by

Cecilia Reynolds

Beth Young

)

Detselig Enterprises Ltd.

Calgary, Alberta

Cecilia Reynolds
Brock University

Beth Young
University of Alberta

Canadian Cataloguing in Publication Data

Main entry under title:

Women and leadership in Canadian education

Includes bibliographical references.
ISBN 1-55059-116-9

1. Women in education – Canada.   2. Educational leadership –
Canada.   I. Reynolds, Cecilia, 1947-   II. Young, Beth, 1948-

LC1767.W65 1995   370'.82   C95-910426-7

© 1995 by Detselig Enterprises Ltd.
210, 1220 Kensington Road N.W.
Calgary, Alberta T2N 3P5

Printed in Canada   SAN 115-0324   ISBN 1-55059-116-9

Preface

I want to say thank you to the editors for initiating the idea of producing this book and to all the contributors for their part in its publication. I anticipate that others will share my appreciation, especially those who are interested in the practice and study of educational administration in Canada.

Each chapter portrays some of the realities experienced by women in Canadian education who accept responsibility for leadership in various kinds of professional spheres. Collectively, the writers ask questions from many points of view to gain greater understanding of what this means to the women themselves, to their families and colleagues, and to their places of work and study. In this volume the researchers report the ways they have wrestled with the problems inherent in undertaking such studies along with the knowledge gained about women and leadership.

Most importantly, these researchers explore the seldom-defined beliefs and rules affecting women and men and the educational institutions in which they study and work. Grappling with the exploration of the pervasive and the invisible is a daunting task. As a result of their efforts, we are given a fresh picture of Canadian education, one rich with tantalizing possibilities.

Naomi Hersom

Contents

Section One: Why All This Fuss About Gender, Educational Administration and Leadership?

Section Two: Experiences of Women Educational Administrators in Provincial Contexts

Section Three: Leadership Issues for Teachers and Others

Acknowledgments

Putting together this collection has been an exciting and challenging endeavor. We are grateful for the assistance and support of many people throughout the project. In particular, we appreciate the enthusiastic cooperation of the writers who contributed chapters to this volume. And we feel honored that Naomi Hersom, one of the our contemporary pioneer women in Canadian educational administration, has graciously agreed to join with us in this collection by writing a Preface to it. Our own work has been greatly enriched by discussions and joint research projects with those students in our graduate programs and courses who share our interest in gender equity issues and feminist scholarship related to educational leadership and administration. We would like to thank those colleagues across the country who have encouraged us to prepare this collection. Thank you, as well, to Tracy Biernacki for her skills in helping to produce the manuscript. We also acknowledge Ted Giles who saw the value of this collection. Finally, we thank Ted, Jennifer and James Reynolds, and Sam Rees for the support that makes our lives more fun and our work more possible.

Detselig Enterprises Ltd. appreciates the financial assistance received for its 1995 publishing program from the Department of Canadian Heritage and the Alberta Foundation for the Arts (a beneficiary of the Lottery Fund of the Government of Alberta).

Contributors

Claudine Baudoux est Directrice du département d'administration et de politique scolaires de la Faculté des sciences de l'éducation de l'Université Laval. Elle est détentrice d'un doctorat en éducation (administration scolaire) de l'Université de Montréal. Ses nombreuses recherches et publications portent principalement sur la problématique de l'égalité des sexes par rapport aux carrières des éducatrices au Québec.

Juanita Epp earned her Ph.D. in Educational Adminstration at the University of Saskatchewan. She is an Associate Professor in the Faculty of Education at Lakehead University, where she combines her interest in teacher participation in administrative processes with race and gender issues in education. Her publications have appeared in various national and international journals.

Hope-Arlene Fennell serves as Associate Professor in the Faculty of Education at Lakehead University, where she pursues a program of research about women as educational leaders. She completed her Ph.D. in Educational Administration at the University of Saskatchewan and is the author of articles that have appeared in several Canadian and international journals.

Barbara Gill has a Ph.D. in Educational Administration from the University of Saskatchewan. She has taught in several different school systems and universities throughout her career. At present she is a faculty member and Graduate Director for Educational Administration at the University of New Brunswick in Fredericton.

Thomas D. Gougeon is currently an Associate Professor in the Department of Educational Policy and Administrative Studies at the University of Calgary. He has a Ph.D. from Washington State University. Reports of his research on cross-gender and cross-cultural communication in schools have appeared in numerous academic and professional journals.

Vivian J. Hajnal completed her Ph.D. at the University of Saskatchewan, where she now serves as an Assistant Professor. Her current research projects include an investigation of the institutionalization of change efforts and an examination of education finance in the province of Saskatchewan. She has written and published on a variety of topics.

Carol E. Harris is an Associate Professor with the Department of Communication and Social Foundations at the University of Victoria, where she specializes in leadership studies and organizational theory. She has an Ed.D. from the University of Toronto. She combines her interests in the fields of music and administration, teaching and writing in both areas.

Barbara Hoffman is working on her Ph.D. in Educational Policy and Administrative Studies at the University of Calgary. She is doing an ethnomethodological study of women's leadership in adult education settings. She has an M.Ed. from the University of Alberta and is a teacher of second languages at both the secondary and post-secondary levels.

Linda LaRocque is an Associate Professor in the Faculty of Education at Simon Fraser University, where she did her doctoral work. Linda's research focus is the development, through collaboration, of shared working knowledge which supports the improvement of teaching and learning, and she has published on this topic in various journals and books.

Hanne B. Mawhinney is a faculty member and program director in the Faculty of Education, University of Ottawa. She completed her Ph.D. at the University of Ottawa. Her research related to the politics of educational policy-making and inter-agency collaboration initiatives has been published in various international periodicals.

Fay Jean Myers has recently completed a Masters of Education (Educational Administration) at the University of Saskatchewan. She has taught in high schools and more recently in a college, where she has also done administrative work. At present, she runs her own tourism promotion business in northeastern Saskatchewan.

Ruth Rees is Associate Dean in the Faculty of Education at Queen's University and the Coordinator of the Eastern Ontario Principal's Preparatory Courses, where she has pursued her long-term interest in issues of gender and equity related to the administration of both schools and universities. She has a doctorate in Education from the University of Toronto.

Cecilia Reynolds is an Associate Professor in the Faculty of Education at Brock University and a former Director of Brock's Women's Studies Program. Since receiving her doctorate in Education from the University of Toronto, she has continued to conduct research and publish work on gender equity concerns in education, including cross-generational and cross-cultural perspectives.

Roberta Russell is the Head of Canadian Studies in the Department of Canadian Heritage with the federal government, where she has worked in a variety of positions. She has a doctorate in Education from the University of Ottawa. Her doctoral research examined the relationship between gender, organizational socialization, and power in organizations.

Alison Taylor is completing a doctorate in Sociology of Education at the Ontario Institute for Studies in Education (University of Toronto). She also holds degrees in education and business. She has contributed articles discussing employment equity policy in education to various national and international journals.

Elizabeth Tucker has a doctorate in Education from the University of Toronto. She has taught administrative theory and concepts to graduate students and is currently conducting research into alternative schools and their leadership and administrative practices and also delivering seminars to educators and business people.

Kathie Webb is completing her doctorate in Educational Policy Studies at the University of Alberta. Her doctoral study focuses on teacher knowledge and the implications for teacher development, and she has several publications forthcoming on her research. Before arriving in Canada, she taught secondary school for 17 years in New South Wales, Australia.

Beth Young is an Associate Professor in the Department of Educational Policy Studies at the University of Alberta, where she completed her Ph.D. in Educational Administration. Her research and publications relate primarily to gender issues in Canadian educational administration, focusing on women's careers and on a feminist critique of our existing knowledge base.

Introduction

This book brings together, for the first time, the work of men and women across Canada who place gender at the centre of their analysis while exploring questions about administration and leadership in education. It will be of interest to researchers, practitioners, and students in education, women's studies and other fields. It presents material on the leadership experiences of women in this country in a wide range of educational institutions and offers feminist perspectives in an area where they have been faintly heard until now.

The impetus for compiling a collection of this type came from the experiences of the editors. In the 1980s, each of us completed what could be called "feminist" doctoral dissertations in two different departments of educational administration in two large Canadian universities. We both subsequently began teaching both graduate and undergraduate students and working in school systems in regard to "gender issues in education." We soon realized that, while each of us and a number of our Canadian colleagues continued to write and do research in gender and leadership, most of the published materials available to students and school practitioners were from the United States, Britain or Australia.

To pull together Canadian scholarship on this topic, we issued a call for papers in 1992 and initiated a collaborative review process by which contributors commented on each other's work. The results of that collaboration appear as the three sections of this book: a. why all the fuss about gender, educational administration and leadership?; b. experiences of women educational administrators in provincial contexts; and c. leadership issues for teachers and others.

Feminists have challenged "traditional" views of administration and leadership in school systems. Indeed, they have persistently questioned "men's hold over the way the world is seen, felt, known and understood. This means challenging not only how women see themselves but also how men perceive themselves and their social relationships" (McCrindle & Rowbotham cited in Spender, 1980, p. 9). Historically, in both theory and practice related to educational administration, however, their challenge has been largely ignored.

There are several possible reasons for this. One reason is that, until relatively recently, only a very small percentage of those who worked as educational administrators or who conducted research in this field were women (Blackmore & Kenway, 1993; Shakeshaft, 1989; Sheriff & Campbell, 1981; Young, 1990). Another reason is that here, as in other areas of school life, gender roles and a gendered division of labor was accepted rather than seen as problematic (Reynolds, 1994). Also, although a "critical" perspective on schools emerged in the 1960s, more attention was given to race, class and ethnicity than to gender.

Finally, "the pressures of modernism and scientization have required a science of administration" (Foster, 1985, p. 2). Educational administration, in this country and elsewhere, has aligned itself with management studies and industrial psychology and sociology. As in these fields, research in educational administration has "always contained a tension between the goals of providing a service and critical analysis" (Tipton, 1985, p. 44). For all of these reasons, many theorists and practitioners in this field have suffered from what Ferguson (1984) has called "radical deafness" toward nonapproved questions such as those posed by feminists and others, and they have also been relatively blind to the experiences of women.

In many respects, this book illustrates that we are still "not there yet" (Young, 1990) with regard to equitable policies and practices for women in school administration. We also do not sufficiently understand the complex relationships between gender, educational administration and leadership. However, the data presented in the following chapters and the diverse views of the authors help us to consider where we might be headed.

References

Blackmore, J., & Kenway, J. (Eds.). (1993). *Gender matters in educational administration and policy.* London: The Falmer Press.

Ferguson, K. (1984). *The feminist case against bureaucracy.* Philadelphia: Temple University Press.

Foster, W. (1985). *Critical theory and critical practice: A perspective on educational administration.* Paper presented at AERA, Chicago.

Reynolds, C. (1994). The educational system. In N. Mandell (Ed.), *Feminist issues: Gender, race and sexuality* (pp. 272-293). Toronto: Prentice-Hall.

Sheriff, P., & Campbell, J. (1981). Room for women: A case study in the sociology of organizations. *Sociologie et Societes, XIII*(2), 113-130.

Shakeshaft, C. (1989). *Women in educational administration.* Newbury Park: Sage Publications.

Spender, D. (1980). *Man made language.* London: Routledge and Kegan Paul.

Tipton, B. (1985). Educational organizations as workplaces. *British Journal of Sociology of Education, 6*(1), 35-53.

Young, B. (1990). Not there yet: Women in educational administration. In Y.L Jack Lam (Ed.), *The Canadian public school system: Issues and prospects* (pp. 85-102). Calgary: Detselig.

Section One

Why All the Fuss about Gender and Educational Administration and Leadership?

Introduction

It is frequently stated that our schools mirror the society which they serve. It is also often claimed that if we are to change anything in our society, the best place to start is in our schools. Feminists believe that being male or female should not alter any individual's access to, experiences within or outcomes from education. A feminist critique of our educational system allows us to see inequities based on gender, even when such inequities may also include race, ethnicity or other factors as well as gender. Such critique "makes a fuss" about aspects of the knowledges and practices which continue to exclude or devalue women and girls. It leads to new ways of seeing things and new questions about the world around us and how we might change it.

In the first section we ask why such a fuss has been made about the relationship between gender, educational administration and leadership. The answer lies partly with the larger feminist critique which argues that women should be seen by themselves and by others as capable of making "meaning" in the world. It should be pointed out, however, that there are many types of feminisms and much diversity within the political category "woman." We begin this section then, by considering how feminist understandings of various types have encouraged us to rethink ideas about administration and leadership. We question what the existing literature offers and what frameworks have emerged to guide both theory and practice.

Another answer to the question about why there is a fuss, however, lies with the experiences of women who have actually become administrators in schools. Partly because of the feminist critique just mentioned, more and more women in recent years have become graduate students in educational administration programs in Canada and have taken on administrative roles. Some of these women have not been satisfied by their experiences and have made a fuss in order to change structures and practices which they feel are discriminatory.

Yet another answer to the question about why there is a fuss, is the recent linkage between post-modernism and feminism which suggests new alternatives we all can pursue with regard to "gender justice" within education. Like earlier initiatives, these approaches begin with a call to rethink concepts, for example, the concept of "authority." In important new ways, however, these approaches offer opportunities to each of us to act within our own spheres of influence to change the "discourses," the everyday social patterns which affect us all.

In Chapter One, Cecilia Reynolds explains that feminist literature on administration and leadership can be grouped into four categories: 1. womanless administration and leadership; 2. women administrators as focus; 3. barriers and strategies for women administrators; and 4. reconstructing the discourse of administration and leadership. She lists examples of work in each category. She also examines feminist claims about epistemology, ontology and theories of human nature. These claims challenge basic assumptions upon which traditional practices and research in educational administration have been based. She concludes that sustained work is required in each of the four categories identified in the chapter if we are to continue to refine feminist frameworks which will enrich our understandings and improve our practices.

In Chapter Two, Juanita Epp draws on the data from her study of female students in fifteen different graduate programs in educational administration across Canada to describe the insidious deterrents these women have faced – incidents associated with a male oriented competitive culture in educational administration classes, androcentric bias in texts and materials and unequal access to resources. These women suggest how school life could be improved for women students in educational administration. The author concludes by identifying a number of "defeating assumptions" which may hinder attempts to realize such improvements.

In Chapter Three, Ruth Rees defines systemic discrimination and draws on her own experiences as an Associate Dean in a Faculty of Education in Ontario to provide examples of how such discrimination works. She clarifies how institutional practices, criteria for promotion, hiring and tenure, and the inequitable allocation of resources can and do work against women's best interests. She suggests several ways to counter these forms of systemic discrimination.

In Chapter Four, Barbara Hoffman links postmodernism and feminism to critique the concept of "authority." She delineates how patriarchal and Hobbesian concepts of authority work to disadvantage women and she suggests new directions for feminist work in reconceptualizing authority.

1

Feminist Frameworks
for the Study of Administration and Leadership in Educational Organizations

Cecilia Reynolds

Historically, organizational theory owes much of its early development to the work of Max Weber (1957) and his analysis of bureaucracy. Another seminal figure was Frederick Taylor (1947) and his work on "scientific management," and yet another was Elton Mayo (1933) and his theories about "human relations." In the historical development of this field, not only have women researchers and theorists[1] been relatively few in number, the very concept of gender has remained largely invisible. For example, most people are surprised to discover that the workers in the famous Hawthorne Experiments conducted by Mayo in the 1930s in the First Assembly Test Room were all women and that the workers with whom they were compared in the Bank Wiring Room were all male. Gender was not a factor Mayo used in his analysis.

In his book *Organizational Analysis: A Sociological View* (1970), Charles Perrow states:

> Structure, technology, environment, goals – these are the concepts that have been stressed in this book. Leadership, interpersonal relations, morale and productivity – these concepts have not been stressed. The difference is one of perspective. (p.175)

What Perrow, perhaps unwittingly, enunciates is the dominant perspective that has enjoyed a long history in the field of educational administration. That view has relied heavily upon organizational theory – i.e., the concern for structure, (e.g., bureaucracy), technology (e.g., scientific management) and environment and goals (e.g., human relations). "Other" perspectives, such as the many that have developed over the last two decades, have had to do so in opposition to this dominant view (Young, 1994).

One such perspective has been that of feminism. This chapter considers a number of feminist studies on administration and leadership in organizations such as schools. A model for articulating the stages of development in pursuing gender-balanced curriculum developed by McIntosh at the Wellesley Centre for Research on Women (cited in Rosser, 1992) has been employed here to organize this diverse literature into four categories: 1. womanless administration and leadership; 2. women administrators as focus; 3. barriers and strategies for women administrators; and 4. reconstructing the discourse of leadership and administration.

Unlike McIntosh's model, however, the categories used here are not seen as "progressive" – i.e., continually improving; nor are they seen as "developmental" – i.e., as stages in a process of growth. Rather, the categories are employed to organize this literature and help us think about similarities and differences within it. The overview helps us understand how feminists consider such foundational concepts as epistemology, ontology and theories of human nature in ways which differ from those traditionally employed by theorists and practitioners in educational administration. It also encourages us to think about what has been done in this area to date and what directions for future work might be desirable.

Womanless Administration and Leadership

In 1981, Judith Adkinson published an influential article in the *Review of Educational Research* which documented that much of the literature on women in educational leadership and administration had been directed to pointing out the relative absence of women. Indeed, Elizabeth Byrne's (1978) *Women and Education* in England and Patricia Schmuck's (1975) *Sex Differentiation in Public School Administration* in the United States made that point.

One category of feminist work in this area has been and continues to be focused on making clear that sex/gender is an issue with which we should be concerned. Much of the work in this category looks at statistics on the distribution of men and women in school administration. Schmuck's (1990) *Women Educators. Employees of Schools in Western Countries* is one example and it shows clearly that in many countries this pattern of women's low participation in official administrative roles in education has a long history. Ruth Rees' (1990) report to the Canadian Education Association *Women and Men in Education: A National Survey of Gender Distribution in School Systems* shows the Canadian pattern.

While much work on the dearth of women in official administrative roles has focused on numerical data and has been published by teacher federations or unions, or by local school boards, some of it has looked at the historical contexts which help explain the patterns. Tyack and Hansot's (1982) *Managers of Virtue* is one such example for the United States. Two Canadian examples are the unpublished theses from the University of Toronto by Shirley Stokes (1974) *The Career Patterns of Women Elementary School Principals in Ontario*, and my own work, Reynolds (1983) *Ontario Schoolteachers 1911-1971: A Portrait of Demographic Change*.

Often studies begin by showing the pattern of women's under-representation in administration and then move on to focus on the experiences of women administrators or that which identifies barriers and strategies for women administrators – the next two categories described here.

Women as Focus

Some of the earliest feminist work in the area of gender and organizations looked directly at women's experiences and asked what we could learn about leadership and administration from that data. Rosabeth Moss Kanter's (1977) *Men and Women of the Corporation* is one example. Margaret Hennig and Anne Jardim's (1977) *The Managerial Woman* is another example. These studies were largely based on interviews and sought to understand and explain women's experiences as workers in large organizations.

In educational administration, the collection edited by Margaret Berry (1979) *Women in Educational Administration* is one example of work which focused on women's experiences. In the collection edited by Sari Knopp Biklen and Marilyn Brannigan (1980) *Women and Educational Leadership,* a number of concepts and theories about leadership and careers were questioned in light of women's experiences.

This emphasis on women's experiences was strongly supported by Carol Gilligan's (1982) *In A Different Voice.* Gilligan showed how many theories, such as Kholberg's theory of moral development, had been based solely on the experiences of men and how, when we listened to women and acknowledged their differences in experiences, we needed to reconsider such "androcentric" theories. While Gilligan's early work was not directly addressed to leadership or administration, it continues to have a strong influence on feminist studies in this area and encourages questions about how women's experiences differ from those of men.

In Canada, Nina Colwill's (1982) *The New Partnership: Men and Women in Organizations* considered differences in men's and women's experiences within organizations. My own work on school principals in Toronto, (Reynolds 1988 and 1989) addressed differences in men's and women's experiences in schools. So too, did the work of Beth Young (1992).

There were also a number of feminist works which looked at the historical experiences of women as teachers and administrators and which raised questions about the androcentrism of structures, practices and beliefs commonly accepted within Canadian schools and elsewhere. Among these were Alison Prentice and Marjorie Theobald's (1991) *Women Who Taught* and Ruby Heap and Alison Prentice's (1991) *Gender and Education in Ontario.*

One agenda in much of this feminist work which has focused on women's experiences has been to elicit the personal narratives of women in an effort to break long held silences and redress omissions in historical records. Another, and somewhat different agenda, has been to challenge a hegemonic "dominant white, male view" (The Personal Narratives Group 1989, p. 3) of the world. Both agendas can be found in Geraldine Finn's (1993) *Limited Edition: Voices of Women, Voices of Feminism* which draws on the self-declared experiences of Canadian women from a wide variety of fields and backgrounds.

Critics of work in this category argue that it often places too much emphasis on individual action and does not pay enough attention to social structures. It sometimes presupposes that people make "rational" choices which account for their destiny. This can lead to a "blaming" of women for not choosing to become administrators and a belief that their difference as women means that they are "deficient" and probably would not make very good leaders. Much work in the next category – barriers and strategies for women administrators – grew out of such a critique.

Barriers and Strategies for Women Administrators

Within this category, work on women in organizations focuses on their differences from men. The emphasis is on internal and external barriers which hinder them from achieving the same levels of "success" within organizations as enjoyed by men. Often, research identifies barriers and then a list of strategies for overcoming them is constructed. Women are encouraged to strive for administrative roles and not to blame themselves for difficulties they might encounter in the process.

In *Outsiders on the Inside: Women and Organizations*, edited by Barbara Forisha and Barbara Goldman (1981), the message was clearly that women in the United States could expect hostile treatment as they tried to make strides within organizational hierarchies. The argument, however, was that for the good of the organization, women's more nurturing abilities should be brought to bear. In their influential work, *Breaking the Glass Ceiling: Can Women Reach the Top of America's Largest Corporations?*, Ann Morrison, R. White and E. Van Velsor (1987) claimed that structural barriers impeded women's progress through the ranks in most organizations and, while they might reach lower levels, they were highly unlikely to move into top roles such as becoming presidents or chief executive officers.

Some studies explained that one of the main reasons for this lack of "success" for women was their role in families. Jennie Farley's (1983) *The Woman and Management: Career and Family Issues* is one example and Terri Apter's (1985) *Why Women Don't Have Wives: Professional Women and Career Success* is another example.

Other works, however, focused on discriminatory structures and practices which operated within most organizations to keep most women "in their place." In this direction, Anne Spencer and David Podmore (1987) edited *In a Man's*

World. Essays on Women in Male-dominated Professions about women's experiences in Britain. In the United States, Kathy Ferguson (1984) wrote *The Feminist Case Against Bureaucracy* which outlined how the bureaucracy itself kept most women and many men from reaching top levels of power. In Canada, Hilary Lips (1981) in *Women, Men and the Psychology of Power* described how women were disadvantaged by the current power structures within most organizations.

Work in education looked at women's career patterns and barriers to equality. Two American examples were Flora Ida Ortiz's (1982) edited volume *Career Patterns in Education: Women, Men and Minorities in Public School Administration* and Elizabeth Fennema and Jane Ayers's (1984) edited work *Women and Education: Equity or Equality?* In Canada, two edited volumes served somewhat the same agenda – Jane Gaskell and Arlene McLaren's (1988) *Women and Education* and Freida Forman, Mary O'Brien, Jane Haddad, Dianne Hallman and Philanda Masters' (1990) *Feminism and Education. A Canadian Perspective.* Also, a publication from the Federation of Women Teachers' Federations in Ontario (1991) *"Go for it!" Barriers to Women's Promotion in Education* is a good example of work in this category.

Perhaps the most widely known work in the category, however is Charol Shakeshaft's (1989) *Women in Educational Administration.* In its three sections and based on much of the literature as well as Shakeshaft's own research in the United States, this volume looks at why there are so few women managers in schools, how we might get more women in those roles and what a "female culture" of administration might be like. Unlike some of the other studies in this area, Shakeshaft began to question whether women should "fit in" the "man's world" of administration or whether that very world should be transformed.

Only relatively recently, however, have feminists struggled with questions about perpetuating dualisms based on an emphasis on difference. In *Making a Difference. Psychology and the Construction of Gender* edited by Rachel Hare-Mustin and Jeanne Marecek (1990) in the United States, we see that the hegemony of psychology as a discipline has served to foster a paradigm in which the entire discourse around gender in organizations is grounded in the dualism "men and women." Within such a discourse, only two forms of argument are possible. One is to argue for "no difference" (as have such researchers as Eleanor Maccoby and Carol Nagy Jacklin (1975) in *The Psychology of Sex Differences*) and run the risk of beta bias – the minimization of differences. The other form available is to argue for "difference" (as have such researchers as Carol Gilligan (1982) *In a Different Voice*) and run the risk of alpha bias – exaggerating differences and perhaps even fostering essentialism – a view in which "female difference is naturalized and (re)produced" (Kenway, 1993, p. 88). To move "beyond difference," many feminists have argued that we need to begin the difficult process of reconstructing the very discourse of organizations, including aspects of that discourse which address leadership and administration.

Reconstructing the Discourse of Administration and Leadership

In 1989, Joan Cocks from Britain wrote *The Oppositional Imagination. Feminism, Critique and Political Theory*. In 1991, Patti Lather from the United States published *Getting Smart. Feminist Research and Pedagogy with/in the Postmodern*. In 1993, Diane Richardson and Victoria Robinson from Britain edited *Thinking Feminist. Key Concepts in Women's Studies*. What all three of these books have in common is that they illustrate how some feminist researchers propose to reconstruct discourse as a route to social change.

Such works argue that we must recognize "genderization" processes within organizational cultures and we must understand the politics of feminism. Both of these arguments require that we move beyond a paradigm in which difference of women from men is the focus. Attention is drawn to the fact that the category "woman" is

> a complex, unstable, and shifting *political* category (rather than a category of 'natural' history) which organizes women's subordination in complex and often contradictory ways in conjunction with other equally diverse and shifting orders of dominance and control. (Finn, 1993, p. 326)

We are reminded in these works that struggles for change will not only be those which occur between men and women. Rather, struggles "among women are both inevitable and indispensable to feminism, as are similar struggles within individual women themselves" (Finn, 1993, p. 326).

Two Australians have made major contributions to attempts to understand gender in organizations in a way amenable to feminists wishing to carry out work in this category. Richard Bates (1986) in *Management of Culture and Knowledge* and Bob Connell (1987) in *Gender and Power* work within what has been called a "critical culturalist perspective of administrative and organizational theory" (Blackmore, 1993, p. 28). Here, gender and sexuality are said to be used within a systematic, yet socially constructed, set of power relations. Various kinds of femininity and masculinity may develop but "values, ideologies and structures associated with dominant theories of administration and associated cultural practices favor certain images of masculinity at any one time" (Blackmore, 1993, p.29).

Explorations of the details of how this happens for teachers and students are found in Kathleen Weiler's (1988) *Women Teaching for Change*, an American study of the experiences of several feminist secondary school teachers. Jennifer Gore's (1993) *The Struggle for Pedagogies. Critical and Feminist Discourses as Regimes of Truth* is another contribution to this form of work and is based on her own teaching experiences at the university level in Britain. Bronwyn Davies' (1993) *Shards of Glass. Children Reading and Writing*

Beyond Gendered Identities, describes experiments with children from elementary schools in Australia. Another example of work in this category is the Australian collection edited by Jill Blackmore and Jane Kenway (1993) *Gender Matters in Educational Administration and Policy*. Here, we find a variety of reports on studies aimed at furthering our understanding of how gender works in school discourses and how we might begin to reconstruct those discourses.

Canadian examples of work in this category include Beth Young's discussion of major themes in the academic discourse of educational administration (1994) and my own description of the possibilities and challenges facing Women's Studies in Canadian universities (Reynolds, 1994).

As we have seen in this discussion, feminist writing and research on administration and leadership in educational organizations is diverse. Feminists have used a number of frameworks to guide their analysis. They have drawn upon developments in a wide range of disciplines, such as history, psychology, sociology and others. Important similarities can be noted however in the definitions of epistemology and ontology and theories of human nature which they have employed. For example, one of the main agendas is to posit that women are meaning-makers. To understand this common theme we need to consider some defining concepts.

Epistemology, Ontology and Theories of Human Nature

Webster's (1981) defines epistemology as "theory of the nature and grounds of knowledge with particular reference to its limits and validity" (p. 381). Gibson Burrell and Gareth Morgan (1979) claim that epistemological assumptions form the basis of the social science upon which studies of organizations are based. They describe only two types of epistemologies – positivist and anti-positivist. They contend that positivists seek verification or falsification of "truth" and accept that the growth of knowledge is essentially a cumulative process in which new insights are added to an existing stock of knowledge and false hypotheses are eliminated" (1979, p. 5). Anti-positivists, according to Burrell and Morgan, reject the utility of a search for universal laws or a single "truth" and argue that the social world must be understood subjectively through the views of the individuals under study.

Sandra Harding (1983), however, argues for the recognition of three forms of epistemology – empiricist, functional/relativist and Marxist, each of which she sees as inadequate in dealing with the question of why the sex/gender system in our society has only recently come to the attention of social scientists. Empiricists, she states, accept natural talents and historical facts as givens because they fail to analyze the changing social relations which have made possible a more adequate view of sex/gender systems now than in the past (p. 317). Functional/relativists, on the other hand, give us no way of sorting beliefs about sex and gender on moral grounds and reduce all knowledge claims to the realm of desired outcomes. In her third type of epistemology – Marxist, Harding says that knowledge can be seen as the mental superstructure which acts upon and in turn is acted upon by the material substructure. In such an epistemology, the regularities of social life can be

> understood only from the politically activated perspective of those dominated by the division of labour by class . . . From this perspective male bias in the history of thought and social life exist, but it is simply the ideological conse- quence – an epiphenomenon – of attempts to maintain the division of labour by class . . . there cannot be distinctive "women's experience." (1983, p. 320)

Sandra Harding proceeds to declare that what is needed is a feminist epistemology which acknowledges women's experience and rejects the claims of the universality of male experience. Such an epistemology would be "able to understand sex/gender as an organic social variable which has become visible to us only because of changes in historical social relations" and which is "sensitive to the differences as well as the commonalties of women's labours across class, culture and race divisions" (1983, p. 321).

Whether or not we agree with Burrell and Morgan or Harding's catego- rizations of epistemolgy, their discussions raise important questions about the bases used for knowledge claims in the study of organizations and the methods used to advance such claims. Mary Evans (1982) defines a feminist theorist as someone who attempts a coherent analysis of her situation and that of other women (p. 67). Kathy Ferguson (1984) points out that "feminist theory is not simply about women . . . it is about the world, but seen from the usually ignored and devalued vantage point of women's experience" (p. xi).

Based on these definitions of feminism, it is possible that anyone, male or female, who endeavors to work toward an expanded epistemology which includes women's experience and which questions changes in the sex/gender system over time, could be considered a feminist researcher. Also, as Hester Eisenstein (cited in Fildes, 1983) points out, theorizing is not just something undertaken by academics but is

> always implicit in our activity and goes so deep as to include our very understanding of reality . . . We can either accept the categories given to us . . . or we can begin to develop a critical understanding of our world. (p. 64)

In attempting to develop such an understanding of the world of organiza- tions, Burrell and Morgan (1979) point out that theorists have entered into a debate about "the very essence of phenomenon" (p. 1) – i.e., about ontology. Burrell and Morgan posit that there are two sides in this debate – nominalist and realist.

Nominalists, claim Burrell and Morgan, assume that

> the social world external to individual cognition is made up of nothing more than names, concepts and labels which are used to structure reality . . . The "names" used are regarded as artificial creations whose utility is based upon their convenience as tools for describing, making sense of and negotiating the external world. (p. 4)

Realists, on the other hand, assume that the social world is a real world made up of tangible and real structures which exist whether or not they are labelled or perceived. Crucial structures, often beyond our awareness and for which we have no "names," exist independently of the individual. Individuals are born into a social world which has a hard and concrete existence.

Mary O'Brien (1981) also talks about ontology. She identifies two historical positions upon which ontological assumptions have rested. Plato, in the idealist tradition, assumed that ideas had supremacy and that they preceded experience. Mind and body were dichotomized and it was mind that gave meaning. Since in Plato's time women were deemed to be tied more directly to their bodies by biology than were men, meaning-making through rationality was seen as a male activity in which women could not participate. Marx, in the materialist tradition, saw history as grounded through action in the material world. It was the unity of work and thought which led to change. Marx, however, did not count as work much of women's activities and for this reason he did not see women as being able to contribute to historical change in any major way.

Feminists such as Dale Spender (1980), Deborah Tannen (1990) and Ruth King (1991) have written extensively about the importance of a critique of language which reveals the many ways in which that symbol system has served to silence women's voices in the past and to negate their experiences and limit their thinking. Like the nominalists described by Burrell and Morgan (1979), they recognize the power of names and the act of naming. As O'Brien declares:

> The relation of the individual to cultures and to collectivities has always been a central concern of political theory. It is now a central concern of women, but women find this problem even more complex because the culture which must provide us with the experiences, the questions and the theories and methods which we use as tools for understanding is a male dominant culture. (1981, p. 5)

One feminist agenda then is to posit that women are meaning-makers, whatever position one takes with regard to ontology. One challenge for feminists is how to develop views of that meaning-making which are not limited by the tools provided in traditional social science, a field in which men have traditionally dominated the act of naming. Another challenge is that feminists must do so within existing social structures, structures which historically have been created and maintained largely by men rather than by women. Yet another part of the challenge is that because women have historically been classified as "embodied" beings rather than "rational" beings, feminists need to challenge the traditional supremacy afforded to rationality and the higher value placed on mind rather than body. To see women as meaning-makers, feminists must view women as historical actors in the material world. As Naomi Scheman (1983) suggests, feminist research embraces the belief that

> our emotions, beliefs, motives and so on are what they are because of how we are related to the others in our world – not only those we share a language with,

but those we more intimately share our lives with . . . we can learn something about where we are and where we ought to be going by looking at the practices that form our lives as women, by taking them seriously, listening to what we do and finding the voices with which to speak what we hear. (p. 241)

Such feminist agendas for research and writing with regard to women as meaning-makers relate to the third set of assumptions which Burrell and Morgan (1979) claim are at the base of all research on organizations – theories of human nature. Burrell and Morgan describe two views of human nature which lead to two types of methodologies in research. One view, determinism, posits that human beings respond in predictable ways to their external world. Thus, a nomothetic methodology treats the social world as hard, real and external to the individual and searches for regularities, relationships and underlying themes which can foster claims about "laws" which govern social interactions. The other view, voluntarism, posits that human beings are the creators of their environment and leads to ideographic methodologies which treat the social world as personal and subjective and seeks to improve our understandings of the ways in which individuals create, modify and interpret the world in which they find themselves.

Feminists, however, often pose the possibility that we may be simultaneously able to partially create and be partially created by the social and natural worlds in which we live. Thus, many feminist researchers combine determinism and voluntarism and nomothetic and ideographic methodologies in order to work toward theories of human nature which include both women and men as human. Many feminists also strive to expand our thinking about humanity beyond traditionally genderized concepts and theories (i.e., concepts and theories which dichotomize individuals and explain their experiences based on sex and/or gender). The task of feminism, according to Carole S. Vance and Ann Snitow, is to

describe and analyze how cultural connections are made between female bodies and what have come to be understood as "woman" or "female sexuality." Gender in this view is a product of culture not biology, even though biological and anatomical markers are used to assign individuals to gender groups. Feminism's dual purpose – to defend women as they currently exist and to examine the way men and women have been created – creates a paradox because the object of protection and defence (woman) is also the object of scrutiny and criticism – that which we hope to eliminate. Feminism defends women's right to be. Yet feminists also know that such characteristics are not natural, or essential, or better. (1984, p. 131)

Considering Gibson Burrell and Bareth Morgan's (1979) claims about the different assumptions upon which work on organizations has been conducted, we can clearly see that they have set up opposing categories. Some feminist work on administration and leadership accepts and reflects these categories. Some feminist work, however, openly challenges the dualistic nature of what Burrell and Morgan have put forward as categories of thought and methods.

Summary

To advance the development of feminist frameworks used in the study of administration and leadership in educational organizations it seems that work in *each* of the four categories used in this chapter is required.

In the first category – womanless administration and leadership – it is important that we continue to monitor patterns of participation by women in formal administrative roles, such as in elementary and secondary schools as well as colleges and universities. That monitoring might also expand to other decision-making roles in education, such as work in provincial ministries or on school boards. What we may also want to pursue is information about the differential participation by men and women in less official leadership capacities. We may want to learn more about how "followers" and subordinates see gender as a factor which affects leadership and administrative outcomes and processes. It may also be important to consider "which" women and men are being promoted, that is, what femininities and masculinities are being viewed as appropriate for school leaders.

In the second category – women administrators as focus – we need to expand our knowledge about the experiences of different categories of women in different types of settings over time. We may want to study First Nations women, women of color, lesbian women, or differently-abled women's experiences. We also need to situate personal narratives within historical contexts which help us to understand why people make the meanings they do out of the worlds which they encounter and help to construct. We may also want to systematically collect information about the experiences of different categories of men both as leaders and as followers. We may want to look at the experiences of less-officially acknowledged leaders, both male and female, to consider how gender is a factor in their leadership styles and in the outcomes they achieve.

In the third category – barriers and strategies for women administrators – we need to consider how barriers may change over time and how they may be linked together in larger systems which prohibit substantial change. We need to consider "survival" strategies within specific historical social contexts. We also need to know more about men's changing family responsibilities and work roles. We need to gather data on how employment equity or affirmative action initiatives impact on women and on men in education.

In the fourth category – reconstructing the discourse of educational administration and leadership – much work remains to be done. As yet we know relatively little about "gendered relations" in Canadian schools or how we might proceed to alter them. We also need to know more about ways in which a "hegemonic masculinity" may affect women and men as they attempt to take on formal administrative or informal leadership roles in our schools at various levels. We need to understand relationships between such things as ideologies, everyday practices and official policies. We need to consider why people, both males and females, often "resist" reform efforts regarding gender equity.

Feminists, in the field of educational administration, as in many others, must walk a tightrope between fatalism and romanticism. We need to understand the world as it is, but not lose our capacity to dream about what it might become.

Notes

[1]A notable exception is Mary Park Follett who wrote *Creative Experience* in 1924 (New York: Longmans, Green). She made an important differentiation between authority and power and is credited by some as having introduced the concept of human relations before Mayo and others furthered that branch of research.

References

Adkinson, J. (1981). Women in school administration: A review of the research. *Review of Educational Research, 51*(3), 311-343.

Apter, T. (1985). *Why women don't have wives: Professional women and career success.* New York: John Wiley and Sons.

Bates, R. (1986). *Management of culture and knowledge.* Geelong: Deakin University Press.

Berry, M. (Ed.). (1979). *Women in educational administration.* Washington: The National Association for Women Deans, Administrators and Counselors.

Blackmore, J. (1993). 'In the shadow of men': The historical construction of administration as a 'masculinist' enterprise. In J. Blackmore and J. Kenway (Eds.), *Gender matters in educational administration and policy* (pp. 27-48). London: The Falmer Press.

Blackmore, J., & Kenway, J. (Eds.). (1993). *Gender matters in educational administration and policy.* London: The Falmer Press.

Biklen, S.K., & Brannigan, M. (Eds.). (1980). *Women and educational leadership.* Lexington: Lexington Books.

Burrell, G., & Morgan, G. (1979). In search of a framework: Assumptions about the nature of social science. In G. Burrell and G. Morgan (Eds.), *Sociological paradigms and organizational analysis.* London: Heineman.

Byrne, E. (1978). *Women and education.* London: Tavistock.

Cocks, J. (1989). *The oppositional imagination.* New York: Routledge.

Colwill, N. (1982). *The new partnership: Women and men in organizations.* Palo Alto: Mayfield Publishing Co.

Connell, R.W. (1987). *Gender and Power.* Sydney: Allen and Unwin.

Davies, B. (1993). *Shards of glass. Children reading and writing beyond gendered identities.* New Jersey: Hampton Press Inc.

Evans, M, (1982). In praise of theory: The case of women's studies. *Feminist Review, 10,* 61-74.

Farley, J. (Ed.). (1983). *The woman in management: Career and family issues.* Ithaca, NY: ILR Press.

Federation of Women Teachers' Association of Ontario (1991). *'Go for it!' Barriers to women's promotion in education.* Toronto: FWTAO.

Fennema, E., & Ayer, J. (Eds.). (1984). *Women and education: Equity or equality.* Berkely: McCutcheon Publishing.

Ferguson, K. (1984). *The feminist case against bureaucracy.* Philadelphia: Temple University Press.

Fildes, S. (1983). The inevitability of theory. *Feminist Review, 14,* 62-70.

Finn, G. (Ed.). (1993). *Limited Edition: Voices of women, voices of feminism.* Halifax: Fernwood Publishing.

Forisha, B., & Goldman, B. (1981). *Outsiders on the inside: Women in organizations.* New Jersey: Prentice Hall.

Forman, F, O'Brien, M., Haddad, J., Hallman, D., & Masters, P. (Eds.). (1990). *Feminism and education. A Canadian perspective.* Toronto: OISE Press.

Gaskell, J., & McLaren, A. (Eds.). (1988). *Women and education.* Calgary: Detselig.

Gilligan, C. (1982). *In a different voice.* Cambridge, Mass.: Harvard Press.

Gore, J. (1993). *The struggle for pedagogies. Critical and feminist discourses as regimes of truth.* New York: Routledge.

Hare-Mustin, R., & Marecek, J. (Eds.). (1980). *Making a difference. Psychology and the construction of gender.* New Haven: Yale University Press.

Harding, S. (1983). Why has the sex/gender system become visible only now? In S. Harding and M. Hintikka (Eds.), *Discovering reality.* Dordrecht: D. Reidel Publishing Company

Heap, R., & Prentice, A. (Eds.). (1991). *Gender and education in Ontario.* Toronto: Canadian Scholars Press.

Hennig, M., & Jardim, A. (1977). *The managerial woman.* New York: Anchor Press/Doubleday.

Kanter, R.M. (1977). *Men and women of the corporation.* New York: Basic Books.

Kenway, J. (1993). Non-traditional pathways: Are they the way to the future? In J. Blackmore and J. Kenway (Eds.), *Gender matters in educational administration and policy* (pp. 81-100). London: The Falmer Press.

King, R. (1991). *Talking gender. A guide to non-sexist communication.* Mississauga: Copp Clark.

Lather, P. (1991). *Getting Smart. Feminist research and pedagogy with/in the postmodern.* New York: Routledge.

Lips, H. (1981). *Women, men and the psychology of power.* New Jersey: Prentice Hall.

Maccoby, E., & Jacklin, C. (1975). *The psychology of sex differences.* Stanford: Stanford University Press.

Mayo, E. (1933). *The human problems of an industrial civilization.* New York: The Macmillan Company.

Morrison, A., White, R., Van Velsor, E., & the Center for Creative Leadership (1987). *Breaking the glass ceiling: Can women reach the top of America's largest corporations?* Reading, MA: Addison-Wesley.

O'Brien, M. (1981). *The politics of reproduction.* Boston: Routledge and Kegan Paul.

Ortiz, F. (1982). *Career patterns in education: Women, men and minorities in public school administration.* New York: J. F. Berin Publishing Inc.

Perrow, C. (1970). *Organizational analysis: A sociological view.* Belmont: Wadsworth Publishing Company.

Personal Narratives Group (Ed.). (1989). *Interpreting women's lives.* Bloomington: Indiana University Press.

Prentice, A., & Theobald, M. (Eds.). (1991). *Women who taught.* Toronto: University of Toronto Press.

Rees, R. (1990). *Women and men in education: A national survey of gender distribution in school systems.* Canadian Education Association.

Ontario schoolteachers 1911-1971: A portrait of demographic change. Unpublished thesis.

Reynolds, C. (1983). Ontario schoolteachers 1911-1971: A demographic portrait of change. Unpublished master's thesis, University of Toronto.

Reynolds, C. (1988). Schoolmarms and tokens. *Orbit, 19*(1), 5-7.

Reynolds, C. (1989). Man's world/women's world: Women's roles in schools. *Women's Education des femmes, 7*(3), 29-33.

Reynolds, C. (1994). Doing women's studies: Possibilities and challenges in democratic praxis. In J. Novak (Ed.), *Democratic teacher education* (pp. 47-62). Albany: SUNY Press.

Richardson, D., & Robinson, V. (Eds.). (1993). *Thinking feminist. Key concepts in women's studies.* New York: The Guildford Press.

Rosser, S. (1992). A gender-balanced curriculum. *The Teaching Professor, 6*(5), 1.

Shakeshaft, C. (1989). *Women in educational administration.* Newbury Park: Sage Publications.

Scheman, N. (1983). Individuals and the object of psychology. In S. Harding and M. Hintikka (Eds.), *Discovering Reality.* Dordrecht: D. Reidel Publishing Company.

Schmuck, P. (1975). *Sex differentiation in public school administration.* Virginia: National Council of Administrative Women in Education.

Schmuck, P. (Ed.). (1990). *Women educators. Employees of schools in western countries.* Albany: SUNY Press.

Spencer, A., & Podmore, D. (Eds.). (1987). *In a man's world: Essays on women in male-dominated professions.* London: Tavistock.

Spender, D. (1980). *Man made language.* London: Routledge and Kegan Paul.

Stokes, S. (1974). *The career patterns of women elementary school principals in Ontario.* Unpublished master's thesis, University of Toronto.

Tannen, D. (1990). *You just don't understand. Women and men in conversation.* Toronto: Ballantine Books.

Taylor, F. (1947). *Scientific management.* New York: Harper.

Tyack, D., & Hansot, E. (1982). *Managers of virtue.* New York: Basic Books.

Vance, C., & Barr Snitow, A. (1984). Toward a conversation about sex in feminism: A modest proposal. *Signs, 10,* 126-135.

Weber, M. (1957). *The theory of social and economic organization,* trans. by A. M. Henderson and T. Parsons. New York: The Free Press.

Webster's New Collegiate Dictionary (1981). Springfield, MA: G and C Merriam Co.

Weiler, K. (1988). *Women teaching for change.* South Hadley, MA.: Bergin and Garvey Publishers Inc.

Young, B. (1992). On careers: Themes from the lives of four western Canadian women educators. *Canadian Journal of Education/Revue Canadienne de l'éducation, 17*(2), 148-161.

Young, B. (1994). An other perspective on the knowledge base in Canadian educational administration. *Canadian Journal of Education/Revue Canadienne de l'éducation, 19*(4), 351-367.

2

Insidious Deterrents: When Educational Administration Students are Women

Juanita Ross Epp

It would be unfair to give the impression that women enrolled in educational administration programs in Canadian universities experience nothing but grief. That is simply not the case. Most of the women whose experiences formed the basis of this report painted a very positive picture of the programs they were in or had just completed. However, it would be equally unfair to ignore the reported "insidious deterrents" which made the educational administration programs just a little more difficult for women than it was for men – even through the women outnumbered men (Government of Canada, 1992).

The purpose of this study, conducted as a mail survey of department heads and female students across Canada in 1992 and 1993, was to see how educational institutions had adapted to the influx of female clientele. The responses suggested that the presence of women in educational administration programs had indeed challenged the discipline's male-oriented roots but had failed to significantly alter program content or procedures. However, women students were eager to make recommendations for the future.

Into the 90s

The survey of Canadian institutions granting M.Ed. degrees in Educational Administration was carried out in December of 1993. Fifteen educational administration department heads provided program information. Although none of these institutions had any special incentives in place for attracting women students, one institution (University of British Columbia) provided financial assistance for women and at the University of New Brunswick the provincial government paid tuition for women working toward a Principal's Certificate. Five of the institutions studied offered special courses specifically pertaining to women (Ontario Institute for Studies in Education [OISE], University of British Columbia, University of Alberta, University of Calgary, McGill University). Others allowed students to use women's studies courses as electives (Queens) or integrated women's issues into core courses (OISE). Seven institutions had an internship option available to both genders and two had a mentoring program which was also open to both males and females. All but one institution had an inclusive language policy and all of them had harassment policies. One institution (University of Calgary) had modified residency requirements for people with families. Although changes were small, and some institutions were more responsive than others, attempts were being made to make institutions more inclusive.

Perhaps the most important change was in the number of women professors in Educational Administration departments. In small departments it was as high as 50 percent (in New Brunswick, for example, one of the two professors of Educational Administration was female). In other institutions the percentage ranged between 10 and 30 percent. The total number of reported educational administration professors in Canada was 130. Of these, 30 were female. Institutional responses indicated that, although the numbers were still low, the ratios were much improved and the hiring of more female professors was anticipated. Students, on the other hand, complained that the numbers were not increasing quickly enough and that female professors were not always valued by the institution:

> It was unfortunate that the one professor in my Ed. Admin. program who was superbly organized, stimulating and current remained in status a sessional lecturer (Respondent 86).

Program Aspects Valued by Female Students

Contacting women students was sometimes difficult as some institutions were prevented by ethics policies from furnishing names and addresses and, in order to ensure anonymity, students who did respond did not identify the institution they attended. Thus, although responses were received from all provinces except Prince Edward Island (where there is no graduate program in Educational Administration) and Newfoundland, there is no way of knowing whether or not the sample was representative. I did hear from 151 graduate students in educational administration across Canada and their responses are included in the following report.

Many students reported essentially positive experiences marred by the odd negative incident. These positive experiences were usually related to specific aspects of the programs. For example, women students appreciated "female content" – core courses which included sections on women's issues, women's studies electives or the special "women's courses" sometimes provided within educational administration departments. Some of these were: Women in Education (University of British Columbia), Ethics and Equity (OISE), Gender

Issues in Educational Administration (University of Alberta), Women in Higher Education (McGill), Women, Education and Social Policy, Education and Feminism and Women in Education (University of Calgary).

Students recognized the importance of these courses in their own development:

> The Women's Studies course allowed me to see that I could approach things from a more qualitative angle and that this was "legitimate" within the teaching research community. Up until that point in time my critical thinking skills . . . were all very linear (Respondent 104).

Although one student reported that she had never had a female professor, advisor or committee member, (Respondent 145), others who did appreciated the presence of female role models. They felt their concerns were more likely to be addressed if instructors were women:

> Having a professor who demonstrated genuine care and understanding was a real bonus. This female professor listened to our problems, shared similar incidents and provided encouragement (Respondent 142).

Often the female instructors were linked to qualitative research styles which was valued by female students:

> Having a woman as my advisor, and a woman who was interested in and had studied in qualitative research methods also added a certain dimension to my studies I may not have experienced otherwise (Respondent 102).

> (My experience was) a positive one. I was able to prepare a qualitative research proposal based on women – from a woman's perspective (Respondent 26).

> The best course I took was one on qualitative research. It recognized that women's experience is different. No other courses even paid lip-service to such an acknowledgment (Respondent 98).

Respondents also commented on the importance of reflective practice, adult learning styles and exposure to new ideas, all of which were, of course, not necessarily related to gender:

> Women's issues often got discussed, as the program I am in often used reflective practice (Respondent 94).

> I had no difficulty with the theoretical base being male dominated. I did, however, have difficulty with the lack of attention to adult learning principles either as courses or in practice (Respondent 148).

Positive experiences, then, usually included some of the following: a. an opportunity to take women's studies or women in educational administration courses as options; b. an opportunity to study qualitative research methods; c. an exposure to reflective practice; and/or d. positive experiences with female professors. Women students who had exposure to some of these elements were affirmed in their own practices. They considered their experiences to be worthwhile and extremely positive. However, there were other students who had not been so fortunate.

Insidious Deterrents

Hall and Sandler's (1982) work on "chilly climate" focused awareness on various subtle factors which served to discourage and demoralize women in post-secondary education. Women were overlooked and undermined in many aspects of education, especially in those disciplines which had traditionally been male dominated (Edson, 1988), and Canadian institutions of higher learning have not been immune to it (Dagg & Thompson, 1988). The respondents in the current study reported similar experiences. Positive feelings about the educational process were often tempered by *insidious deterrents*. Insidious deterrents were those day to day comments or incidents which made female students feel uncomfortable or unwelcome. They usually centred around a male oriented competitive culture, gender bias in texts, materials or traditions, and unequal distribution of resources. Although these interact and overlap, they will be treated here separately.

A Male-Oriented Competitive Culture

Although many women felt welcomed and encouraged by professors and by fellow students, there were those who were disturbed by a "competitive culture in educational administration classes" (Respondent 116):

> Instructors allowed the loudest and the first out of the gate to dominate. . . . Some females matched them and others were left to reflect (Respondent 132).

Two students used almost identical phrases to state that both "Chauvinism" and "the old boy's club" were "alive and doing well" (Respondents 15, 141).

One indication of male bias was the use (or non-use) of gender-inclusive language. Although nearly all the departments surveyed had some form of inclusive language policy, its use was not necessarily the norm. Students noted that the pronoun "he" was commonly used to refer to an administrator. Fewer than 10 percent reported consistent use of inclusive language and some claimed never to have heard inclusive language used at all.

Although many women students were pleased (and surprised) to find their professors both supportive and understanding, other professors were obvious in their non-support. The least problematic were those who were simply old fashioned:

> The women's perspective (was) excluded from many discussions, not by intention or overt bias but rather from lack of knowledge and understanding of the issues (Respondent 122).

> The professor often focused on the practicing male administrators' perspective and the traditional hierarchical structures (Respondent 86).

Some women felt ignored by professors who were more attentive to male students (Respondent 105) or directed lectures to the males in the class (Respondent 15):

> Two of the five professors I had made it very clear that women weren't welcome in their classes (Respondent 90).

One woman noted that when the term papers were returned, the professor knew the names of the eleven men in the class but had not bothered to learn the names of the three females: "He didn't know our names, but he had personalized the males in the class" (Respondent 137).

Some women felt they were ridiculed or intimidated (Respondent 59):

> Female students are unable to contribute as their opinions are dismissed, and at times ridiculed (Respondent 72).

> Much of the time I felt humiliated and valueless (Respondent 90).

There was also difficulty when women chose to use feminist methodology or to use women's issues as a part of their research:

> A colleague . . . wrote a paper on women's ways of knowing and received a very low mark. Her professor told her that the research she cited was just a bunch of crackpot theories and not worthy of serious consideration (Respondent 90).

Women students often saw the educational administration program as just another hoop to jump through. Unfortunately, they sometimes found that the expectations of those holding the hoops were inconsistent. Some professors expected women to "behave more like men, to be more boisterous, more competitive" (Respondent 67):

> He put me down for not being more vocal and aggressive. When I asked for assistance he told me you either "had it or didn't" (Respondent 121).

Others were encouraged to remain silent, and to be more ladylike:

> One professor is obviously uncomfortable with women in the program and puts down those who are assertive and do not share his personal viewpoint (Respondent 101).

> I feel that when I question an idea I'm seen as challenging, nagging, nit-picking etc. When men challenge, their status increases and they're seen as engaging in intellectual dialogue (Respondent 116).

The competitive male-oriented culture was not solely the responsibility of the professor. Women students sometimes felt that male students "dominated discussion" (Respondent 101) and that there was too much "male puffer which was artificial and counter-productive" (Respondent 116). They noted that "Men talk(ed) more often, at greater lengths, in large groups with louder voices" (116) and interrupt(ed) women when speaking (Respondent 59):

> I found latent prejudice coming from fellow male students. In such cases, the young men found my views "female" and did not always attend to them (Respondent 35).

Gender rifts were sometimes associated with affirmative action policies which were being implemented in the school systems. Male students felt that affirmative action "limited their opportunities" (Respondent 122):

> Offhand comments about my (or other women) being in the courses because we were going to be hired or promoted were frequent and (professors) commiserating with the male students took place (Respondent 55).

The perception that females had the advantage was not necessarily directed at female classmates but at women in general:

> There was an anti-affirmative action atmosphere, though women in the course were accorded respect in discussion and during their presentations. So the difference was between women as an anonymous group and women as individuals (Respondent 122).

> I think we trust women we know very well and treat them like "exceptions," but we don't trust women in general (Respondent 23).

The women knew that the perception of a female advantage was only that – a perception. They did not find job hunting any easier because of their gender and they resented comments which implied that they had the advantage. Statistical examinations of appointments show that they were right in their perceptions (Rees, 1991; Epp, 1993).

The competitive culture of the educational administration classes became more than an annoyance when women felt that marks and marking systems were being affected by gender. In some instances they felt blatantly discriminated against:

> The presentations of males (were) far poorer than those of females, yet males (got) higher marks (Respondent 7).

> One gave lower marks to young women because, as he stated "They hadn't paid their dues" and so didn't deserve the same mark that an older male administrator would get (Respondent 90).

Although they were angered by these practices, women students seldom complained because the pervasive acceptance of the traditional thinking discouraged it:

> The atmosphere that permeates the entire faculty of education is one of sexism and the power of the "old boys network." The problem goes beyond the Ed. Admin. program to the entire faculty and the entire university (Respondent 90).

> I'm tired and discouraged and frustrated by the inequities I view and experience. There is a need for sweeping changes in order to rectify the present situation (Respondent 1).

These women felt that they could not formally express their concerns since complaints may have jeopardized the goals which had sent them to the institution in the first place:

> This is not what I expected higher education to be about. I have not filed a complaint because I fear reprisal (Respondent 60).

The sense of not belonging and needing to fit a pattern was not the experience of all women, but for some, lack of support from male professors was compounded by the fact that women's experiences were rarely recognized or legitimized, as was evident in the gender bias in texts and materials.

Gender Bias In Texts, Materials And Traditions

In spite of special courses addressing women's issues and efforts to include women's experiences in existing courses, androcentric bias in texts and materials persisted. By the 1980s, nearly one-third of the articles in the *Educational Administration Quarterly* (EAQ) were written by women and gender-exclusive language was rare. However, other, more subtle, areas of bias remained. The theories and instruments of research continued to be based on male experiences and the inclusive language used in reporting sometimes served to mask androcentric bias to make it appear less prevalent (Epp, Sackney & Kustaski, 1994, Shakeshaft & Hanson, 1986).

Although recent texts were likely to include chapters on women and their contributions, this did not necessarily ensure these issues would be dealt with in class:

> In our Theories of Educational Administration course, the two male professors deliberately excluded the text chapter on "Women in Educational Administration." They denied that women have different experiences from men in their careers and adamantly refuted the "white male privilege" concept (Respondent 60).

When women's issues were discussed they were often brought to the class by the women themselves through their comments or presentations:

> In the courses taught by men, the professors make no special effort to study women as educational leaders. They are, however, very receptive when women students introduce theories and reports by women. The seeds are there but we still have a way to go (Respondent 10).

When women's issues did surface, there were both positive and negative reactions. Although many male professors and students made positive comments about how the women's presence "created a better dimension" to the course (Respondent 94), there were ugly experiences as well. In several instances "experiences and perspectives of female style of leadership were not legitimated" (Respondent 56) and sometimes the content about women focused on the negative (Respondent 43). For example:

> Male students groaned or verbally expressed their lack of patience about hearing women's issues expressed. In all cases, when this feeling was given by males in the class, discussion ceased in favor of their feeling. One professor "blamed" the woes of education on women's ways of doing things – saying (women) "had a lot to answer for" (Respondent 55).

The possibility of differences between male and female leadership styles were sometimes discussed but most students felt that their courses had not been modified to reflect the experiences of female students. One respondent mourned: "I sometimes longed for a female perspective on theories" (Respondent 39).

The people who "longed for the female perspective" were those who were most aware of feminist pedagogy and were disappointed when they were treated like "outsiders" (Respondent 56):

> (I) basically felt like a "fish out of water." The female perspective is not considered worthy of consideration (Respondent 72).

> As a woman in educational administration you often feel "schizophrenic." Your feminine "sense of being" is constantly "at war" with the functionalist, objectivist, quantification of what educational administration is. The values of "humanness" are swept under the carpet as "status quo" values of maleness are held high (Respondent 67).

Male orientation in texts and materials did not surprise the women who had already experienced it in the workplace. Some of these women had returned to university in the hopes of using the additional qualifications to overcome barriers to their advancement in the school systems. They felt that the changes should have begun in the schools, to be followed up in the universities:

> If school districts/teachers associations were pushing for these changes, perhaps universities would be more responsive (Respondent 101).

Others found the university more accepting than the school system. It offered a sense of equality which was not duplicated in the world in which they were seeking work:

> I don't find that (this university) holds me back, rather it's the reality of our non-accepting, male dominated society that I am weary of (Respondent 33).

For them, the courses served as a haven in which the realities of the world could be examined and discussed – if not corrected. Although they felt supported and protected this did not always translate into support in the "real world." Some students felt doubly betrayed when the positive reinforcements of the good marks and academic encouragement did not translate into continued support in getting an administrative position:

> No-one told me that I shouldn't be in the M. Ed. program, but again, not a soul encouraged me. I almost had the sense that they thought I would never get an administrative position (Respondent 1).

> Awareness has increased . . . However, reality still seems to support the old boys network and pseudo males in the workplace (Respondent 62).

In order to become administrators women needed the support of both the university and the school system. Earning a place in one did not necessarily mean the automatic support of the other.

Unequal Distribution of Resources

Female students felt that they had fewer financial resources than the men in their classes. There was also an unequal distribution of household chores and childcare duties. Women students were often working full-time, caring for a home and family, and taking educational administration classes at the same time. They also lacked institutional and professional resources. The men were more likely to have secretarial help, were in a better position to pay a typist or research assistant, and had more time to spend on the research itself:

> We tend to perceive our environment from different experiences because we do not have the privileges (personal, social and professional) that are automatically granted to men (Respondent 38).

> The burden of family care still seems to fall on women . . . Conversely, many of the men comment(ed) on how fortunate they were that their wives were "holding down the fort" and driving their children to various activities while they were occupied at class (Respondent 76).

> The males in the classes never faced the same obstacles as I did. They had wives to look after their children, help them with homework etc. to perform all the endless household tasks etc. These responsibilities fell squarely on my shoulders. I did my own typing and research too! (Respondent 1).

Graduate school is yet another undertaking for women who are probably already responsible for more activities than their male counterparts, yet they are expected to perform on par with them.

For most women these insidious deterrents were little more than a nuisance. They could overcome negative treatment by male professors, ignore their classmates' remarks and try not to let their perceptions of injustice affect their experiences. When deterrents were isolated occurrences, they were of little consequence.

> You learn to live with the system. You cannot change it, and it will not accommodate you (Respondent 131).

However, in some cases deterrents were repeated often enough to damage the students' sense of purpose and belonging and to destroy the self-confidence and determination necessary for the women to succeed:

> I took only two courses and then discontinued the program because of the irrelevance of the courses to anything I would be doing. One professor wasted my time with personal anecdotes "ad nauseam" and very little or no content and (the other) allowed for no deviation from the "right way" (Respondent 5).

Women were not quitting administration programs because individual professors made inappropriate comments. They were not falling apart each time a fellow student made an unkind remark, but sometimes they did find themselves in a washroom dissolved in tears for no apparent reason. They sometimes didn't recognize their own dissatisfaction. As one student commented:

As I was responding to this I came to the realization that my experience in this program has been in many ways a very negative one (Respondent 117).

In spite of the insidious deterrents, there was evidence of growth and change and students were eager to recommend ways in which the female experience in educational administration could be made more positive.

What do Women Educational Administration Students Want?

Women students identified what they valued in educational administration programs – the opportunity to take courses of special interest to women, the inclusion of women's issues in regular course work, the exposure to qualitative research and the opportunity to work with women professors. Their suggestions for improvement included changes to courses and in quality of instruction.

Recommendations Concerning Course Content and Program.

a. Incorporate women's issues as a component of existing courses so that all students, male and female, can be exposed to them (Respondents 72, 91, 104, 43, 149). Include more research about and by women. Required readings should include references to positive contributions made by women's ways of administering (Respondents 79, 56, 27, 19, 72, 121, 104, 33, 6, 74, 41, 136, 149):

> The entire educational system needs to be re-conceptualized to incorporate the lives and experiences of women. Education consists of an initiation into an existing body of knowledge. This existing body of knowledge is (currently) defined by males (Respondent 1).

b. Make special courses on women's issues available (Respondents 97, 73, 77, 67, 36, 132, 136). These should include assertiveness training (Respondents 47 and 69).

c. Use alternative methods of teaching. Use role-playing of conflict management (Respondent 73), case studies (26), and in-class sharing sessions (36). Invite female administrators to speak to classes about the special issues faced by women administrators (33, 6, 73, 149, 144). Use special seminars (67, 82), panel discussions (73), and speaker series (73) to augment course content.

d. Provide for networking and mentoring. Encourage a network of contacts in the school systems for beginning administrators and encourage formal and informal mentorships (Respondents 50, 76, 64, 107). Students could "shadow" practicing administrators (79) or have access to an experienced administrator (104). Students could go through the program with a cohort of other students (108) and/or be matched with senior graduate students (43) who could provide information about classes and job opportunities (58).

e. Use innovative scheduling to improve access for people with children (Respondents 72, 88, 60). There could be more flexible deadlines (66, 91, 17), relaxed residency requirements (76), or arrangements made with school systems to allow time off work to attend classes (17, 104). Alternative delivery methods such as teleconferences (97) and off-campus courses would reduce the need to commute (66).

f. Provide daycare (Respondents 134, 36, 56, 87, 12, 35, 59) and financial aid to encourage women to take the full-time programs (134, 86, 67, 64, 17, 2, 12, 76).

Recommendations Concerning Instructors.

a. Employ more female professors (Respondents 84, 111, 59, 14, 74, 79, 67, 72, 149, 150) to provide more role models (68, 103, 1), and "demonstrate equality" (97, 86). Female professors should be "women-affirmative, but not necessarily aggressive" (39) or "career women – mothers and teachers who can appreciate how difficult it is to juggle both a career and a family" (7), not "consultants" (54) or those who have "bought into the traditional way of being and doing" (116).

b. Provide "awareness opportunities" (Respondent 38) for male instructors such as "seminars, similar to cross-cultural training" (133, 72). Professors could also be trained in teaching adult learners (148, 106).

Implications

Women educational administration students responding to this survey showed great ability and initiative. They had already overcome societal expectations and impressed their school boards before they came into the university programs. Once there, the lucky ones were encouraged by female role models, felt included in course content and were exposed to reflective practitioning and qualitative research. However, some encountered hostility from professors and other students, were exposed to a competitive, sometimes unfair grading system and felt marginalized throughout their experience.

There would be little value in trying to identify "good" places for women to take educational administration programs as most institutions had made serious attempts at inclusion. Unfortunately, progressive admission policies, flexible hours and inclusive policies had not prevented insidious deterrents from being handed out by individuals. Policies cannot prevent professors from marginalizing female students, from omitting the "female content" or from placing higher value on traditional androcentric structures. This is not to say that inclusive policies are not important. Difficult as they are to implement and impossible as they are to enforce, they are a necessary foundation for change. However, the existence of such policies could lead to some defeating assumptions.

One defeating assumption, as pointed out by the responses from these students, was that the existence of policies would automatically lead to a warmer climate for female students. Many people, men and women alike, have the impression that these are "1970s issues" (Respondent 53) but the chilly climate has not gone away and it remains as a factor in the recruitment and retention of female educational administration students.

Another defeating assumption is the perception that, as our current professors age and retire, they will be replaced by younger, more sensitive people. Age and gender have little to do with enlightenment, and our future professors are being trained in the educational administration programs of today. Without exposure to issues regarding gender, race and other factors and discussion of the implications, there will be little difference between the professors of today and their replacements of tomorrow. It is essential that these issues be addressed in current educational administration classes.

It would also be defeating to conclude that a balanced gender ratio would adequately address these issues. Female students appreciated the opportunity to do qualitative research, to be treated to adult learning practices and the chance to learn reflective processes. Exposure to these processes affects the way our students think, teach and respond and could eventually have a strong impact on schools and school practices. Issues of inclusivity are not only the concern of a few women having a bad experience in an educational administration program. The way we teach in our educational administration programs will have a profound affect on the way schools are run and the way children learn.

The final defeating assumption is also related to that sense of futuristic importance. Although on the individual level, professors may feel that they are not in a position to intervene in school systems, what is taught and how it is taught can have a profound effect on school personnel decisions. The women students in this survey spoke of an entrenched anti-female attitude which discouraged female teachers from seeking administrative training. Not every educational administration student will become an administrator but most of them will become leaders in educational communities. To neglect to expose them to notions of equality and to deprive them of the opportunity to reflect on those issues is to further discourage those willing to seek change and to put our stamp of approval on the status quo. Universities do exert influence on the school system and have the potential to be catalysts in the change process.

This study illuminated the cold fact that women students were not always treated with the same respect afforded to their male counterparts. The modest recommendations made by these women students were not demands for special treatment for women, rather they were demands for equal treatment. If universities could honor those demands for all people, they would be setting the tone for a just and equitable society in our future.

References

Dagg, A., & Thompson, P. (1988). *MisEducation: Women and Canadian universities.* Toronto: OISE Press.

Edson, S. (1988). *Pushing the limits: The female administrative aspirant.* Albany: State University of New York Press.

Epp, J. (1993). Leadership Qualities Valued in Principal Selection. *Canadian School Executive. 12*(10), 31-36.

Epp, J., Sackney, L., & Kustaski, J. (1994). Re-assessing levels of androcentric bias in the Educational Administration Quarterly. *Educational Administration Quarterly, 30*(4), 451-471.

Government of Canada (1992). *Profile of higher education in Canada.* Ottawa: Department of the Secretary of State, Minister of Supply and Service, Canada.

Hall, R., & Sandler, B. (1982). *The classroom climate: A chilly one for women.* Project on the status and education of women. Washington: Association of American Colleges.

Rees, R. (1991). The Ontario principals' qualifications course: Towards employment equity? *Journal of Educational Administration and Foundations, 6*(1), 37-52.

Shakeshaft, C., & Hanson, M. (1986). Androcentric bias in the Educational Administration Quarterly. *Educational Administration Quarterly, 25*(1), 68-92.

3

Systemic Discrimination in a University

Ruth Rees

Overview

The purpose of this chapter is to reveal, through example, some types of *systemic discrimination* experienced within one Canadian university. My overall aim in writing this is to prevent the university community from becoming complacent that systemic discrimination is no longer an issue. Rather, this chapter underscores the concerns of a woman academic that systemic discrimination *is* in evidence in at least one university in Canada and suggests that the university community should systematically redress those causes of discrimination.

Some Definitions

Judge Abella in 1984 in the Royal Commission Report was the first to define systemic discrimination within a Canadian context. And as her definition is used in Supreme Court case law decisions, that definition acts as a starting point: "systems and practices [which] we customarily and often unwittingly adopt . . . affect a certain group unfairly or adversely" (p. 9). Abella observed two basic antecedents to discrimination:

a. a disparately negative impact that flows from the *structure of systems* designed for a homogeneous constituency; and

b. a disparately negative impact that flows from *practices* based on stereotypical characteristics ascribed to an individual because of the characteristics ascribed to the group of which he or she is a member. [my emphasis]

The former usually results in *systems* primarily designed for white able-bodied males; the latter usually results in *practices* based on white able-bodied males' perceptions of everyone else.

In both cases, the institutionalized *systems* and *practices* result in arbitrary and extensive exclusions for persons who, by reason of their group affiliation, are systematically denied a full opportunity to demonstrate their individual abilities (Abella, 1984, pp. 9-10).

The Canadian Human Rights Act Employer Guide (1981) explains systemic discrimination as *policies* as well as practices based on organizational rules and assumptions or past traditions; systemic discrimination is a by-product of systems established for some other purpose – past institutionalized privileges, where these privileges have become imbedded in laws and regulations, in informal rules, in social roles, and in behavior and structures of organization.

Using these and others' explanations, I developed the following operational definition of systemic discrimination as a framework for my writing: any *institutionalized* (not individual) structures, policies, practices, customs and attitudes which disadvantage individuals who are members of certain groups (self-defined). These treatments may be both directly discriminatory and also discriminatory in their effect. Also its negative or discriminatory effect, impact or result either limits the opportunities of a group from participating fully in the life of the organization or, more dramatically, actually excludes that group from participating in the organization. As examples, having no women on promotion committees has been identified as limiting women employees' opportunities for promotion; and the former height criterion for police officers was said to restrict most women from even applying for those jobs.

Although systemic discrimination affects all four designated groups (women, aboriginal people, visible minorities and persons with disabilities), this paper focuses only on systemic discrimination evidenced toward women academics, and one university faculty woman in particular. As Abella and others have pointed out, each targeted group has its unique problems and warrants unique solutions. Consequently, the suggestions for eradication of systemic discrimination advanced here are intended for that one designated group: women academics. There is no presumption that the examples given below are able to be generalized or comprehensive; rather they provide evidence to support the claim that systemic discrimination exists within an academic community.

The unfortunate result of systemic discrimination is that it affects only those people who are perceived by those in power as being different (i.e., those who are not the majority group or the group that has traditionally been the dominant group). Accordingly, *The Canadian Human Rights Act Employer Guide* argues that preventative programs should focus on the macro – the *structural causes* of discrimination, embedded in the criteria and evaluation schemes which comprise systems of hiring, personnel management and performance measurement, rather than the micro – such as trying to find out *who* is culpable. Abella claims that we should be focussing on the effects or the outcome of remediative treatment or affirmative action within the workplace as the test of true institutional change as we move towards employment equity. Sheppard (1993) says that affirmative action or equity programs designed to remedy systemic discrimination encompasses institutionalized changes and/or special legislative measures aimed at redressing inequalities in society at large. If one believes in the systems framework of organizations (as I do) however, all perspectives are necessary; changes in the context, changes in the inputs, changes in the processes and changes in the climate must *all*, ultimately, take place in order for noticeable changes in outputs.

Instances of Systemic Discrimination

This next section describes some examples of systemic discrimination that I have experienced within the last three academic years as an Associate Dean in an Ontario university. In my university, a medium-sized full-service university within Canada, approximately 26 percent of its full-time faculty in 1994 are women. Yet only 16 women of 126 faculty or 13 percent are in middle management positions; and 3 women faculty out of 15 or 20 percent are in upper level management positions (one woman of the seven vice-presidents and two women out of the seven deans). Even in my faculty where 69 percent of the undergraduate and 71 percent of the graduate program are comprised of women students, only 18 percent of full-time faculty are women (1994-95 data). I was the first female Associate Dean in the twenty-five year history of the faculty, and the only female in the faculty's administrative structure.

Before I begin, I wish to reiterate that I believe that no *one* person is culpable. As systemic discrimination is institutional, I believe that it is the organization which is responsible; it is the organization which allows these discriminatory actions to occur and to perpetuate.

My reflections commence when I was interviewed for the position of Associate Dean. I was interviewed by a committee of seven men and was asked about the "special" attributes that I would bring to the position *as a woman*. I informed them of the frequent occurrences of discrimination toward women which I had experienced or had heard were occurring in the faculty. The group's immediate response was one of disbelief; later, however, I learned that some of those committee members sought out other female faculty to verify my statements. With that auspicious beginning, I thought that it might be useful and revealing to keep a diary of personal experiences.

Later, having read some literature on women academics' experiences of systemic discrimination, I reflected on my own personal experiences. I identified three distinct types of systemic discrimination. I labelled them as: discriminatory institutional practices; discriminatory criteria in promotion, hiring, tenure and review; and inequitable resource allocation. Each category is clarified by examples from my own experiences and from the literature.

Discriminatory Institutional Practices

The most apparent example of systemic discrimination is the use of exclusionary language within the faculty. For example, women students and staff are frequently called 'girls' by both male faculty and support staff, in classes and in general discourse, despite a Dean's request to all faculty, several years ago, not to use gender-exclusive language.

On a number of occasions during my tenure as Associate Dean my gender seems to have made a difference. For example, I was not made the Acting Dean on either a temporary or year-long basis, as was the usual practice for men. I was not allowed to attend senior management meetings in the Dean's absence, although other (male) Associate Deans have attended on different occasions.

Literature on women in *academe* supports my contention that such practices exclude women faculty from "powerful" positions where policy is set (Aisenberg & Harrington, 1986; Caplan, 1993; Chamberlain, 1988; Robbins & Kahn, 1985). To quote Caplan (p. 180):

> Rarely are women made department heads, deans or other top administrators, and, despite being placed on many working committees, infrequently do they hold positions on the powerful ones or on funding bodies or editorial boards.

Kahn and Robbins (1985) observed that women academics have disproportionate demands made of their time for committee work. Furthermore, Hyle (1993) pointed out that much of this committee work to which women academics are assigned is meaningless and unimportant. In my university, representation has been requested on all committees, and especially on the selection/review/promotion/tenure committees. I would agree that the few female faculty members are over-worked or over-used in terms of their internal community service. Accordingly, I applaud a recent report by the Faculty Advisor on Employment Equity which recommends to senior administration that committee work should be taken into consideration when women faculty are applying for tenure and promotion.

The paucity of women in middle and senior management in this university supports Finkelstein's (1981) point about a lack of female role models. Indeed on many occasions, I have felt "on parade" and was even advised by a male colleague not to be the *first* woman Associate Dean, but the second. The first, I was informed, would be subject to pressure for exemplary performance, and my failures would be generalized to all women. Finkelstein makes similar observations. What I sorely miss, however, is a network of female colleagues with whom to share common problems. Rather than turning inward to the university community, I now seek support and feedback from colleagues in other institutions.

For three consecutive years, I asked to attend a well-known management training program for university administrators. The senior university management committee (committee of the president, vice-presidents, and deans) refused my request for two reasons: first, because I was "too new in the job"; and second, because the professional development fund had been expended (an associate dean of another faculty was awarded funds towards his professional development). I expressed my dissatisfaction with the decision and was told that the procedures had just been changed within the university: professional development of management was now decentralized to the Dean's level. From a larger central fund then, professional development funds "devolved" to a much smaller departmental fund. Not only had the rules been changed for the (one) female applicant, but the resources were reduced and became more restricted.

At Faculty Board with a male as chairperson, men have been allowed to talk more than once to a topic; when women try, Robert's *Rules of Order* have been invoked as the reason for denying women's voices. Fuehrer and Schilling (1985) and Lewis (1993) have commented upon this silencing of women academics.

Despite my repeated attempts, I have been excluded from Old Boys' clubs which are operational both within the university and within the faculty. While "the boys" sometimes go out drinking or dining, play golf, or have a quiet weekend together, any overture on my part for informal networking has been turned down. Furthermore, I have been reminded of my children at home. As documented in the literature (Epstein & Coser, 1981; Kahn & Robbins, 1985; Lewis, 1993), here too, women are excluded from the informal social networks where decision-making occurs.

Status-levelling (Finkelstein, 1981) and stereotyping (Kanter, 1977; Yoder, 1985) have occurred when I have been positioned anywhere near the secretary's desk; most strangers ask if I am the secretary, and male faculty members invariably comment upon my secretarial skills. As well, I am referred to by my first name (by students, staff and faculty) (something, however, which I do not mind) or as Mrs. (something which I *do* mind) while the other Associate Dean is invariably addressed by his title. Robbins and Kahn (1985), too, observed this inequity. Furthermore, when my husband and I attend university functions together, strangers address *him* as Associate Dean.

When a publisher requested that I undertake a national research project, one of my male colleagues suggested that I should share it with a male colleague. He believed that the findings would be more readily accepted if it were co-authored by a male. (I thanked him for his viewpoint, but remained as the single author.) Yet his comments are not unfounded: Geis, Carter and Butler (1986) wrote in a similar vein, saying that women's scholarship has been hampered because of some editors' reluctance to publish papers in which women are the single or senior author.

I have argued with senior university administration that our policy of decentralization sometimes works adversely for the non-dominant groups within the university. A case in point has been associated with the recent changes to the opening and closing times and dates of school and, in particular, elementary school. In our county, secondary students are transported to school prior to elementary students. Parents of elementary school children must provide before-school care for their children because their work commences at 8:30 am. Rather than centralizing the university's flexible starting-time policy to accommodate the parents/care-givers of elementary children (usually women), the university has stated that flexible start-times are at the discretion of each Department Head. As the majority of the Department Heads are older males, what has happened in practice is that several women who have asked to start later have been turned down. Several more are too intimidated to ask. As Associate Dean, I made sure that those people affected within our faculty were accommodated; but unfortunately, this support was not forthcoming throughout the university.

Criteria in Promotion, Hiring, Tenure and Review

The second category of systemic discrimination within the university is criteria or standards which have adversely affected women academics in the hiring, selection, promotion, review and/or tenure processes. As before, several examples can be drawn from my experiences and the experiences of other women described in the literature.

Despite university policy requiring that search committees be heterogenetic in composition, no woman member was on the search committee for the Associate Deanship when I applied.

Different questions were asked of the male applicant than the female applicant in the interview for the Associate Dean. Moreover, questions at the interview were asked of me about "women's issues/problems/concerns" in the faculty, and not of the male competitor. Again, all standard personnel selection procedures dictate that the same questions be asked of all candidates to ensure fairness. Perhaps the university philosophy of decentralization has prevented the articulation of such a centralized policy.

In my faculty, criteria for promotion, tenure and review appear to change with the group of individuals who are going forward – being norm rather than criterion referenced. If one academic has a very strong record, for example, others are "competing" with that individual, rather than being compared to an established standard. As I see it, the game plan currently is to determine who else is going for promotion, tenure or review at the same time, in order to determine one's own degree of success.

The literature has reported the prevalence of vague and ambiguous criteria for evaluation by review/promotion/tenure committees (e.g., Graham, O'Reilly, & Rawlings, 1985). Other instances documented by these same authors are where department heads have neglected to notify female faculty of the date on which those dossiers are due; where department heads have neglected to act in a timely fashion to secure external reviews of the women candidates' qualifications for promotion and tenure; and where the committees have distorted the interpretations of external reviewers' evaluations unfavorably or have even ignored these positive evaluations.

Recently, a female faculty member applying for early tenure articulated the latter concern; she (and I) deemed her dossier to be exceptional, but the committee did not. I knew the contents of her file and from my reading, the referees were very positive. But because the woman was untenured, she would not file a formal grievance. She believed that her dossier had been evaluated from an anti-women perspective. Hyle (1993) writes of the same thing occurring to other women academics.

Newly-hired women for both contract and tenure-track faculty positions have been offered less as starting salaries than were their male counterparts. This issue is not new to our faculty; others, such as Acker (1987), have pointed out this situation. Not only did this happen to me, but I saw it being applied during my tenure. As Graham, O'Reilly and Rawlings (1985) attest, I too believe that the salary recommendations have been made without considering the unique experiences and backgrounds of these women.

Women in non-traditional faculty positions are concerned that their review/tenure/promotion committees are inappropriately structured and that their work will be scrutinized and assessed by those who are not their peers. This concern has been voiced by our university faculty association and by Fuehrer and Schilling (1985) who note the problem of "peer" reviews due to a lack of *de facto* peers because of their different sex, attitudes, backgrounds and experiences. Some female faculty members have also mentioned to me that their administrative and committee responsibilities which they *were asked* to take on are now, at review/tenure/promotion time, being undervalued or dismissed.

The recruitment and hiring of new faculty have been carried out in a very *ad hoc* manner within our faculty, despite the existence of a university-wide hiring kit. In my term of office, I attempted to ensure that selection committees were truly representative and were seen as being representative by discipline, and that the committee agreed upon and put in writing the criteria for selection *before* they read any applications.

Inequitable Resource Allocation

The third category of systemic discrimination is the inequitable allocation of resources. A number of examples within that category are provided below.

Previously, senior university management requested that departments compare the salaries of women and men academics and report any discrepancy within rank. Unfortunately, no determination was made as to what was considered a significant salary differential. Consequently, salaries which I considered as unequal (and favoring the men) were thought of as "comparable" by my senior colleagues.

The registrar has tabulated that male faculty members initiate about 95 percent of the special requests (regarding class scheduling and room allocation) made to her office. Moreover, male faculty members have made more change-of-room requests to the Registrar's Office than have women faculty.

I and several of the other female graduate faculty have argued that we, as advisors, have been assigned more graduate students than our male colleagues. This inequity toward women academics has been observed by Chamberlain (1988) and by Robbins and Kahn (1985).

Another concern raised in the same literature is that women faculty have heavier teaching loads than men. But as Associate Dean, I tried to ensure that this was not the case. I assumed that all faculty's teaching assignments are written down, available for public scrutiny.

I have undertaken the development of an orientation program for new faculty. Now, a list of resources which any incoming academic can expect to receive and a list of other resources they can qualify for, such as start-up grants, is available. I did this as a reaction to my feelings of distrust of "the system" and because I believed myself to be powerless when I first arrived at the faculty. I had no mentor or network to show me "the ropes" or to ensure that I was allocated what other (male) colleagues received. By opening up and regularizing this process, I hope to inform and hence empower others.

In our facility, the administrative wing of the building, housing twenty-two women and three men, had only one women's washroom and two men's washrooms. Even the physical structure of that wing of the building was discriminating against women! I had another female washroom installed last year.

The literature offers three more examples demonstrating the inequitable allocation of resources within the university. The first is that women faculty have been assigned less desirable and less permanent office space than men faculty (Graham et al., 1985). Secondly, women have less access to secretarial and technical support than men (Hyle, 1993; Robbins & Kahn, 1985). And lastly, women have less access to graduate students and doctoral fellows who can assist with research and publications (Robbins & Kahn, 1985). To date, however, I have neither observed nor recorded any such discrimination here.

As Abella stated, however, equality in employment does *not* necessarily mean that all parties must be assigned equal amounts of resources or are necessarily given the *same* opportunities. To Abella, equality in employment means treating people the same, despite their differences [in some instances], and [in other instances] it means treating them as equals by accommodating their differences. (p. 4)

I wish to expand on this latter point. To say that women should have access to or should be given the same as what men have, implies that the one (male) standard is the appropriate norm with which to compare these two groups (Eckart, 1983). Rather than assuming a male norm, as Eckart (1993), Fuehrer and Schilling (1985) and others attest, the controls/standards/ criteria must take into account the different experiences of *both* women and men. By doing so, the "out group" (i.e., women) has a greater chance of being understood and accepted. Accordingly, women might be more readily accommodated as part of the more-inclusive "in group" or the "one group" (my terminology).

To reiterate then, to apply a single standard based upon the male *status quo* gives a false impression of equality. Moreover, this single male standard is said merely to perpetuate rather than to eradicate systemic discrimination (Robertson, 1990; Taub, 1995). "Indeed, it has been suggested that in some circumstances, it is the essence of equality to make distinctions between groups to accommodate their different needs and interests" (Sheppard, 1993, p. 6). The concern, now, is who will determine these new standards. How will these new standards be determined? Who will apply these standards? And, how inclusive will these standards be not only for white women, but for the other three groups (aboriginal people, visible minorities and people with disabilities) who are also currently under-represented within the academy?

Conclusion

As should be clear from the examples above, I and other women academics have been subjected in different ways to discriminatory attitudes, behaviors, policies, practices and structures. While I am uncomfortable in documenting these examples, I feel the anger that Lewis (1993) referred to. I am trying to be a fully participating member of the academy and to be all that I can be. But these discriminatory practices described here have worked to continuously reinforce the belief that I am working within a system that extols and upholds stereotypes, rather than attempting to eradicate them. That system is working against the best interests of myself and other women academics.

My five suggestions for institutional change are from the macro rather than the micro perspective. The first four are intended for the university; the last one is for women academics. The first is for the university to acknowledge that systemic discrimination exists, i.e., that the *effect* of our institutional policies, practices, structures and conventions have impacted adversely on, in this particular case, women academics. The second is that the institution should articulate the objective of the eradication of those discriminatory policies, practices, structures and conventions. The third suggestion is one that is stated in the Federal Contractor's Program: senior management should have in their letters of appointment the responsibility and the accountability for employment equity. And the fourth suggestion is to reconstruct policies, practices, structures and norms based upon new assumptions, which use more objective (not male-based) evidence and criteria, and which come from improved understandings of their different backgrounds. "It seems clear that most gender differences are socially created and therefore may be socially altered" (Epstein, 1988, p. 231). "We make our realities; therefore, we can also change them. If we can see discrimination, we may be able to combat it," (Hyle, 1993, p. 21). Instead of the university merely perpetuating discriminatory social norms, the university must take the responsibility for bringing about these social changes. In addition to these institutional changes, my fifth suggestion is to reiterate to those women in the academy and to those of us in (albeit few) positions of educational leadership the recommendation of Aisenberg and Harrington (1988, p. 142):

> As a general strategy, we would emphasize the importance of women's continuing to press for positions in the profession as if their holding public authority *were* the norm, continuing to claim authority as rightfully theirs.

Time has demonstrated that systemic discrimination, by its very nature, will not disappear of its own accord. "Too much is personally at stake for most people in the universities to end discrimination against women. It will not end voluntarily; it must be required" (Pottker, 1977, p. 407). Every policy, institutional custom and traditional practice should be scrutinized for its potentially adverse impact. Differences within gender groups should be accommodated. Structures require reconfiguration. In order to call itself an employment equity organization, the university must root out systemic discrimination very methodically and deliberately. Can it set the example for society and sorely-needed social change? To move toward becoming the *inclusive institution*, first it must move away from perpetuating systemic discrimination.

References

Abella, R.S. (1984). *Report of the commission on equality in employment*. Ottawa, ON: Government of Canada.

Acker, J. (1987). Sex bias in job evaluation: A comparable worth issue. In C. Bose & G. Spitze (eds.) *Ingredients for women's employment policy*. Albany, NY: SUNY, 183-196.

Acker, S., & Piper, D.W. (1984). *Is higher education fair to women?* Guilford, Surrey, ENG: SRHE & NFER-Nelson.

Aisenberg, N., & Harrington, M. (1988). *Women of academe. Outsiders in the sacred grove*. Amherst, MASS: U of Massachusetts Press.

Canadian human rights act. Employer guide. (1981). Ottawa, ON: Canadian Human Rights Commission, 13-14. ERIC #ED222629.

Canadian Human Rights Reporter. (March, 1992). The Ontario Human Rights Code.

Caplan, P. (1993). *Lifting a ton of feathers. A woman's guide for surviving in the academic world.* Toronto: U of T Press.

Chamberlain, M.K. (Ed.). (1988). *Women in academe. Progress and prospects.* New York: Russell Sage Foundation.

Dagg, A.I. (1993). Academic faculty wives and systemic discrimination – Anti-nepotism and "inbreeding." *The Canadian Journal of Higher Education, 23*(1), 1-18.

Eckart, D.R. (1993). Discrimination, Feminist narratives, and policy arguments. *Women and Politics, 13*(1), 19-37.

Epstein, C.F. (1988). *Deceptive distinctions. Sex, gender, and the social order.* New York: Russell Sage Foundation.

Epstein, C.F., & Coser, R.L. (Eds.). (1981). *Access to power: Cross-national studies of women and elites.* London: George Allen & Unwin.

Epstein, C.F., & Goode, W.J. (Eds.). (1971). *The other half. Roads to women's equality.* Englewood Cliffs, NJ: Prentice Hall.

Finkelstein, C.A. (1981). Women managers: Career patterns and changes in the United States. In C.F. Epstein & R.L. Coser (eds.), *Access to power: Cross-national studies of women and elites,* London: George Allen & Unwin, 193-210.

Fuehrer, A., & Schilling, K.M. (1985). The values of academe: Sexism as a natural consequence. *Journal of Social Issues, 41*(4), 29-42.

Gallant, M.J., & Cross, J.E. (1993). Wayward puritans in the ivory tower: Collective aspects of gender discrimination in academia. *The Sociological Quarterly, 34*(2), 237-256.

Geis, F.L., Carter, M.R., & Butler, D.J. (1986). *Seeing and evaluating people.* Newark, DEL: The Office of Women's Affairs, University of Delaware.

Graham, D.L.R., O'Reilly, P., & Rawlings, E.I. (1985). Costs and benefits of advocacy for faculty women: A case study. *Journal of Social Issues, 41*(4), 85-98.

Hyle, A.E. (1993). Women and the community of higher education: Invisibility through institutionalization? Paper presented at the annual meeting of the American Educational Research Association. Atlanta, GA.

Lewis, M.G. (1993). *Without a word.* New York: Routledge.

Kahn, E.D., & Robbins, L. (1985). Social-psychological issues in sex discrimination. *Journal of Social Issues, 41*(4), 135-154.

Kanter, R.M. (1977). *Men and women of the corporation.* New York: Basic Books.

Morgan, N. (1988). *The equality game: Women in the federal public service (1908-1987).* Ottawa: Canadian Advisory Council on the Status of Women.

Pottker, J. (1977). Overt and covert forms of discrimination against academic women. In J. Pottker & A. Fishel (eds.), Sex bias in schools. *The research evidence.* Cranbury, NJ: Associated University Presses, Inc., 380-407.

Powell, G.N. (1993). *Women and men in management.* 2nd ed. NY: SUNY.

Rees, R. (1990). *Women and men in education: A national survey of gender distribution in school systems.* Toronto: Canadian Education Association.

Robbins, L., & Kahn E.D. (1985). Sex discrimination and sex equity for faculty women in the 1980's. *Journal of Social Issues, 41*(4), 1-16.

Robertson, H.J. (1990). *The myth of gender-neutrality*. Toronto: Science Teachers' Association of Ontario.

Sheppard, C. (1993). *Study paper on Litigating the relationship between equity and equality*. A study paper prepared for the Ontario Law Reform Commission. Toronto: Government of Ontario.

Taub, N. (1985). Dealing with employment discrimination and damaging stereotypes: A legal perspective. *Journal of Social Issues, 41*(4), 99-110.

Vizkelety, B. (1987). *Proving discrimination in Canada*. Toronto: The Carswell Co. Ltd.

Ward, K.B., & Grant, L. (1985). The feminist critique and a decade of published research in sociology journals. *The Sociological Quarterly, 26*(2), 139-157.

Ward, K.B., Gast, J., & Grant, L. (1992). Visibility and dissemination of women's and men's sociological scholarship. *Social Problems, 39*(3), 291-298).

Yoder, J.D.(1985). An academic woman as a token: A case study. *Journal of Social Issues, 41*(4), 61-72.

Zimmer, L. (1988). Tokenism and women in the workplace: The limits of gender-neutral theory. *Social Problems, 35*(1), 64-77.

4

A Feminist Perspective:
A Postmodern Critique of Authority

Barbara Hoffman

Underpinnings

Feminism and postmodernism seem to have much in common. Both challenge the epistemology that has created a subject/object dichotomy which has had a major effect on the status of women in Western culture. Only subjects can constitute knowledge, so the exclusion of women from acting as subjects has reflexively subverted their inclusion from rationality and the characterization of the underlying metanarrative of truth. Feminists reject such a definition of knowledge because it is the product of the fundamental dualism between male and female that has made rationalism a specifically masculine mode of thought. A feminist critique extends a postmodern critique of rationalism by revealing its base in gender distinctions.

Postmodernism offers a critique of the view of representation as reflecting reality (rather than as constitutive of social reality) and of the idea of "man" as the centred subject of such representation. Strathern (1987, p. 288) says that a feminist task needs to destroy the authority of other persons who determine feminine experience. She argues that in men's accounts, women are seen as "the Other," while the institutions and persons who represent patriarchy are often concretized as "men."

For postmodernists, knowledge is not acquired through the abstracted separation of subjects and objects, but rather, is constituted collectively through discourse. That is to say, facts are never given. We can only know in the sense that we constitute meaning for our experiences. Thus, our common sense presuppositions about the "real" depend upon how the "real" is described, how it is put into discourse, and how the discourse is interpreted. The public world is rendered specifically as discourse, as a political account. The individual ceases to be centred in an a priori "self," but becomes a locus for the intersection of various signifying systems. The individual's perspective (situatedness) becomes an important consideration in determining how knowledge is constituted.

What positions knowers in society is constituted in accordance with their values, ideas and feelings. These are produced by their cultural circumstances. They all interact to constitute each other in a reflexive relationship. A variety of circumstances constitute the different perspectives of knowers. For Foucault, there are no subjects or objects, only individuals caught in a network of historical power relations. This perspective has been particularly useful for examining ways in which authority is constituted by patriarchal discourse.

Postmodernism posits that we can only know the world through a process of cultural detoxification; through examining the network of socially established meaning systems that constitute the discourses of our culture. In order to do this, we must unmask the deceptions of naive realism and identify what the hidden systems are that constitute our perceptions of social reality.

In this sense, perspective mediates, so that in disciplines, for example, we cannot separate structure from content. While knowledge produced within a discipline may seem perfectly adequate to insiders, it can seem quite contradictory to others. This has implications for our conceptual configurations of authority.

Patriarchal and Hobbesian Concepts of Authority

Many feminists maintain that the historical and current conceptualization and practice of authority needs to be reconfigured. One such attempt is made by Jones (1993) who looks at authority through the lens of gender, conceptualizing traditional authority as sovereignty, which privileges connections between authority and masculinity.

In her analysis, gender is constituted as "a code of meaning in and through which actual experiences are constructed" (1993, p. 29). Furthermore, Jones posits that the dominant political discourse around citizenship and political participation has been conceptualized in a specifically gendered way. Joan Scott supports this position when she states: "emergent rulers have legitimized power as masculine" (1988, p. 47).

Using sovereignty as an analytical category, Jones claims that from about the fifteenth century AD, political authority in Western discourse was conceptualized as supreme power, which was understood as the ability to command obedience. Furthermore, sovereignty (either secular-kingship, or religious-the Church) implied a notion of obligation to superiors. Such obligations were not self-imposed, but followed distinctions of rank and duty that the social order embodied. In this manner, the modern Western conceptualization of authority rested on the monopolization of sovereignty in one source.

Jones argues that early in the seventeenth century, the father's right to rule in the family was still held to be natural, but that a shift occurred. Since the father had natural authority over his sons, the king, as father of his people, was also credited with equivalent power. In this manner, the biological aspect of paternity was linked to sovereign authority. Political authority was constituted to be a naturally hierarchical and paternal construct wherein discourse practices created command-obedience relationships.

According to Jones, the social theories of Thomas Hobbes served to unsettle patriarchy as the foundation for modern states. Hobbes based his theory on the assumption that the state of nature was a perfect state of equality, wherein all individuals existed in isolation from each other. Their individual pursuits were motivated by a combination of inquisitiveness and personal insecurity that sometimes pitted individuals against each other. Equality meant that all individuals were in the same state of insecurity. The insecurity was the necessary result of the natural state and the natural equality of all individuals. Hobbes argued that humans need a sovereign, a common power to keep them in awe and to direct their actions towards the common good. That is, individuals could enjoy a peaceful life only under the condition of political domination entered into by a social contract.

Feminist Responses to Male Constructs of Authority

Postmodernism presents cultural understandings as the product of previous representations; past events are given meaning, not existence, by their representation in history. Di Stefano (1983) criticizes Hobbes' theory of the individual as a masculinized representation of self that denies relatedness. Pateman (1988) argues that even though the foundation of authority in the Hobbesian state rested on a social contract that signaled the end of rule by the father, patriarchalism continued to thrive in the form of a "sexual contract." By means of it, men claimed the right of command over the use of women's bodies, in exchange for protection.

A paradox seems to exist, however, for contemporary feminists because on the one hand they reject authority while on the other hand they demand authoritative status for their own discourse. A feminist critique of authority entails a transformative project that dislodges current understandings of what authority is and engages in a quest for new conceptualizations of the characteristics of authority. Feminist critiques ultimately point to the hierarchical structure of cognitive authority that allows the perspective of some to determine the shape of knowledge for all. The construction of a "canon" is a process of selection by the few for the many. Feminists try to restructure knowledge, but must work within a complex set of practices for structuring traditional forms of knowledge, particularly in the academy, for example, in departments of Educational Administration in universities. As Angelika Bammer asked: "How are we to go about the business of dismantling the masters' houses while we are trying to get computers for the offices we have set up inside them?" (1991, p. 237).

Restructuring Discourse

Language has always been a central issue for feminists. We have seen how women have been excluded by the "oppressor's language," so one concern is to gain mastery over it. However, adopting the language of the other side does not necessarily change the configuration of power. Can we use language in ways that will enable us to effect changes in the existing hegemonies of class, race and gender? Hekman (1990, p. 163) posits that Derrida's (1987) rejection of epistemology and his attack on the metaphysics of presence have much to offer feminists. Deconstruction destroys the notion of absolutely grounded truth. There are multiple truths and multiiple readings of them. According to Hekman, the deconstruction of the polarities in western epistemology (which has led to the disprivileging of women) is essential to a feminist reading of any text – including those centring on authority.

Harding (1991) notes that given the crucial differences among women, it is unreasonable to expect any unified feminist theory about authority. We need not be concerned about making statements about objective knowledge and true propositions about women working in positions of leadership. Rather, she suggests that our discourse should address "knowing how" rather than "knowing that." This position is supported by both Derrida and Foucault, who reject a politics grounded in an appeal to absolute moral principles of absolute knowledge and truth. Foucault (1988, p. 267) argues that relinquishing the absolute does not mean refraining from making judgments or offering critiques. Rather, the political program that emerges is based on the contingent interpretation of the moment, not as an ideology that is universally grounded.

Feminists must seek to disrupt the categories of knowledge/power that serve to oppress them and others in their daily practices. We must consider questions of good and right administrative action in the situatedness of everyday life. We need to challenge current characterizations of administrative practices, policies and even the discipline of administrative science which regards organizations as independent of the individuals who constitute them. We must denounce the "science of administration" which outlines research agendas based on "objective" surveys of production outputs and performance variables, which defines strategies for maximizing output, efficiency and control, and which imposes the will of a few over many others because of "expert knowledge."

Organizations exist only because of human action and will. Administration is about power because conflict occurs in organizations when individuals hold opposing values or must choose among values that are accepted by the group but are incompatible with their own. Administrators must come to understand these complexities and lead through their commitment to ethical and wise decision-making. Administrative studies must be based on the examination of people trying to realize their ends in specific school settings where community is established and maintained through discourses that accommodate a plurality of values and voices.

We need to look at how authority is socially constituted in particular settings such as our schools, colleges, and universities. We need to examine specific instances of what is constituted by us to be male dominance. We need to examine critically the policies and the histories of policies that define our "truth" as different from that of males. We need to create our own discourses about our situatedness in the ethical dilemmas of leadership in everyday practice.

Harstock (1987) argues that in order to overcome our inferior status, women must constitute ourselves in a way to overcome our marginalization. Derrida (1979) emphasizes that feminism should not seek to replace one truth with another, but rather, should inscribe a new structure of multiple truths, of multiple voices. His aim is not to erase difference, but to displace the polarity of difference by revealing a multiplicity of differences. This is in agreement with Foucault, who argues that new ways of thinking arise from the spaces between the concepts of the old episteme. There is a need for feminist research to uncover and redefine the situatedness of leadership – to displace administration as a set of preconceived practices that establish and maintain control.

One of the aspects of Foucault's perspective on knowledge/power is that it is not localized in one social sphere, whether economic or political. Rather, it is diffused throughout the multitude of institutions that constitute society, including educational settings. Thus elements of subordination are constituted by the plurality of structures and discourses that pervade all aspects of educational administrative practice. We need to look at everyday practices such as how staff meetings are structured, how agenda are prepared, how we choose the varying registers we use for communicative purposes, how we establish policies (i.e., in whose interest), how budget allocations are determined, how staffing needs are established (whose interests are being served), how procedures are established for dealing with disturbances or complaints, how inclusive our decision-making is, and how we define ourselves as leaders.

How can we attempt to do this? First, we need to understand how the feminine has been constituted as inferior through a "critical ontology of ourselves." Secondly, the feminist task requires re-evaluating and disrupting the rules that define the feminine as inferior or as "the Other." The silences and ambiguities of such discourses provide us with opportunities to restructure them. Thirdly, we need to examine and restructure the daily events which reflexively lead to our interpretations of power and authority in such a way that a feminist authority would constitute the feminine, the masculine, and authority in a different, pluralistic way. Fourthly, we must come to understand how to arbitrate value conflicts that occur in our educational communities by understanding how language both confers and cloaks power. Finally, we need to study the roads to administrative power and authority, to better understand how a feminist reconfiguration might be shaped.

References

Bammer, A. (1991). Mastery. In J. E. Hartman & E. Messer-Davidow (Eds.), *(En)Gendering knowledge: Feminists in academe* (pp. 237-258). Knoxville: The University of Tennessee.

Derrida, J. (1979). *Spurs/eperons*. Chicago: University of Chicago Press.

Derrida, J. (1987). *The post card: From Socrates to Freud and beyond.* Chicago: The University of Chicago Press.

Di Stefano, C. (1983). Masculinity as ideology in political theory: Hobbesian man reconsidered. *Women's Studies International Forum, 6*, 633-44.

Foucault, M. (1988). *Politics, philosophy, culture*: Interviews and other writings, 1977-1984. L. Kritzman (Ed.). New York: Routledge.

Harding, S. (1991). Who knows? Identities and feminist epistemology. In J. E. Hartman and E. Messer-Davidow (Eds.), *(En)Gendering knowledge: Feminists in academe* (pp. 100-115). Knoxville: The University of Tennessee Press.

Harstock, N. (1987). Re-thinking modernity modernism: Minority vs majority theories. *Cultural Critique, 7*, 187-206.

Hekman, S. (1990). *Gender and knowledge: Elements of a postmodern feminism.* Boston: Northeastern University Press.

Jones, K.B. (1993). *Compassionate authority: Democracy and the representation of women.* New York and London: Routledge.

Pateman, C. (1988). *The sexual contract.* Stanford: Stanford University Press.

Scott, J.W. (1988). *Gender and the politics of history.* New York: Columbia University Press.

Strathern, M. (1987). The case of feminism and anthropology. *Signs: The Journal of Women in Culture and Society, 12*(2), 276-292.

Section Two

Experiences of Women Educational Administrators in Provincial Contexts

Introduction

Much of the work on gender and educational administration and leadership has sought to give "voice" to women and to help us understand their experiences from their perspectives. The focus of such work has been on those few women who have become administrators or officially recognized leaders within their organizations. Since we are trying to understand the complexity of a phenomenon, small sample sizes and interview techniques which reveal narratives and "thick descriptions" of experiences have been widely used. Researchers have attempted to listen closely to women and to interpret and explain how they make sense at a micro level of the many macro level forces which affect their daily realities. Among those macro level forces, policies designed to improve the participation of women in official leadership roles have come under scrutiny and questions about the impact of such policies have been considered from the perspectives of women themselves.

In this section we consider "stories" of the experiences of a number of women administrators in several different provincial contexts. We ask what we can learn about gender and leadership from those who have taken on official roles of administration. We also explore differences that women might bring as administrators and how their presence impacts upon the organization. We learn about barriers they have encountered and consider the various strategies they have used to overcome roadblocks. One recurring theme is the persistence of a masculine image of the "tough" and adversarial administrator. Another theme is the use of humor in order to "survive." There are also identifiable "feminine roles" expected of them because they are women, and they talk about combining their public and private realms of activity. What also becomes clear is the isolation these women feel as administrators and the many contradictions they encounter.

In Chapter Five, Barbara Gill assesses the impact of an Assessment Program for educational leadership candidates in New Brunswick and a recent provincial policy which provided women candidates with free tuition if they chose to enter the required training for school administration at the elementary and secondary school level. She draws on data from interviews with 29 women who have recently undergone such training to reveal the barriers they actually encountered as they attempted to become school administrators. She concludes that while a few women may enter school administration, a glass ceiling blocks the route for most women teachers.

In Chapter Six, Claudine Baudoux shows a historical pattern of decline in the number of women in educational administration in the province of Quebec since the late 1950s. Drawing on data from an extensive study by GRADE, a multi-disciplinary research team, she delineates hypotheses related firstly, to required feminity, and secondly, to systemic discrimination which may explain this decline. She also outlines how most women in Quebec elementary and secondary schools have been excluded from administration and describes various survival strategies some women administrators have employed.

In Chapter Seven, Alison Taylor takes a close look at the impact of employment equity policies in Ontario school boards. From an in-depth interview with one woman secondary school principal, she describes the disjunctures that exist between policy and practice and the contradictory effects of the equity policy upon this woman. She argues that it is important that women understand why they feel ambivalent as they take on administrative roles in education.

In Chapter Eight, Fay Myers and Vivian Hajnal draw on the data from interviews with nine women who are leaders in the upper management levels of Saskatchewan adult educational institutions to discuss factors affecting the development of their leadership styles. The authors raise questions about how women's styles of leadership are affected by such things as early socialization and their multiple social roles.

In Chapter Nine, Hope-Arlene Fennell examines metaphors for leadership provided in her interviews with four women principals identified as exceptional leaders within school boards in Ontario and British Columbia. Her analysis of the metaphors these women employ leads to questions about leadership and power and how gender is implicated in that relationship.

In Chapter Ten, Roberta Russell draws on interviews with 21 female and 22 male administrators in education and public administration in six Canadian cities to identify the "survival strategies" women have employed. She describes how gender and visible minority status are combined for some administrators. She discusses the implications of such strategies as the use of humor and the attempt to find suitable mentors. She concludes that we have much to learn from women leaders who describe a range of techniques for dealing with barriers.

5

Breaking the Glass Ceiling or Sliding Back the Sunroof?: Women in Educational Administration in New Brunswick

Barbara A. Gill

Educational administration is still a male-dominated profession. According to a New Brunswick Teachers' Association study conducted in 1992 (NBTA, 1992), the overall percentage of women in administrative positions has not changed since 1973. Current figures indicate that in 1992-1993 only twenty-six percent of the administrators in both the Anglophone and Francophone school systems combined were women (Table 1).

Table 1
Provincial Percentages of Women Administrators

Administrator	Anglophone		Francophone		Total	
Superintendent	3/12	25.0%	2/6	33.0%	5/18	27.7%
Assistant Superintendent	4/16	18.8%	1/18	12.5%	4/24	16.6%
Supervisor	19/51	37.0%	28/47	59.5%	47/98	48.0%
Principal	55/268	20.0%	37/143	25.8%	92/411	22.4%
Total	81/347	23.0%	68/204	33.3%	148/551	26.0%

Source: Department of Education School Directory, 1992-1993

Women have become vice-principals in growing numbers in New Brunswick. The percentage of female vice-principals has increased from twenty-one percent in 1988 to thirty-two percent in 1992. However, at the same time, the percentage of women in the teaching profession has increased from sixty percent to sixty-three percent, so the total number of female vice-principals must continue to rise just to maintain the status quo (Paulette Moore, personal communication, May 1993). In schools with female principals, as the age of the students rises so the percentage of female principals declines, from twenty-four percent at the kindergarten level to nine percent at the senior high level. If the figures are examined by school district it can be seen that the larger percentages of female administrators tend to be in the small, rural school districts.

The Province of New Brunswick is attempting to address the problem. In 1992 the New Brunswick Department of Education unveiled plans to increase the number of women in educational administration. Program summaries from *Excellence in Education* (1992), the New Brunswick Department of Education's plans for the educational future of the province, indicated that the Minister's Advisory Committee on Women's Issues in Education would work with the Department of Education and the New Brunswick Teachers' Association to implement strategies for increasing the number of women in educational leadership positions. In February 1993 the Department of Education announced that tuition costs would be paid for women students, back-dated to Fall 1993, for all courses leading to the New Brunswick Principals' Certificate. However, these bursaries were discontinued in March 1994.

The New Brunswick Centre for Educational Administration (NBCEA) provides the National Association of Secondary School Principals' (NASSP) Assessment Program for educational leadership candidates. In order to attend, participants must be supported by their school boards. Boards pay the costs of the assessment and the cost of hiring substitute teachers for the two and one half days of the assessment. It should be noted that women tend to perform better than men in the assessment process (Schmitt and Cohen, 1990). Other agencies have addressed the issue of the low representation of women in educational administration and attempted to suggest ways of addressing the lack of women in leadership positions (NBTA Women's Issues Committee, 1992). If these initiatives are successful the number of women in positions of educational leadership in New Brunswick could increase significantly over the next few years.

But there is also the possibility of the existence of a glass ceiling for women educators in New Brunswick. The concept of a glass ceiling was proposed by Morrison, White and Van Velsor (1987) to describe barriers which allowed women and minorities to advance only so far in their chosen fields. It is possible that barriers exist which prevent women educators from obtaining positions, or which allow only a certain number of women educators to obtain positions in educational administration. If this is the case, then there is a need to identify these barriers and break them down before many more women can become educational administrators in New Brunswick.

The Study

What are the experiences of women who wish to enter educational administration in New Brunswick? What factors assist women in their search for administrative positions? Are there barriers or obstacles to achieving their goals? Do they feel they are breaking the glass ceiling and moving into positions of educational administration with ease? Or does the low proportion of women in educational administration indicate that, rather than breaking the glass ceiling, a sunroof slides back temporarily to allow only a few through?

In order to answer these questions a study was devised which examined the experiences of a group of women teachers who were searching for or who had obtained a position in educational administration in New Brunswick (Gill, 1994). Women educators who had participated in the New Brunswick Centre for Educational Administration Assessment Program from 1988 through 1992 were contacted by the Centre's Director and asked if they would agree to participate in the study. Twenty-nine women or 67, percent agreed. Each participant was then contacted by the researcher and a time for an interview was set up. The time and location were chosen by the participant. Each participant was promised confidentiality and anonymity. This group of women was chosen for two reasons. Their participation in the NBCEA Assessment Centre could be taken as an indication of their willingness to search actively for an administrative position and, as their school boards were responsible for funding their participation in the Assessment Centre, they were the individuals receiving support in their career goals, at least to the extent of participating in the assessment process.

Of the twenty-nine women educators in the study, twelve (41 percent) were vice-principals and nine (31 percent) were classroom teachers looking for administrative positions. Three (10 percent) were Central Office administrators and three (10 percent) were principals. The other two were Methods and Resource teachers. On average, the participants had sixteen years teaching experience and three years in their current administrative positions. There was at least one volunteer from each Anglophone school district in the province. All school levels were represented and there were volunteers from urban, suburban and rural areas.

Reaching the Glass Ceiling?

When asked directly whether they had faced any barriers or obstacles to obtaining administrative positions, most of the respondents made comments similar to these:

> No. None that I can think of. Even though we had changed superintendents and went from a female to a male it didn't make any difference there whatsoever.

> My principal is very supportive of females being in administration and he tries to encourage people, females in particular, to take positions of responsibility. I really can't think of any.

The general perception among these women was that they had the support of the District Central Office. They had been encouraged to pursue careers in educational administration.

There were a few women who did believe there were barriers and they spoke in these terms:

I think there are barriers right now . . . If you are married and a woman, then you are expected to follow your husband.

. . . right now here we're male dominated although we have women in certain positions, but we're still male dominated.

In applying [for a position] probably. If there were six board members I suspect that there was at least one that felt that this shouldn't be a female administrator, especially the top position, so to speak. Of the others, I think they felt strongly that . . . there should be a male counterpart. That there shouldn't be two females. I don't think they would express the same concern that there shouldn't be two males.

However, further discussion with the women who felt there were no barriers to them personally revealed that there were situations which existed that could work against their obtaining a position or functioning effectively in an administrative position. A vice-principal discussed her wish to obtain a principal's position and her current principal's reaction to her goal.

This is his thirty-fifth year in teaching and I think that he sometimes would question whether I would be forceful enough because he's got a definite attitude of what the boss is that I don't necessarily see the boss being.

A teacher who wanted to become an administrator saw taking university courses as a barrier.

You've got to go back to school and learn all these things . . . I'm not exactly sure that the things that you would learn in university are really sort of applicable to what's in the real situation.

Another participant felt that the attitude of some of her professors at university had been condescending. While the professors might not directly influence the hiring process they could cause individuals to doubt their career aspirations.

A couple of professors that I took courses from I found to be a little bit time set back in the fifties . . . there were a few that I thought even though they're teaching in the 1990s had it in the back of their heads somewhere . . . this is a man's game and we'll pay you lip service and we'll include you in our courses and we'll give you a Masters certificate, the degree and the whole bit . . . but I still sensed very much that a few of them were rather condescending and I don't even think they were aware of it. I really think if I asked them they would consider themselves very enlightened, current up-to-date men.

The perceived need to have contacts among those responsible for hiring was also described as a barrier.

It's very political . . . if you don't know someone on the personnel committee, forget it . . . I see that as an obstacle because I am not a politically oriented person and I see no reason why I should be nice to someone for a year or two just to get a job.

A Central Office administrator described her frustration at trying to get women teachers to apply for vacancies in the district.

But no luck with those three ladies and that's kind of sad. Because they would be excellent people and they just thought, "Well, you know, I just can't do it, I can't listen to the hassles, I couldn't put in the time."

Obstacles and barriers experienced on the job took a number of forms. The most frequently mentioned was the effect of the perception, particularly at the junior high and senior high school level, that women could not cope with all the demands of the position. They were hired because they were women and not because of their talents and therefore were bound to be ineffective. A perception that a senior high school or a junior high school administrator had to be a "tough guy" contributed to this perception.

The only negative thing is the perception around here that women get the job. And maybe that is a barrier for actually carrying out your job more than getting the position because some men have the mind set that women cannot do the job ... but give credit to the men who came up to me after a year and said, "You've proved me wrong. Darned glad to have you around."

In rural areas women administrators, as women in authority, were not always readily accepted.

I find sometimes the bus drivers will bring in discipline problems and I suggest an alternate ... they really don't like taking direction from a female. There's a tendency if the principal is here to take the problems to him because he's a male even though I'm the one that's been on bus duty. And [the principal] sends them in here and they seem to be a little embarrassed ... that they have to bring a discipline problem to a female. So that's probably a barrier.

A principal described her experiences as the only female at principals' meetings. While the male principals offered to help her and were willing to give advice when asked, she sensed their resentment when she offered ideas and suggestions at meetings and appeared to take her responsibilities more seriously than they thought appropriate.

I was the only female at the principals' meeting. I never in my life felt such a strong "old boys network" attitude being displayed although surface conversations and so on were always polite, collegial and "anything I can do to help you" ... it would be rolled eyeballs, or at coffee breaks, "What's with you today, lay off, we don't want to be here all day. This is only a morning meeting."

The perception that a Central Office administrative position was a reward for service was also apparent.

One of the key things was they felt I was very young to get this position and I guess I never thought of myself as being that young. I never thought that administrative positions were for old people. Some people felt that way. That it was a reward after so many years of service. I guess I've never felt that way. That was a shock when people started saying that. But people obviously perceived that. That you paid your dues and there was going to be this reward.

The participants were asked why they felt there were so few women in administration in the province. The most frequent response was that women still took on the major responsibility for the home and family.

> I think in the past, society has led women to take the homemaker role and that you had to put your children first. I don't have any problem with that. I think your family is important and does come first. I think a lot of families expected that women would go into nursing, teaching or secretarial work – all women's jobs. I think it's changing.

The perception that administration was a male profession also held women back from considering a career in educational administration.

> It's not by and large what most teachers see themselves as doing, being administrators. They see themselves as being teachers and I think it's something that most people have the basic kinds of skills probably in teaching to become quite able administrators. Because it's an extension of those same skills that make you a good teacher that make you a good administrator too.

> I still think many women see it as a "guy job," especially principals.

The participants were also asked for their views on the latest government incentive of providing tuition bursaries to women who wished to take courses towards their Principal's Certificate. Most of the women were against it or had ambivalent feelings about it. However, a single parent saw the bursary as a way to finally earn her certificate.

> I am a single parent and I have two children. I'm their total support. I don't get any other outside maintenance support or anything for my children. It's just me. And it's not always easy financially to decide, well gosh, I'm going to go and take this course because my money is pretty tied up, making sure my kids have stuff, my mortgage payment and those kind of things, even this is going to make it a lot easier for me.

A Glass Ceiling or a Sunroof?

The results of this study are consistent with much of the literature. Female teachers spend longer in teaching prior to obtaining administrative positions than do male teachers. The majority of the female administrators were at the vice-principal level, and in kindergarten through grade six. Nine women in the study were appointed in the rural school districts of the province. Similar findings have been reported by Edson (1988) and Shakeshaft (1989) for women administrators in the United States.

The initial denial of the existence of barriers or obstacles by most of the participants was interesting. Similar findings were noted by Schmuck and Schubert (1986) in their study of female principals in Arizona, Oregon and California. In the New Brunswick situation, the denial could mean that there are no barriers. Any woman who has the qualifications, applies for the position and is the best candidate is appointed to the position. Indeed the overall impression of all the participants was that they had the support of their school district central offices. However, these same participants described experiences which could be considered barriers. It is possible that the volunteer sample used in the study represents the "favored women," the ones who are supported and "promoted" by their school district. One of the participants suggested that some behaviors are not acceptable from women administrative candidates:

> I actually worked with another lady who is a lot more aggressive in terms of making it known that she has the ability to be an administrator, is setting out to put herself in all the right positions, is really kind of selling herself . . . and she has had problems, she has yet to get into an administrative role, as a matter of fact we have interviewed for a couple of the same jobs . . . I sometimes wonder if she's too aggressive, too demanding and almost telling people that they've got to give her the job, that she's sort of overselling.

One participant suggested the reason so few women indicated directly that they had experienced barriers was that it was considered inappropriate to admit to problems. It may be that barriers and obstacles exist, but the participants did not identify them as such. Schmuck and Schubert (1986) noted similar examples. Having stated there were no barriers, their participants described situations on the job where the perceptions of some colleagues and community members could make the job more difficult. It is possible that these perceptions are an indication of a pervasive culture that says, "This is not a job for women." It is never spoken, never articulated, but is always there in the background. The influence of this pervasive culture has been around so long that it seems a normal way of thinking. The result is a "two-pronged effect" dissuading women from applying for administrative positions and dissuading communities from appointing women to administrative positions.

Many who opposed the government bursaries for women in New Brunswick felt that such incentives reinforced the perception that women could not make it on their own. They saw the bursaries as contributing to the belief that women were appointed to administrative positions because they were women and not because they were the best candidates. There is evidence in the study presented here that indeed there is a pervasive attitude in this province that educational administration is a male profession. Barring a few exceptions, many people believe that men make better administrators than women. There is a view that, particularly at the high school level, the principal must be a tough male, able to maintain control and exert authority. This suggests a certain kind of control and authority, based on "power over" and "fear of." Whether this conception of leadership is appropriate for schools in the 1990s must be examined.

Conclusions

Do the results of this study suggest that women educators have made real gains in the last five years? Has the glass ceiling been broken? Or are the gains made merely temporary advances which will disappear at a later date – the sliding back of a sunroof which can be closed again at any time?

Women educators are making progress. They are being encouraged to train for and apply for leadership positions by central office administrators, principals and colleagues. Publications from the Department of Education indicate the provincial government's support for increasing the number of women in educational administration. Many strategies exist for women to become familiar with administration and what it entails. The women in leadership positions are bringing a variety of skills and talents to the positions and a "new look" to administration. While they spend longer in teaching before becoming administrators, they bring a wealth of knowledge and experience to these positions as a result.

The participants in this study suggested a number of strategies for helping women teachers learn more about administration. One idea was to encourage having different teachers to take on the principal's responsibilities when that individual is away. This is one way to introduce women to the role of principal and what it entails. Another suggestion was to rotate administrative positions every few years in order to allow more interested teachers the chance to experience these roles with the knowledge that they were not making a lifetime commitment.

> I think it would be a great sense of empowerment and also, it's easy enough to sit in these positions and criticize sometimes but let's all have a chance to do it and then I think we'd realize a whole lot better the kinds of pressure people are up against.

Programs such as Leadership 2000 can give women teachers the confidence to believe in themselves and their abilities to hold administrative positions. All school districts should implement such programs.

Also, the networking process which takes place gives women holding administrative positions or women interested in becoming administrators an opportunity to meet other women with similar interests.

Yet the glass ceiling cannot truly be said to be broken yet. The strategies which exist to encourage women to enter administration are not uniformly available in all school districts. There is a danger that in tough economic times the strategies which help women become administrators will fall victim to budget cuts, as happened with the tuition bursaries. Barriers and obstacles to women becoming educational administrators do exist. They exist in the form of attitudes which claim that women cannot or should not do the job, particularly at the junior high school and senior high school levels. They exist in the form of the image of an effective school administrator as a "tough guy." They exist in the form of societal expectations that women will shoulder the major responsibility for homemaking and child rearing.

Women must be valued for the skills and talents they bring to administration rather than being compared to traditional concepts of administration. We need an overall commitment on the part of government to bring women into leadership positions. We also need to see those government policy statements translated into action at the school district level. Until school administration is seen as a woman's rightful place, the sunroof will only slide back to admit a few and the glass ceiling will not be broken.

References

Department of Education (1992). *School directory.* Fredericton: Department of Education.

Edson, S. (1988). *Pushing the limits: The female administrative aspirant.* Albany, NY: State University of New York Press.

Excellence in education. Fredericton: New Brunswick Department of Education.

Gill, B. (1994). *Educators and visionaries: Women in educational administration in New Brunswick.* Research Report for Grant No. UNB 24-66. ERIC Document Reproduction Service No. ED 368 035.

Morrison, A., White, R., Van Velsor, E., & the Center for Creative Leadership (1987). *Breaking the glass ceiling: Can women reach the top of America's largest corporations?* Reading, MA: Addison-Wesley.

NBTA Women's Issues in Education Committee (1992). *Toward fair hiring procedures in New Brunswick.* Fredericton: New Brunswick Teachers' Association.

Schmitt, N., & Cohen, S. (1990). *Criterion-related validity of the National Association of School Principals' Assessment Centre.* Reston, VA: NASSP.

Schmuck, P., & Schubert, J. (1986). *Women administrators' views on sex equity: Exploring issues of information, identity and integration.* Paper presented at the Annual Meeting of the American Educational Research Association (Washington, DC, November 13-15, 1986). ERIC Document Reproduction Service No. ED 309 457.

Shakeshaft, C. (1989). *Women in educational administration.* Newbury Park: Sage.

6

Diminishing Participation by Women as School Administrators in Quebec

Claudine Baudoux
(translated from French by Mark Dobbie)

What explains the fact that, in Québec, in the last thirty years, there has been a progressive decline in the proportion of administrative positions filled by women in schools? The situation was well known by the end of the 1960s: in a letter published in the March, 1968 issue of *Chatelaine*, an anonymous woman deplored the fact that so few women held high-ranking positions in education.

In the educational community itself, women teachers were the first to complain of the restricted access to administrative positions and of the additional effort necessary to attain them. In 1975, principal Marjolaine Ducharme took the trouble to translate an article, from an American journal, about the absence of women candidates during the hiring process for administrative positions in schools (McIntyre, 1975), and to have it published in the Quebec journal for administrative personnel *Information*, but there was no response. However, with the notable exception of a 1978 report from the *Conseil du Statut de la Femme* [Counsel on the Status of Women], the gender-related disparity between teaching and administrative personnel, went pretty much without notice, or was judged to be socially irrelevant, for a long time. In the 1980s, women researchers, and the Conseil supérieur de l'Éducation as well, concerned themselves with the relative numbers of men and women principals and vice-principals, both in religious and in secular schools, and pointed directly to the relative absence of women administrators in the school community as a whole (Thivierge, 1981; Clio, et al., 1982; Létourneau, 1982; Dumont and Malouin, 1983; Conseil supérieur de l'Éducation, 1984; Dumont and Fahmy-Eid, 1986).

Introduction to the Study

It was necessary for us not only to establish a systematic portrait of the distortion between the proportion of women teachers and that of women administrators, and of the gradual disappearance of the latter, but also to attempt an explanation of the phenomenon itself. That phenomenon is both complex and paradoxical, given its occurrence at a time when society has been advocating the principle of the equality of the sexes. The situation is all the more surprising, considering that one would usually expect there to be less discrimination in the public sector than in the private sector. In fact, however, statistics prove that access to positions of authority is more difficult for women teachers than for women working in job sectors that are reputed to be more discriminatory. The situation is even more surprising in an educational system that has the responsibility of presenting school girls with role models. What is the explanation for such apparently discriminatory behavior on the part of the government and on the part of local administrations?

Is such possible discrimination the result of unequal treatment stemming from social relations between the sexes? Social relations between the sexes are not constant: they undergo partial distortion and daily erosion. They disappear or undergo metamorphosis imperceptibly or suddenly. That is why GRADE, a multi-disciplinary research team[1], deemed it useful to study the phenomenon of the diminishing participation of women as school administrators in Québec. The scientific interest of the research is all the greater because we are dealing with a profession where women were formerly in the majority.

We wanted to set ourselves apart from traditional models of analysis that centre on individual progress in organizational hierarchies. These models postulate the social equality of the men and women, but diverse forms of discrimination exist. Such discrimination may take the more direct form of refusal to promote a woman because of her sex, or it may be of an indirect, systemic nature, affecting groups rather than individuals, and becoming obvious only after the fact. It may have a historical basis, and indicate the persistence of stereotypes and prejudices. Both types of discrimination, direct and systemic, may be rationalized by decision-makers. A school board, for example, might allege that women teachers applying for administrative roles are too few in number, or that women do not possess the level of credentials required. The problem with this type of reasoning is that the reasons given, even if they were true, might only be so because the women teachers involved have been less encouraged to apply than men, or because, for legal or for social reasons, they have been prevented from acquiring a level of credentials equal to that of their male colleagues.

We now come to the postulates underlying our research. The first postulate deals with the social construction of the sexes referred to as gender. We consider men and women as social constructs. The second postulate is that relations between the sexes are the most fundamental structural element determining admission to administrative positions. In this spirit, we define the organization not as a "thing" but instead as the constantly reactivated product of social relations. Organizations depend first and foremost on the subordination of certain groups. They are in fact the product of several contradictory relationships: between social groups; between organizations and the government; between organizations and their own personnel; between the personnel of different organizations. As such, they are not free of the disorder and conflict, latent or overt, inherent in social relations.

The third postulate is that social relations between the sexes cut across society as a whole. Daune-Richard and Devreux (1986a) have shown that the places occupied by the sexes in different social spheres are reproduced according to the same logic, even though this logic may assume different forms. The relationship between the sexes (including male domination) is a fundamental social relationship assuming a structural role across the whole of society.

The fourth postulate is that social relations linked to sex and gender change over time. Strategies become more refined and, by their existence, prevent the formulation of typical patterns of behavior for men and women. The reproduction of these social relations is not a simple duplication, but rather a complex and continuous process. It is important to analyze not only the perseverance of the phenomena related to the relations between the sexes, but also the transformations of this perseverance. In spite of the persistence and the reproduction of social relations, there does in fact exist a dynamics of social relations that is both changing and contradictory.

We used these postulates to formulate hypotheses. The first is of a historical nature: it states that the gradual disappearance of women administrators is related to transformations that occurred in the educational sector throughout the span of three decades, from 1954 to 1984, and that *each important structural change had a negative effect on women*, if not in the short term, then in the longer term.

The second hypothesis specifies the existence of two roles for women: a formal role, related to employment itself, and an informal role, related to how work is carried out. It suggests the existence of a sexualization of administrative tasks in the educational sector. The feminization of women administrators and the reproduction of the father-mother couple in schools are seen as responses to the necessity of performing tasks by applying qualities that stem traditionally from the private sphere. In our view, *decision-makers, without saying so openly, demand that women administrators possess the qualities that they, the decision-makers, attribute to women*: they appreciate the presumably feminine qualities necessary in professions related to raising babies or to the education of children, and in any profession where helping and caring for people, including hierarchical superiors, is required. In spite of the rapid change in the social status of women in Quebec, certain constants in the functions they are expected or permitted to fulfill remain: functions of service, subordination, and collaboration. Even some administrative positions involve conciliatory duties, a broadening of maternal functions. It is our hypothesis that the dual task of getting the work done and doing it "as women" is an implicit requirement imposed by schools organizations.

The third hypothesis relates to *sexual discrimination*. It states – leaving aside the direct discrimination that continues to be present in organizations – that systemic discrimination takes at least two forms: 1. the choice of criteria that constitute barriers to women candidates, and, at the opposite extreme, 2. different judgments according to sex based on the same criterion. Underlying such discrimination is the general habit of rendering women invisible.

Since we wanted to study the effects of the relationship of domination on representations and practices, and the evolution of the interactions between practices and representations, along with their possible contradictions, we have given preference to a multireferential approach (i.e., an approach calling upon several disciplines, several methods and several paradigms). We have had recourse to several disciplines: administration, history, sociology, anthropology, and psychoanalysis.

It was a matter, among other things, of studying what theories in the area of administration say about the behavior of women as administrators, to enable us to verify whether there exists, as is sometimes stated, a typically feminine approach to administration. At the same time, it was necessary to distinguish clearly between the use of authority in a given position and the access to that position, which remains the focus of our research.

Anthropological analysis enables one to apprehend the elements in organizational culture, in its imaginative centre and its symbolism, that block women's careers. Attention to the symbolic dimension of language is also involved.

The phenomena of authority, authorization, relationships with the father and mother, and with knowledge and power, may be interpreted in the light of what psychoanalytical theories say. In particular, psychoanalysis applied to the organizational context, as developed by Enriquez (1983; 1987), in a non-sexist way, can contribute to a better understanding of the phenomena we wish to study.

We situate government policies and the evolution of roles and practices in their social and cultural context. We place the struggles and strategies of the men and women actors in a historical perspective and set in relief not only the mechanisms by which women working in education have been placed in a minority position, but also their struggles and contributions that have gone unrecognized. We have chosen to break the period of our observations into three decades articulated at three important dates: 1954-55, 1964-65, and 1974-75. In its historical aspect, the research follows the structural development of the educational system in Quebec and its effect on the presence of women in decision-making structures. It examines the evolution of the role and tasks of people in positions of authority in educational establishments, and the evolution of related social representations as well.

The research proceeded through several different stages:

1. During an exploratory stage of the research, we attempted to verify the following;

   i. to what extent women principals and vice-principals have the same access to resources as their male counterparts, based on variables of a professional order; and

   ii. whether tasks are differentiated on the basis of sex (Baudoux, 1986a).

2. In parallel, in 1986, we organized a colloquium entitled "Gestion de l'éducation au féminin" [Educational Administration: the views of women], in which about a hundred women, for the most part administrators or teachers, from all levels of the educational system, took part (Baudoux, 1986b).

3. We established a statistical portrait of change in the composition of personnel according to sex, at the elementary and secondary levels.

4. At the more specific level of organizational administrative practices, the selection process reveals itself to be critical. In an exploratory study combining interviews and analysis of documents, we attempted not so much to quantify discriminatory practices (i.e., to know to what extent administrative practices in educational establishments were wanting in one way or another), as to list, systematically and as exhaustively as possible, the various obstacles preventing access to administrative positions that women are likely to encounter during the selection process.

5. With the permission of the Commission d'accès à l'information [Access-to-Information Commission], we analyzed the records of white-collar workers at the Ministry of Education (denominalized PERCOS record). This allowed us, for example, to discover an emerging trend for school boards to grant temporary administrative positions to men rather than to women.

6. The selection process is often examined by researchers according to its explicit form and criteria. Few have shown, however, at stage 4 (Baudoux et Girard, 1990), that these apparently objective criteria are defined in various ways and valuated differently by committee members. In addition, the criteria vary from one school board to another, and even from one hiring process to another. It is therefore necessary to use the indirect method of comparing, according to sex, the characteristics present among all teaching personnel with those among accepted candidates, in an attempt to capture certain, usually implicit, criteria and certain latent characteristics demanded of women and men candidates.

7. We also conducted interviews with women and men school principals, active and retired. We also interviewed individuals possessing special knowledge, based on their previous experience, their research, or both.

Our research has both a synchronic and a diachronic perspective. The diachronic perspective, making use of statistics, quantitative data, and interview materials, allows us to single out certain factors that may have caused the progressive disappearance of women from positions of authority. The synchronic perspective makes use of a variety of methods: interviews, questionnaires, analysis of documents, etc.

The Reversal of Statistics

What is the general situation with respect to the declining proportion of women administrators in elementary and secondary schools? Table 1 shows the relative numbers of men and women in administration at the preschool, elementary, and secondary levels, in public and private schools, Catholic and Protestant, from 1958-1959 to 1984-1985. There is a constant decline in the proportion of women administrators at the elementary and secondary levels for the entire period. It would have been interesting to be able to go back before 1958-1959 to learn in which year this proportion was at its highest. For lack of data, we cannot determine whether 1958-1959 was a peak year, or, instead, part of a declining tendency, either recent or of long standing.

Practices Excluding Women

At the organizational level, what are the practices than can exclude women? It is worth remembering that all organizations, regardless of type, need inequality, and that gender difference gives those in power the advantage of justifying a hierarchy of the sexes and using it in regard to roles, tasks, and salaries. But on the subject of this gender difference, we agree with Delphy (1991) and Guillaumin (1992) in stating that women are not excluded from power because they are different, but that women are established as different because they are excluded from power. Society does of course have various mechanisms that allow for the credibility of the meritocratic principles that are supposed to govern institutions. Some exceptional women do get through the many structural obstacles that stand in their way. But several manifestations of social relations between the sexes do keep many women away from the more powerful positions, including those in educational administration.

Table 1

Changes in the Composition of Administrative Personnel According to Sex, from 1958-59 to 1984-85, Including Public and Private Sectors, Catholic and Protestant Schools, Preschool, Elementary and Secondary Levels

Year	Men	Women	Total	Percent Women[2]
58-59	1278	1833	3111	59
59-60	1424	1974	3398	58
60-61	1443	2008	3451	58
61-62	1695	2152	3847	56
62-63	1936	2318	4254	54
63-64	2080	2309	4389	53
64-65	2561	2388	4949	48
65-66	2197	1980	4177	47
66-67	2873	2142	5015	43
67-68	3193	2277	5470	42
68-69	3398	2175	5573	39
69-70	5195	3020	8215	37
70-71	5374	2764	8138	34
71-72	5798	2641	8439	31
*72-73	–	–	4264	–
*73-74	–	–	4435	–
*74-75	–	–	4534	–
75-76	3191	1481	4582	32
76-77	2958	1289	4247	30
77-78	2946	1209	4155	29
78-79	2924	1128	4052	28
79-80	2900	1088	3988	27
80-81	2925	1067	3992	27
81-82	2834	1030	3864	27
82-83	2802	985	3787	26
83-84	2784	929	3713	25
84-85	2678	852	3530	25

*The Ministry of Education did not compile statistics for these years.

The Required-Femininity Hypothesis

A women has to have more qualities. I'm asked to be competent technically, in my relations, to be good with children, to be everything. A man's competent because he's a man; they don't ask him to be as good because he's a man. Women get asked to act like mothers, men get asked to act like fathers . . . A man has administrative things to take care of. A woman gets involved in school life, gets to know the children. They ask the same of a women as of a man, but expect her to go overboard. Men get allowed to interact with the kids in ways that women could never get away with. (Josiane)

The images of mother and couples and the notion of the complementarity of the sexes spring up everywhere in our findings. Although a majority of women administrators did wish to express their "femininity," and many of them actually do so, the interviews studied show that they tend to give pride of place to professionalism and competence in matters within the school environment and also in external relations. Women administrators, since they are obliged to do more and frequently have their authority contested, tend to compensate by concentrating on the work at hand. Such qualities commonly attributed to women as being dependable and concerned with quality, in addition to their own involvement and determination, help them to "prove themselves" in a difficult environment. Women being involved to too great an extent is occasionally deplored by men administrators and even by some women administrators themselves.

Employers' expectations for women are linked to what they presume women's roles in the private sphere to be (ways of working or of behaving at work, patience, diplomacy, attentiveness, physical appearance). At the elementary level, since 1975, the image of Joan of Arc has occasionally been put forth. However, it is the figure of the mother that predominates at all educational levels, most notably at the secondary level.

According to our results, women head schools with younger students and with students suffering from a variety of handicaps. In addition, they are consulted less often formally than informally, in the latter case fulfilling the role of secret advisor. Furthermore, they apparently project themselves as less authoritative, look after issues related to teaching, and face greater expectations of showing their allegiance to authorities and of accepting manifestations of paternalism.

The image of the mother is particularly striking in the world of education, especially at the secondary level. That does not mean that women teachers who are also mothers are privileged when it comes to being recruited for administrative positions. In fact, there is even a certain taboo in schools with respect to the family: women are not supposed to bring their family cares to work and they are recruited for positions of authority less often because of a fear that the work environment will be upset by their absences resulting from sickness in the family.

It is more a question of symbolic maternity, exercised with students or with teaching personnel ("my children," "my teachers," even "my men" can be read in the texts of interviews studied). It was already the case that nuns were to be solicited as spiritual mothers (Spielvogel, 1990). Certain characteristics were appreciated in women candidates during the selection process. For example, being the oldest child in the family (second mother), was valued at all three educational levels; being head of a religious or charitable group was valued at elementary and secondary levels; not fearing to use words charged with emotional content when making speeches was valued at the secondary level.

If maternal femininity is being sought after to such an extent, especially at the secondary level, the phenomenon can be linked to the implicit or explicit search for father-mother "couples" to head educational establishments. Statistics indicate that the reproduction of the father-mother couple usually occurs according to a hierarchy leading to traditional placement of the sexes: men as principals, women as vice-principals in charge of teaching. Men vice-principals wind up in the professional sector, as though there were no professional sector for women.

Characteristics associated with the feminine gender are also valued in women during the selection process, especially at the secondary level. Appreciation is granted to those who are relatively silent and to those who consider it is their job to be indirect rather than direct.

This confinement of women to stereotyped roles also explains their lack of success during recruitment. While administrators hired between 1964-1965 and 1974-1975 appear to have had recourse to attitudes and behavior of a somewhat "macho" nature, those hired during the last decade studied showed attitudes and behavior transcending sexual roles and occasionally linked to traditional femininity. There is thus a manifestation of reversibility of gender among administrators during the last two decades covered in our study, caused in part by the decisions of selection committees. It appears that male administrators, in contrast to their female counterparts, now have the advantage of being able to count on their masculine traits (paternal authority) as well as their feminine traits (flexibility, etc.), having perceived the new value of the latter through contact with theories of management.

The Systemic Discrimination Hypothesis

We have a two-part hypothesis with respect to systemic discrimination. During the selection process, decision-makers may:

1. choose criteria or procedures that systematically eliminate women; or, on the contrary,

2. using the same criterion, judge men and women differently (a phenomenon of reactivated prejudices and stereotypes).

Differing Judgments According to Sex, Based on the Same Criterion

On many points, female candidates are judged differently than male candidates. This is especially true at the secondary level, where problems occur not only with selection, but also with encouragement offered to get people to apply, and with the phenomenon of favoritism.

Another recurring theme is an underlying one: the fear of women. Perhaps this fear should be thought of as paradoxically linked to the search for the mother: women's focusing on competence may in fact interfere with their advancement, as a result of some men reacting to it, negatively, as dangerous (i.e., as not suited to the image they usually have of "femininity"). If it is not a question of the mythical danger of the Amazon, then it could be that, not far from the mother, looms the archaic mother that must be warded off.

Many of our quantitative findings, too numerous to be included in their entirety in this chapter, (Baudoux, 1994) indicate a veritable fear of career-oriented women. Compared to the way male candidates are received:

– specialized training in school administration is seen in a poor light when it comes to female candidates at the elementary level, while general training in administration is not;

– women who actively seek an administrative position at the secondary level, or who apply without being asked, face relative ostracism, whereas having ambitions, but not showing them, is to their advantage;

– women who consider that they hold power in their teaching job are less likely to be hired than their male colleagues;

– taking initiative at work in a very visible way brings lower regard to female candidates than to male candidates at the secondary level;

– being well known in the work place is less of an advantage for female candidates at the secondary level; actions that bring visibility to women teachers at the secondary level, such as delivering important speeches, appear to meet with appreciation only if they are legitimated by male mentors;

– manifesting a desire for mobility, on the part of a woman, is not well regarded at the secondary level;

– women administrators with a strong involvement in their schools are sometimes not well respected.

What is the explanation for the fear of women illustrated in the following excerpts from interviews?

Lately, I went through something awful. There was an opening for a Directeur des Services Éducatifs [Director of Instructional Services]. We got together to talk about our priorities. One of the men principals said that his only priority was "sex," and that he didn't want a women that year. I couldn't believe it. There was no way I was going to argue with him, out of respect for myself. I didn't want to waste my time on someone so stupid. I wasn't about to scream because he had the nerve to say such a thing. All I said was: "Can I count on the support of the men principals, because I'd like to apply for the job. I'm a woman; are you going to go along with Mr. X if I apply? Because I'm not going to apply without your support." The room was like ice. People were very uncomfortable. M. X's idea was rejected. *That man is afraid of women.* He said there were too many women in the school district (Josiane. Our emphasis.)

There's rivalry between men and women administrators about the challenges facing us. I'm the only woman vice-principal in the school [among men vice-principals] and the principal is a woman. I'm not saying that it's done on purpose, or that it's selfish or cruel, but my life [at the school] is based on rivalry. *They're afraid of me.* Sometimes they make little wise cracks. The women principal told me so; "we bother them" (Irma. Our emphasis.)

There are lots of competent, qualified women in the school district who could apply for a top position. But they don't do it, even if their competence is recognized. In a "macho' school district, *even if you're competent, it's really, really threatening, because the men are afraid of falling behind.* (Gina. Our emphasis.)

These quotes certainly indicate that men are afraid of stronger competition, not only amongst themselves, but also between men and women.

This perspective enables one to understand why women in educational organizations, both candidates and functioning administrators, whether they realize it or not, are still somewhat "under surveillance." They are asked to prove their loyalty more often than are men administrators. Apparently, they are more often on the receiving end of paternalistic behavior (advice, criticism), regardless of educational level; they are supposed to be more sensitive to taboos concerning the family, at the secondary level; they are expected to seek the company of authorities and to participate in social activities related to their career.

Criteria that Exclude Women

Systemic discrimination can be accomplished by means of criteria that systematically exclude a given social category. This type of systemic discrimination occurred most of all in previous decades, when competition for administrative positions was especially fierce. Its effects could be catastrophic for some potential candidates who are female. The rejection of applications from women could take the form of favoritism such as giving preference to candidates who were also executive members of social clubs for men only, under the pretense that such clubs could give financial support to extracurricular activities. Such discrimination could also show up in the way that previous experience in administration was taken into account, since there seemed to be a preference for giving temporary administrative appointments to men. Such appointments were made without the involvement of a selection committee.

The marginalization of women was accomplished through criteria for training and experience. Women teachers had less training, but more experience: emphasis was placed on training. Whether such practices were intentional or not, every time the average amount of training of women teachers reached a new level, a corresponding increase in requirements occurred automatically in the following year. Moreover, for women teachers, increased training did not always translate into improved access to administrative positions: at the end of the 1960s, women teaching in elementary schools were more likely to have a university education than their male colleagues, but they found themselves at the elementary school level simply because they were women. In the same spirit, requirements for experience were based on the experience of men teachers alone. All of these criteria acted as filters to exclude a large number of female applicants.

Selection Procedures that Exclude Women

When we began our research, we were convinced that there were proportionately fewer women teachers applying for administrative positions than men teachers. School administrators, male and female, as well as university professors working in the area of school administration that had been on selection committees, were all of that opinion. Our results clearly show that this was not the case. As we have no reason to doubt the experience of those just mentioned, we must conclude that the elimination of female candidates occurs mainly during preselection (i.e., at the stage where it is determined who will be called in for an interview).

It must also be emphasized that close to a third of positions are filled without a selection committee being formed. This situation is to men's advantage: selection committees do discriminate against women, but not as much as favoritism (without a selection committee), especially at the secondary level. Criteria for favoritism reflect a number of prejudices and concerns about women. For example, preference is given to women candidates who

1. are more focused on their work (less likely to be married, less likely to be mothers, who bring fewer cares for their families to work, and who consider life at work to be more important than life at home;

2. have greater experience or training (professional, non teaching-experience, training in administration);

3. are more unassuming (having less power in their place of work, receiving less recognition for their actions, less self-confident);

4. are more deferential (who are the object of remarks about their appearance, who seek the company of authorities);

5. are more "masculine" (acting with less tact while at work, excelling less at conciliation, less attentive to non-verbal expression, less inclined to seek consensus at meetings, less skilled in personal relations. Before 1964, women teachers with training in administration and heading economic,

political, religious or charitable organizations, were more likely to be hired in the absence of a selection committee.

The composition of selection committees was also discriminatory, since almost all of them were composed exclusively of men or had men in the majority, in spite of the strong numerical presence of women in the educational sector. Thus female candidates were interviewed in a context less favorable to them than to male candidates. It also bears repeating that, according to statistics from the Department of Education, temporary administrative positions were offered most often to men teachers, who usually were confirmed in the following year.

Practices that Render Women Invisible

One of the ways in which discrimination continued to be expressed was through practices seeking to erase the presence of women. Numerous examples exist. Differences in access to positions of authority was of little interest to those in the educational milieu. Reports presented to educational commissions deal little, if at all, with the discrimination that young women faced. In discussions bearing on the lack of inspectors, there was no consideration of the possibility of hiring women. Statistics according to sex are lacking for much of the 1970s. It was most of all through symbolic means and through the absence of feminized language that the presence of women was obliterated. This "forgetting" about women had an effect on their access to resources (smaller schools, thus smaller salaries, smaller staffs, and fewer services) and on their daily work (less frequent consultation emanating from school boards, and an advisory capacity within the school).

The Strategies of Women Administrators

Given their subjection to unequal treatment, women administrators have had recourse to a variety of strategies of survival, accommodation, and activism. Although these strategies are rarely clear and coherent viewed from outside, they do represent an expression of choice and a grasp of the chances afforded to men and women acting within a given set of constraints. These strategies are not the mechanical result of submissive behavior or of the powers that be; nor are they completely predictable, but, on the contrary, they are contingent. Women do not all apply the same strategies, nor in the same circumstances. Women have their own gender-determined perspective on educational organization, depending on the idiosyncratic coloration given them during primary and secondary socialization, on structural perspectives of mobility, and on the culture of their work place. Depending on circumstances, women may adopt an attitude of resignation or of mobilization. In this way, and through the opportunities they consider to be more or less favorable to their objectives, women administrators become differentiated from one another.

It bears repeating that many women administrators resign from their positions and return to teaching. To our great regret, we were unable to reach this group of people. It may be assumed, however, that the questioning of their authority, on a regular basis, and the continual challenges arising from sexual stereotypes lead some women to abandon administrative positions.

Those Who Accept The Status Quo

I never noticed any reaction to me because I was a woman. Sexism is all through society. You might find it with men administrators or with some women who find themselves wronged in relation to a man. We've both got to prove ourselves. (Éliane)

In general, we help each other out a lot as administrators. We tell one another just about everything, including what we hear people say about the school. I feel very comfortable with the men administrators, I don't feel any discrimination. Maybe I've found the right way to assert myself by using my personality. (Fanny)

You earn your place at the table little by little. You raise a point; it's accepted or rejected. With some men, after they speak, it's as though they hadn't said anything. Others get a lot more respect, and the same goes for women. (Nina)

If I went back into administration, there would be twenty-five men and two women; I wouldn't be happy with so few women, I'd prefer half and half. I feel good when I feel truly represented. But I never felt unwelcome, even if I was the only woman. Affinities went more with age than with sex. (Hélène)

Although many women administrators often experience discrimination, many of them refuse to admit it. It is well known, in this regard, that the strongest denials of oppression come from the victims of oppression (Mathieu, 1985). This refusal may take one of two forms: disavowal (refusal to recognize oppression) or negation (denial that an idea or sentiment, beginning to arise from one's discomfort, applies to oneself). A form of disavowal may be observed with Nina and with Hélène (there is no discrimination), and a form of negation, with Éliane and with Fanny (there is sexism throughout society, but not towards me; I don't feel any discrimination, but maybe it's because of my qualities).

Many studies have shown that, at the beginning of their careers, women do not perceive the obstacles set in their way. Such obstacles are in fact insidious and only reveal themselves when women administrators compare the way they are treated (when they are aware of it) with the way men administrators are treated. Éliane seems to consider the sexes as socially equal and, with this way of looking at things, finds that women may occasionally be sexist with respect to men. As happens with many women, far from giving up on the fulfillment of their aspirations, women administrators target themselves, hunting down their tiniest fault (Fahmy, 1992a), going so far as to accuse themselves of sexism!

Negation allows one to avoid the traumatic and humiliating experience of seeing oneself as oppressed. With respect to women administrators in particular, Erickson (1984) explains the negation of discrimination as a survival mechanism. If women administrators were aware of the discrimination against them, they would have to face up to it and take steps against it, endangering their careers and their everyday relations in the organization.

> When you accept an administrative position, I think, first of all, you have to get away from ideas of fighting against men. You might tell yourself "Yes, I'd like to help," but I don't have to carry the weight of the women's movement on my shoulders. but, of course, I'll help whenever I can. (Sidonie)

> I've never asked myself "will being a woman hurt me?" I often say that I don't have the time to be a feminist. (Yolande)

> And my male colleagues told me: "It's funny, with you we never got the feeling we were being censored. You laughed with us." And I think that's important; as women, we have to fight for things, but not just anything. Fighting against colleagues because they tell stories, because it's a bit sexist, I don't think that's the way to improve things for women. (Sidonie)

This strategy of refusing feminist behavior, whether intermittently or not, is used by women administrators who do not want to become conscious of the fact that women are seen first and foremost as women, independently of their talents and efficiency.

> As a woman on the school board, at meetings chaired by a man, maybe others have felt differences, but I've never felt that favoritism was shown to men's ideas, maybe because I'm very involved in all questions of administration and teaching. (Hélène)

Conforming with stereotypes, on the part of women, is implicit acceptance of their being treated as though they had given "natural" modes of behavior: as mothers, virgins, seductresses, and mascots (Kanter, 1977). The stereotype of the mother is especially striking in the educational environment, at all levels, but especially at the secondary level. At the elementary and college levels, it cohabits with another extremely common stereotype: the virgin.

Some women resort to strategy, letting men speak first and then repeating several of their ideas, in order to appear competent in the men's eyes:

> At the school board, men are in the majority around the table. *The strategy is to let them speak first.* Because you've kind of got the impression, being in a minority of women, that you're from Mars. Then you start bringing out your own viewpoint, with some of the men's ideas. Then they take you seriously. They think you've got a head on your shoulders, and the idea you slipped in with theirs is accepted. (Corinne. Our emphasis.)

Others use their own bag of tricks (gentleness, pretending to be submissive) as in the case of Nina:

With some directeurs de service [directors of services, assistant superintendents] if you try to talk to them as equals, you've got a 60 percent chance of having your project refused. *So, without saying so, you have to hint "I know it's in your power to say no, but I think it's a good project, and there are loads of reasons why you should say yes." I let him know he's the one with the power.* It's a way of negotiating with him. But I never had to promise to sleep with anybody to get what I wanted. I don't think it happens much between school administrators and school boards members. (Nina. Our emphasis.)

This strategy, if it is widely used, has the disadvantages of making the leadership of women principals less effective and of helping to sustain prejudices against women.

I think that, whether you're a man or a woman, the important thing is to be competent. It is true that, in some environments, when a woman is asked to be competent, she has to be twice as competent. (Rose)

Women work more and get more involved in their work. (Monique)

Women administrators are overall more competent than men, I'm sure of it. (Monique)

You have to work more if you want to be considered as an equal. I think that still holds true in administration. If you're a woman, you have to work more to become known for your effectiveness, for preparing files better... (Bernadette)

A woman always has to be twice as good as a man. (Bernadette)

We have seen that competence is a recurring theme in our interviews of women administrators and that they tend to overestimate the true usefulness of competence. But perhaps it is one of the only means of support left to them. Many women administrators, not being able to have a strong influence on the structural and cultural constraints around them, have recourse to the single thing they can change: themselves. Some try to get the acceptance of men by attempting to interest themselves in the men's activities. Sidonie bears witness to such behavior:

With my colleagues, I have to say that the men tell me: "The funny thing is we didn't have a problem with you because we never had the feeling you were waging a feminist war against us." Well, I've always worked with a majority of men, and I've often said to the male colleagues under my authority; 'Everybody knows you guys have two topics of conversation: there's sports and there's sex. So apart from that, there's not much to be expected." And they'd laugh and laugh. I'm not one to take offense automatically; I've always laughed a lot, so I make a good audience. When you work with a team of men, they talk about sports a lot, most of them. Right now, I like going to hockey games, and I'm pretty much up on everything; when we discuss things outside of work, I know what to say. At first, I wasn't that interested, but I said to myself: "It's something that interests them," and I made an effort to become interested in it. (Sidonie)

Thus, it is women who are obliged to become interested in activities traditionally thought of as masculine, and not the other way around.

Resorting to humor in sexist situations is one of the strategies women administrators use most. Rose, Irma and Zoé bear witness to this:

I'm often helped out by humor in situations where I could take offense at things. (Rose. Our emphasis)

Sometimes they make clever remarks to tease you, but I have my say too; *I kid around like that. At times it isn't easy.* (Irma, Our emphasis.)

The men tease me [with sexual jokes], there are two or three people on my staff, [they] don't flirt with me in a vulgar way, but they take that route to tease me. And *sometimes they don't quite know how to talk to a woman boss. So they'll talk to the woman, instead of talking to the boss. I know lots of women who would feel uncomfortable. But I find it amusing, and I know how to tease too.* (Zoé. Our emphasis.)

Those Who Want to Alter the Status Quo

While women administrators would put themselves in jeopardy if they had recourse to confrontational strategies, they do shape an identity for themselves, as a group, by developing cultural skills geared to rebellion against the patriarchal constraints of the organization.

Women administrators remind people of their authority with the intention of imposing recognition of their legitimate right to occupy an administrative position (frequent reminders of their competence given to parents, police, etc.). With respect to interpersonal relations, they impose certain rules of behavior, at the risk of being labeled as authoritarian or puritanical:

I told them when I first started working with them, that I didn't accept vulgarity. People knew what to expect, and I've always been completely strict about it. I could never stand dirty jokes. And the guys knew it. They've never told any when I've been around. (Bernadette)

The risks that go with confrontational strategies are high. Labeled as intolerant, aggressive, domineering, even as castrators, women in administration who adopt them may isolate themselves and thereby reduce their effectiveness as administrators.

Women administrators are close to men who have changed. Men like that are usually more competent, more capable, more up to date. They seem to have more of the traits we women have. In any case, we get along better. There are men who relate to people. It depends on the individual . . . Others haven't changed . . . (Monique)

On the other hand, others don't make remarks and are very open-minded, they encourage us, give us advice, tell us not to give in and not to let ourselves be stepped on. (Fanny)

Some women try to create an anti-sexist culture for themselves in some of the informal gaps in the organization:

Sometimes when feminist concerns are raised, things get pretty interesting. One thing that I see often, for example, is that men tend to get together with one another at meetings to talk about their concerns; so you always wind up with the men off to one side and the women together. The men here know what to expect from the women and they accept it. Last year, the school had a publicity campaign, and of course our priorities in the campaign centred around the women on the staff. Our former students are women, our present students are women; so we didn't hesitate to promote the female side of things. *We insisted that all the photographs for the publicity show women.* So we chose women teachers, because this is a girls' school. It was done on purpose. The men talked about their existence being neglected in the school, but finally accepted it. So we got to be privileged, and it was great. (Diane. Our emphasis)

I know I can really count on my secretary. She knows when I can be disturbed, but she also knows that I'm receptive and available with respect to any problem that may arise. *We make a great team, because there's a rapport between us and our actions are always headed in the same direction.* (Fanny. Our emphasis.)

As can be seen from the above interview excerpts, and from the various practices of female sponsorship and encouragement that we have noted, women administrators often show their solidarity with other women – secretaries, teachers, and colleagues.

A final strategy, at the organizational level, involves support for equal opportunity programs. These efforts lead to formal actions of a socio-political and legal nature that have a greater impact on women in general. Our results indicate that female candidates who are radical feminists currently have a better chance of being selected, at all three educational levels. Thus, changing organizational realities may be possible through political struggles that concern all women. Feminist administrators, through collaboration and solidarity with the other women administrators and with women teachers, and through collaboration with their male and female allies in the educational milieu may be able to change the milieu. In our view, it is a question of introducing administration from a feminist perspective, and rejecting various forms of social exclusion.

Although one may still observe that many decision-makers ignore the statistics on administrative personnel and suffer from veritable amnesia with respect to the past, in spite of the introduction of equal opportunity programs in the educational milieu, such programs have begun a revolution in the work place. These programs are essential. We need to eradicate discrimination and put an end to prejudice. But it's still a rough road: in 1985, 48 percent of school boards did not believe that it was useful and relevant to set up equal opportunity programs for women, while 265 judged them to be useful (Fédération des Commissions Scolaires [Federation of School Boards], 1986).

An End To Masculinization?

Statistics indicate that equal opportunity programs, though limited to nineteen school boards and twelve CEGEPs[2], have created a favorable environment for the hiring of women administrators. In 1990-1991, (MEQ, 1992), the proportion of women in administration was 28 percent, a rise of 4 percent since the introduction of equal opportunity programs. These figures, however, illustrate a clear underrepresentation of women in administrative positions. In spite of the recent increase accompanying equal opportunity programs, the proportion of women in administration is much lower than that of women in teaching. Thus, vigilance is necessary. We must prevent this small amount of progress from being short-lived, especially, when, as in the 1950s, educational authorities in Quebec appear interested in boys and men alone and show little will to impose equal opportunity programs. Henceforth, people will need to demand the right to a career, regardless of their sex. Educational organizations are products of their culture, and, for that very reason, reflect social discrimination. Official discourse makes claims about abandoning discrimination. The government, the school boards, and the CEGEPs have the responsibility of putting these words into practice. Organizations also produce culture. Accordingly, it is their task to work for a truly diverse environment.

Notes

[1] The GRADE team includes Claudine Baudoux, director; Claire V. de la Durantaye, co-director; Lysanne Langevin; Claudette Lasserre; Sylvie Girard; Céline Desjardins; Flore Dupriez; Martine Matteau. Funding has been provided by the SSHRC and the FCAR, to whom we express our thanks.

[2] Principals and Vice-principals

[3] CEGAP; acronym for Collège d'Enseignement Général et Professionnel [College of General and Vocational Education]. (translators note)

References

Baudoux, C. (1986a). *Directeurs et directrices d'école: Environnement, missions, activités.* Montréal: FQDE.

Baudoux, C. (1986b). *Gestion de l/éducation au féminin.* Chicoutimi: UQAC.

Baudoux, C. (1994). *La gestion en éducation: une affaire d'hommes au de femmes.* Québec: Presses Inter Universitaries.

Baudoux, C.,& Girard, S. (1990). Sélection de candidatures féminines dans les postes de direction d'écoles et de collèges. *Revue des sciences de l'éducation, XVI(2),* 163-183.

Clio, collectif (1982) (Dumont, M., Jean, M., Lavigne, M., and Stoddart, J., second edition, 1985 and third edition 1992]. *L'histoire des femmes au Québec depuis quatre siècles.* Montréal: Quinze.

Conseil du Statut de la Femme (1978). *Pour les Québécoises: Égalité et indépendance.* Québec: Éditeur Officiel.

Conseil Supérieur de L'Éducation (1984). *La situation des femmes dans le système d'enseignement: Une double perspective.* Québec: Gouvernement du Québec.

Daune-Richard, A.M., & Devreux, A.M. (1986). La reproduction des rapports sociaux de sexe. In *A propos des rapports sociaux de sexe.* Parcours épistémologiques. Paris: Centre de sociologie urbaine-CNRS-IRESCO, re-edited 1990, 117-233.

Delphy, C. (1991). Penser le genre: Quels problèmes? In M. C. Hurtig, M. Kail, and H. Rouch (Eds.), *Sexe et genre. De la hiérarchie entre les sexes* (pp. 89-102). Paris: CNRS.

Dumont, M., & Fahmy-Eid, N. (1986). *Les couventines.* Montréal: Boréal-Express.

Dumont, M., & Malouin, M.P. (1983). Évolution et rôle des congrégations religieuses enseignantes féminines au Québec, 1840-1900. *Société canadienne d'histoire de l'église catholique, 50,* 201-230.

Enriquez, E. (1983). *De la horde à l'État.* Paris: Gallimard.

Enriquez, E. (1987). Personnalité et organisation. In D. Dejeux (Ed.), *Organisation et management en question(s)* (pp. 11-29). Paris: L'Harmattan.

Erickson, H.L. (1984). Female public school administrators and conflict management. *Dissertation Abstracts International, 45*(5), 1251-A.

Fahmy, P. (1992a). *Femmes entre vie et carrière. Le difficile équilibre.* Montréal: Adage.

Fédération des Commissions Scolaires Catholiques du Québec (1986). *Rapport de la consultation des commissions scolaires sur la condition féminine.* Sainte-Foy: Fédération des commissions scolaires catholiques du Québec.

Guillaumin, C. (1992). *Sexe, race et pratique du pouvoir.* Paris: Côté-Femmes.

Kanter, R. M. (1977). *Men and women of the corporation.* New York: Basic Books.

Klein, M. (1968). *Essais de psychanalyse.* Paris: Payot.

Létourneau, J. (1982). *Les écoles normales de filles au Québec.* Montréal: Fides.

Mathieu, N.C. (1985). Quand céder n'est pas consentir. In N. C. Mathieu (Ed.), *L'arraisonnement des femmes* (pp. 19-23). Paris: Éditions de l'École des Hautes Études en Sciences Sociales.

McIntyre, K.E. (1975, January). Évolution de certains critères de sélection du principal d'école élémentaire aux États-Unis de 1970 à 1972, translation by M. Ducharme of a text edited in *Principal*, NEASP, LIII, 5, 1974. *Information, 14*(5), 19-23.

Spielvogel, M. (1990). La maternité spirituelle: Une analyse du discours sur la vocation religieuse féminine. In L. Vandelac, F. Descarries, G. Gagnon, J. Daigle, M. de Koninck, N. Guberman, and A. Quéniart (Eds.), *Du privé au politique: La maternité et le travail des femmes comme enjeux des rapports de sexes* (pp. 43-55). Montréal: UQAM.

Thivierge, M. (1981). *Les institutrices laïques à l'école primaire catholique au Québec de 1900 à 1964,* doctoral thesis. Québec: Université Laval.

7

Employment Equity For Women:
Toward A Revolution From The Ground Up

Alison Taylor

Introduction

There continue to be far fewer women than men in educational adminis-tration in Ontario, despite the existence of provincial employment equity policies for women for more than twenty years. Instead of remaining within the policy frame that implicitly constructs women as "the problem," as "lacking in ambition," and as "incompetent," the research used in this chapter moves beyond formal policy statements and statistics to explore the experiences of one woman administrator. In my interview with a female secondary school principal, she discussed her career history and reflected on policies that are designed to promote equitable gender relations. The resulting data are useful in pointing out disjunctures or contradictions between policy and practice, and between individual experiences and broader social realities.

Policy Background

Employment equity for women has been a policy issue for the Ontario Ministry of Education for over twenty years. In 1979, the Ministry established an employment equity unit which encouraged school boards to develop pro-grams, defined as follows:

> An affirmative action/employment equity program is a program of special measures and activities whose aim is to diversify as well as to raise the level of occupational opportunities for women. . . . It involves establishing flexible goals and timetables to ensure that qualified women are included, on an equal and competitive basis, in all employment opportunities, and that they are given an equal opportunity to acquire the necessary qualifications and experience. (Employment Opportunity/Affirmative Action Unit, 1989, p. 2)

Although equity programs were to address all women in education, the focus has tended to be on women in administration.

But still the representation of women in positions of added responsibility is far from proportionate. Table 1 presents recent figures for various administrative positions. We can see that, in 1991, only 15.6 percent of public secondary school principals were women (Ministry of Education, 1993, p. 54). The picture is not greatly improved in elementary schools where women held 26.2 percent of principalships in 1991. This underrepresentation exists despite the relatively proactive stance taken by the Ontario Ministry of Education.

Table 1

Representation of Women in Administrative
Positions in Ontario, September 30, 1991

Position	Percent
Director	5.1
Supervisory Officer	17.9
Elementary Principal	26.2
Elementary Vice-Principal	43.6
Secondary Principal	15.6
Secondary Vice-Principal	27.3

Source: Ministry of Education, 1993, p. 54.

For example, in 1988, the Education Minister requested that school boards establish a goal of at least 30 percent representation of women in all positions by the year 2000. Two years later, the Minister raised this goal to 50 percent representation by women for the positions of Supervisory Officer, Principal, and Vice-Principal. Most recently, in 1992, the Education Act was amended to require school boards

> develop and implement a policy of employment equity for women and other groups designated by the Minister, to submit the policy to the Minister for approval and to implement changes to the policy as directed by the Minister. (Ministry of Education, 1993, p. 12)

It is no longer enough to say that there are too few women in educational administration. Rather, it is necessary to begin to understand how women experience positions of added responsibility within the context of employment equity policy. Only then can we begin to understand the implications for women of equity policy in practice. The articulation of experiences encourages other women to understand their own experiences differently, as they begin to comprehend the social construction of discourses around gender and equity.

The Study

With my expressed purpose of understanding how women experience educational administration in the context of employment equity policy, I set out to speak with a woman high school principal. I was interested in speaking with someone in the secondary panel because women have traditionally found it more difficult to break into administration there. Diane agreed to participate and we arranged to meet at her office at school.

I interviewed Diane[1] on two occasions and collected approximately five hours of taped interviews. Interviews were semi-structured in that I had pre-formulated questions, but the dialogue moved away from this agenda as other issues arose. I also spent a day "shadowing" Diane, that is, following her around the school as she carried out her daily routine.

My analysis involved a process of listening to Diane and then constructing a dialogue between her, me, and other theorists who have thought about similar topics (Rossiter, 1988). Therefore, in this chapter, I interweave theory and data.

Career History

Diane originally became qualified as a teacher in the early 1960s when her father, a high school principal, suggested that teaching would be a good way for her to earn some money to pursue graduate studies. But when Diane entered teaching she found that she enjoyed it, and she has pursued a career in education ever since.

Reflecting back on her entry into educational leadership, Diane remembers certain key events. For example she remembers the encouragement of a principal:

> I can remember vividly his calling me into his office, and this must be 17 or 18 years go, and saying to me: "Look, you've got to get your paper qualifications down . . . because you are going to want to go into administration, this is something you should be considering. And then I started thinking about it and thought: "Yes, I do like this . . . this is something that I'm good at." But if it hadn't been confirmed from outside, I'm not sure that I would have gone into it as quickly.

Diane initially received encouragement from male administrators and later from a support group of women colleagues. She describes the thinking that prompted her to apply for an administrative appointment:

> It not only seemed to be something I wanted to do. It seemed to me it was something I had an obligation to do. That I didn't have the right to sort of sit back and say: "Somebody else can do this and somebody else can speak for women." But that there needed to be role models for the young women in our schools. And also, there were other women that I knew who were taking on

these roles – were willing to do the extra work and responsibility – and were enjoying it.

Diane moved into the vice-principal position in 1983, and after five years in that role she became principal at her present school. She is the first woman principal to be employed by this high school and has made a commitment to herself that she will get her supervisory officer papers next year.

Discourse around Gender

Diane is aware that gender relations are also power relations; she knows that historically men have been leaders, and women, subordinates. In our interviews, Diane talked about different manifestations of male power: male norms in administration, male career paths, and social constructions of masculinity and femininity that pose barriers for women entering administration.

In her discussion of women in administration, Diane focused on the relationships between men and women:

A: . . . [I]f I asked you what you think the barriers were, and maybe are for women entering administration all along the way, how would you answer that?

D: Well, they are very basic societal issues which are power issues in society . . . that men have power and see no reason why they should give up power or share it.

Diane's linking of the power involved in gender relations recalls Catharine MacKinnon's (1987) suggestion that

if gender is an inequality first, constructed as a socially relevant differentiation in order to keep that inequality in place, then sex inequality questions are questions of systematic dominance, of male supremacy . . . (p. 42)

Diane has seen and experienced the manifestation of male power in educational administration. For example, she talks about the way she was perceived by staff when she was vice-principal:

I always believed that before I could establish any kind of real consequences that were going to work with the kids, I had to have a relationship with them. That used to drive my teachers crazy . . . So what they tend to do with vice-principals who do that who are female, is they call it your "social work approach": [mimicking] "We don't need a social work approach in the school, we need a vice-principal!"

In this instance, Diane is probably being compared unfavorably to the male norm of vice-principal as strict disciplinarian. A woman educator in Britain describes a similar phenomenon:

John got the headship, he is 6 ft 2, 15 stone, has a loud voice. He plays – he is a bully – and he plays a very hard line in that school. . . . When it comes to the rock solid crunch, there's always an issue for women about control and discipline, and that's the crunch I'm at now. . . . It's to do with needing to be tough to do this job. And it's all couched in male language. (Grant, 1989, p. 46)

Both Diane's experience and that of Grant's informant suggest that the image of how an administrator looks and behaves is powerfully male in the minds of hiring committees and staff (Acker, 1989).

Similarly, in Diane's present position, she is still confronted with having to fit into the existing "male-stream" system. For example, she talks about the Principals' Group[2] in her board:

> I still feel that the group is too competitive, and that if I share information about myself they'll use it. Because everyone's out for things for their own school ... I get the feeling that many people, when they get into a principal's role ... feel that if you're in that role you have to go it alone. .... Except for a couple, they feel very isolated and don't necessarily want to work together.

This environment contradicts Diane's belief in collaboration and cooperation.

Diane is aware that particular norms predominate because of the position that men have held in the past:

> I think the routes [into administration] used to be: male teacher, male head, male mentor, male principal advocate, then the candidate gets into administration.

And although women are gaining access to some administrative positions, the influence of the traditional routes persists:

> ... [A] very interesting OSSTF [Ontario Secondary School Teachers' Federation] survey ... tried to dispel some myths about women ... [For example,] as many women as men were putting in hours after school, in different things from what men were doing. They weren't doing football coaching, which is visible. What they were doing was coaching academic decathlon or doing extra help with kids ... There's a perception on the part of some males that it's only visible people who should be promoted. And that these other people are intruders and are not qualified because they haven't been coaches; they haven't been mentored by the visible males in the system.

Therefore, it is evident to Diane that the informal job requirements of particular administrative posts (such as vice-principal) indicate male preference, as do the ways in which aspirants are perceived to distinguish themselves.

But, it is also the case that the traditional male-defined career path "effectively limits management posts to women without children or those who are prepared to combine the early years of motherhood with a full-time teaching role" (Grant, 1989, p. 44). In other words, the split between private and public – family and work – is distinctly drawn in the eyes of women like Diane. She maintains that women frequently have to give something up in their bid for administration:

> Some of us see that the women who have been most successful are women who are divorced. And therefore, what they've given up is either a husband or a child often, in order to be successful – because there isn't enough time and energy to handle all those things. Or they've given up both and stayed entirely single.

In Diane's case, she and her husband both worked part-time after their son was born, and she continued to be heavily involved in professional activities. She was obviously aware of the penalties for women who take career breaks. Diane also points out that she has been able to pursue a career in administration because her husband is very supportive of her and has not himself been interested in promotion. She realizes that this is probably not the case for many women:

> You either have to be in a relationship which is very supportive – or you have to get out of it – or you have to give up your position . . . You can't live in a relationship where a spouse is constantly saying: "Why aren't you home? . . . Why is it that you can't take so-and-so to hockey? Why is it that I have to be doing it 50 percent of the time, or more? This is *your* job."

The social construction of wife/mother clearly poses barriers for potential female aspirants. Diane suggests that women often do not apply for positions even when encouraged, because for women, "it's never the right time":

> Women say: "If only I get this behind me, and if we have enough money, and if we have a house." And then, "if my husband is established," and then, "if my kids are old enough," and then, "when my kids are in school." I mean, it's never the right time! And once my kids are in school: "Well, I really like the job I'm doing." So you really, women really have to be pushed.

Shakeshaft (1987) suggests that what appears to be women's lack of aspiration "may actually be an accurate reflection of reality in light of home and family responsibilities and job opportunities" (p. 89). As another woman principal comments: "If [women] apply for the job, they're still going to have to raise the kid!"

It has been suggested (Cunnison, 1989; Oram, 1989) that gender reproductive forces tend to operate because the status quo suits the interests of men and that men are therefore unlikely to initiate change. Similarly, when Diane considers the younger generation of male teachers, she does not see a lot of change in their attitudes, or in society's expectations of them:

> Still, there is an expectation that men will be self-sufficient. They will be people who cannot admit when they're wrong. They will be independent. And women will somehow or another . . . drag them into interacting in relationships so that there's nurturing going on, with children and with women. But that's not something that men – most men – seem to need.

Diane's comments bring to mind similar sentiments expressed by one of the women participants in a study of barriers faced by women in the public service:

> There are three waves of male resistance – the older Old Boys' Club; the contemporary movers who view women as competition; and the future wave of neo-conservative university graduates. The resistance is continuous. (Task Force, 1990, Vol. 3, p. 17)

It is clear that Diane is aware of the problems inherent in existing gender relations; she has lived these. She is conscious of the informal expectations associated with success in a career in education that serve to favor men and exclude women. But while Diane frequently adopts a feminist discourse around gender as inequality, she experiences contradictions when it comes to formulating a politics of change. For example, while Diane observes the power differences between women and men in her context, she would like to believe that men will voluntarily give up some of their power. She comments that there is a need for women to work with men "in order to figure out how we can educate our young men to see that there are advantages in sharing power and sharing roles."

However, it may be argued that the advantages for men of sharing power with women are not compelling in a society in which women's work is so devalued (Casey & Apple, 1989). Probably because Diane's style is to collaborate, she does not think that "taking power" is appropriate. At the same time, she recognizes that collaborative approaches take much longer and may not work. The dilemma for her is how to change the existing power relations without reproducing patriarchal practices. This became an important theme in our discussion of employment equity policy.

Discourse around Equity

Equity Policy: Instrument of Liberation or Oppression?

In Findlay's (1987) analysis of the relationship between the Canadian state and the women's movement between 1966 and 1979, she makes the following observation:

> Overall, although an analysis of the process demonstrates the success of the women's movement in pressuring the state to represent women's interests in the policy-making process, it also demonstrates the success of the state in constructing this representation in a way that controlled women's demands and limited reform. (p. 33)

As Pascall (1986) concludes, social policies have contradictory effects for women: "They cannot be understood in one-dimensional fashion, as instruments of oppression or of liberation" (p. 26).

The often double-edged character of state policy may result in feelings of ambivalence among "target group" members. For example, although Diane wants to improve the situations of women in the workplace, she questions three aspects of the policy:

1. The Ministry's commitment to this goal;

2. The existing policy as an instrument of change, and;

3. The Ministry's implementation of equity policy for women.

For example, in the following excerpt, Diane questions the Ministry's motivations:

A: Why do you think the Ministry decided that employment equity for women was necessary?

D: I don't think [the Ministry] ever would have done it on their own. But it's because of the political force of two very strong unions: The Women's Federation, and the Secondary Teachers' Federation.

A: What do you think then, that the Ministry is setting out to do with employment equity?

D: Say that they're doing something. . . . [A]ll they can do is keep it as a visible issue. . . . I think it's very much a monitoring, you know, keep the lid on but make everybody feel happy kind of situation that the Ministry's in. I don't think they have any really major concerns that they're prepared to . . . They can't do a whole lot about it; they don't have any clout.

Diane questions the ability of employment equity policy to bring about change. For example, she focuses on the Ministry's recommendation that boards adopt hiring "targets and timelines," and the Ministry's incentive funding for affirmative action coordinator positions.[3] On the topic of targets and timelines, she says:

Quite truthfully, I think they don't work. [pause] The reason they don't work is because people don't want them to work . . . I mean, what it does is it creates incredible conflict among the people who are competing for those positions . . . So I would not want to be part of that; I think it's enormously frustrating.

Diane has observed that the enforcement of hiring targets and timelines results in a backlash from males in the system, and that this has to be weighed against the benefit of having more women in the system. She adds that there "is more to the issue than women being in positions of responsibility:"

If you get women in positions of responsibility and they're not supported by their male counterparts, or the male hierarchy above them, then they may as well not be there. They're completely ineffective.

From this perspective, the Ministry's focus on statistics[4] appears to be narrow and overly-simplistic. The emphasis on timelines and targets also produces a situation which is ripe for what Apple (1986) describes as the "exporting of blame" onto women (p. 18). He is referring to the tendency to blame women who are entering the labor market for their difficulties rather than examining the dominant mode of economic organization. In Diane's context, there is a similar tendency to blame women for the disappointment experienced by male aspirants instead of considering the governance and economic policies and practices that are associated with public education in Ontario.

As far as the affirmative action coordinator positions go, Diane feels that there is a potential for abuse:

I haven't had direct experience with boards or administrators who have felt totally positive about those positions. And the only way it works is . . . where that coordinator is directly responsible to the Director, and the Director wants to have the position in place. Otherwise, it's much too convenient to shuffle that person off, and say: "Well look, we have this person. Gee, it's too bad things aren't going well. Obviously, she's not doing her job." And that's not good. That, to me, is no answer at all.

Again, the exporting of blame onto people in coordinator positions is likely.

The potential for abuse of the coordinator positions stems, in part, from the funding arrangements made by the Ministry. Between 1985 and 1989, the Ministry Incentive Fund reimbursed boards for the cost of employing an affirmative action coordinator, for up to a maximum of $20 000 in the first year; $18 000 in the second year; and $10 000 in the third year of a board's participation (Ministry of Education, 1987). As a result, many boards made these positions part-time and discontinued the positions once they had received the maximum available funding (Ministry of Education, 1991, p. 11).

As an alternative, Diane suggested that the Ministry might have given incentive funding to boards to put women into "administrator-in-training" positions:

[Y]ou give some money to the board to release a teacher from part of their teaching schedule in order to shadow a person in an administrative position and do some of the tasks. So it's kind of an additional position of responsibility in the school that the school boards cannot afford .... If the Ministry gave some funding for women only to be put into those positions, without making it too large scale, I think that would have an impact.

In summary, Diane would agree that employment equity policy is equivocal. Targets and timelines do not work, in her view, because

men don't want them to work. They don't want them to work because they don't want to give up anything that they have. And I don't know why, humanly, we would expect that they would.

In fact, the policy is also likely to be seen as problematic by women since it is introduced as a program of "special measures" (EO/AA Unit, January 1989). This wording implies that women need preferential treatment in order to compete with men for administrative positions. Therefore, women's *difference* is emphasized as *inferiority* in the wording of the policy itself.

One of the problems with the concept of employment equity is that the inequity that women experience *in employment* is inseparable from wider social relations. Diane recognizes this, and we can hear her frustration in the following passage:

We're not going to make those great huge steps until we are somewhere in the 22nd century when the roles of men and women are more clearly defined. In the sense that they have either decided by that time that they're going to share the child-raising functions, so that men and women can both work part-time and not lose seniority and all of those things ... I mean, unless all those issues get sorted out, we're dealing with a very small segment of women. We may be 51 percent of the population, but you're dealing with such a small segment of the population, in comparison with the male population, who can apply for positions without going crazy, without going completely insane!

Diane clearly feels that there must be societal supports in place for women before the pool of administrative aspirants will increase. She is aware that employment equity policy is only one tool to be used in the fight to bring about equality for women. And, in fact, the double-edged character of that policy prompts her to consider what is the best way to bring about this change.

Evolution or Revolution?

It is evident that Diane faces a contradiction between her realization that men will not willingly give up power, and her collaborative, non-confrontational style which makes her reluctant to suggest that women must take power. For example, when I asked Diane how to increase the numbers of women without hiring only women, this was her response:

> I don't know. [pause] The two views of history, I guess, is that there is the *revolutionary* view and the *evolutionary* view. And [pause] I'm not the kind of person who wants to see . . . If I had to make a choice between our going to war over these issues and fewer women being in positions of responsibility, I'd choose the fewer women. [pause] I think. Now maybe I'm saying that because things have gone pretty well in this board. [pause] No, I probably wouldn't. I'd choose to go to war [laugh].

Diane's use of the "war" analogy indicates that she views equity issues as very important power issues where the stakes are high, and the relationships potentially adversarial.

The evolutionary and revolutionary views are epitomized for Diane by the approaches taken by her board and another board with which she is familiar. In her own board, Diane does not see the kind of backlash that she observed in ABC board:

> Our directors have been reluctant to take an affirmative action policy to the [school board members] because they're afraid that there will be a backlash against women, and they cited their own hiring statistics. Over the last eight years, for example, our board has done better percentage-wise in hiring women into positions of responsibility than ABC board, which has had an affirmative action plan and officer for, what, ten years now. Plus the enormous backlash that they had.

Diane's board has taken an "evolutionary" approach. They have a plan but "it isn't sort of blasted with the directors"; also, they don't talk about targets and timelines. Diane recognizes that without targets and timelines, you are "completely relying on the expressed goodwill of the people in positions of responsibility above you." However, she feels that women in the board have bargaining power with the director *because* the board is not complying with Ministry policy:

We would go to [Mr. Director] . . . "If you're not going to give us an affirmative action coordinator or policy, then we need money to do this. To run this series of workshops for superintendents and principals on the power issues between men and women."

In Diane's board, it is up to concerned women to initiate change. In their conclusion, Miles and Finn (1982) also advocate a strategy for social change that begins with individuals:

There are . . . two ways of getting rid of a structure. . . . One is to put a bomb under it . . . and the other is to dig around and undermine it till it topples. . . . The revolution which women are making is from the ground up. (p. 303)

Diane is aware of the difficulties with policy implementation and discusses her feeling that the evolutionary approach is the way to go:

You can still do things visibly but you don't have to hit people over the head with them. . . . Even though I pushed very hard to have an affirmative action policy and coordinator in the board, in the back of my mind I was thinking: "You know, if you don't get the right person and if they don't operate in the right way, we're going to have war on our hands." And it's pretty difficult to come back from war to cooperation. And it's very difficult to affect the behaviors of a large majority of men in a positive way when they've been in power positions all along, and they don't understand why they should have to give it up.

Diane's perception of what happened in ABC board reinforces her belief in a more evolutionary approach. She suggests that ABC board implemented the directives of the Ministry with respect to employment equity. In her view, the women in ABC spoke out and said what they wanted to say without concern for the reaction. The affirmative action coordinator reported to the director and targets and timelines were apparently followed. Her perception was that women who entered administrative positions at this time were initially "frozen out" of the principals' group; in other words, a backlash occurred. But, Diane sums up the results of this revolutionary approach over time:

Obviously, a number of the women have been successful in the board and have managed to make a positive contribution, a very strong, positive contribution. Because they have more women superintendents than we do. And I think they have more secondary women principals than we do, proportionately. So they've obviously made their way or they would have been forced out. And I think it's settled down considerably since five years ago. But it was pretty scary at the time.

Diane's characterization of the evolutionary versus the revolutionary approach can be summarized as follows:

• The evolutionary approach is concerned with men's reactions and expects that change will take longer;

• The revolutionary approach is unconcerned with men's reactions and expects change to be immediate.

However, if we think of evolution as working within the system, and revolution as working outside of it (or working to destroy it), the approach of ABC board is not particularly revolutionary! ABC board is simply implementing the Ministry's employment equity policy as it exists; it is complying with the Ministry's recommendations (more than is Diane's board). Perhaps what is revolutionary is that, contrary to what might be expected, a school board is actually taking the voluntary policy seriously.

Diane's characterization of ABC's approach as revolutionary indicates the power in our society of a discourse that presents the demands of previously excluded groups as an infringement on the rights of the dominant group, (i.e., as reverse discrimination). In Diane's discussion of evolutionary versus revolutionary approaches, we are again reminded of her dilemma: how to change patriarchal power relations without adopting patriarchal practices.

Possibility in the Form of Women's Support Groups

The questions surrounding change for women working in the education system are not easy to answer. How does an individual begin to address issues around equity? Most feminist theories would suggest that women should begin with their own experiences and with the contradictions between these experiences and the predominant social discourses. For example, if women are ambivalent about employment equity policy and experience a contradiction between what they are told it is doing and what they see it doing, then this is a valid starting point for evaluation. But women must have the space to discuss and affirm each other's experiences collectively.

For example, Diane recognizes the difficulty that seems to arise for women in mixed-gender situations:

> I would really like to be able to sort out when women can stop meeting by themselves. But the fact of the matter is that the dynamic changes when there are men there. We still seem to feel this need, to both protect ourselves and not say certain things when men are there – like anything that will make us look vulnerable, or look weak, or emotional. There's a need to defer to men, um, it's the "fragile-male-ego syndrome," in my head. If we don't then what will happen to them; they'll fall apart. And there's also the need to be approved by men. So all of those things happen when you take an intact female group and add men to it. I've seen it happen over and over and over again.

Diane's assessment is confirmed by other writers. For example, Lewis and Simon (1986) explore the dynamics in a mixed-gender graduate seminar where female students became increasingly aware of the practices by which they were being silenced and excluded. Smith (1987) also refers to the taken-for-granted authority of the male voice. She suggests that it is only when women begin to treat one another as "those who count" that we will break out of our silence (p. 35).

For Diane, a support group of other women in education has been important for her development. When she first mentioned this group, I asked how it came to be formed:

> Well there was a precipitating event. The principal, who was an extremely well-liked, charismatic leader left . . . and the men planned a "stag" for him, *that* was the leaving party.

She goes on to describe the process of awareness that went on within this group:

> I think the group formed because we felt that women didn't have a voice. And then, it became fairly obvious. I mean, you only had to hit us over the head with it a few times over a couple of years. That, if we wanted to have a voice, we had to have women who were willing to take on positions of responsibility. There was no other way. I mean, we could have our minutes sent to the [department] heads' group and have them deal with it. But the fact of the matter is, unless there was someone there advocating for our points of view, the chances of it being taken up were not all that great . . . . So, it certainly formed because we were completely excluded. There were no females in that administrative group.

I asked Diane how the administration responded to the formation of the group:

> They ignored it because they didn't really know about it. They figured it was another "stitch and bitch" group, I think. Where the women got together and everybody made food – which of course, none of us had time to do – and everyone sat around and talked about insignificant things.

MacKinnon (1982) describes the idea of women meeting together to "critically reconstitute the meaning of their social experiences" in terms of "consciousness-raising" (p. 29). In such meetings, the impact of male dominance may be uncovered through the collective speaking of women's experience. Thus, women may come to a recognition of male power as total, but also as delusion, as women recognize their own part in maintaining male dominance.

The group began in 1973, and although there have been periods when they did not meet, and although the membership has changed, there is presently a group of women that continues to meet once a month. When the group began, all of the women were teaching at the same school, and it seems that most were interested in learning about administration:

> [T]here was a real sense of supporting one another and encouraging one another. Because it was a very strong group of women, very well-qualified, very bright, very interested . . . [A]nd we spent a lot of time learning as much as we could about what we should be doing in order to be good people in positions of responsibility. And as women became appointed, they brought that information back to the group as well. So it was a very interesting support group.

At the time of our interviews, eight of the ten women in the group were in positions of responsibility.

Since its inception the membership has changed, and the function of the group has also changed. Originally, many of the group members were in their early thirties, and the group provided support for them in balancing concerns around having a family with their desire to enter administration. As women decided to apply for administrative positions, the group focused on improving resume-writing and interview skills. They invited a woman elementary school principal to one of their meetings to talk to them about women in leadership and how to get into those positions.

In the late seventies, the group disbanded for a while until there was another "precipitating event:"

> [T]here was a group of us that went off to this "Women and Health" seminar . . . which was a wonderful seminar. It dealt with all kinds of women's health issues. And we started then, looking at it as a more personal thing: being together to meet more personal needs. Because a number of us had already built our skill levels, in terms of interviewing and support and things like that. And so, four or five of us said: "We should meet regularly again. We've got to get a group of women together again."

At that time, Diane and some of the other women in the group were raising young children and were sorting out family issues:

> So that was another reason. We felt we needed some internal support from one another, trying to figure out: "If we're interested in leadership positions, how do we do that – at the same time that we're raising kids, and sorting through some of the family issues?" . . . So we did start to meet in one another's homes again.

It is interesting that the group originally provided career-related support to the women, but its function changed as they realized that personal support was also important and necessary. In other words, they could not partition-off their *private* and *public* lives. Their issues with families were very much connected to their career decisions. For example, when I asked Diane to describe how the group functioned, she replied:

> It really was very much a sharing kind of thing. What's happening here? Here's a problem that I've got. How would we go about solving it? Or just socializing kinds of things. You know, all kinds of personal things are happening in people's lives – people splitting up and getting back together in another formation. And so, sort of helping people sort through their personal things. Both educational and personal support kinds of things.

Professionally, the women in Diane's group support others in the group by encouraging them to apply for positions, offering emotional support if they are not successful, and helping them to prepare for a subsequent bid for the position. They support each other when they meet and also maintain contact between meetings. The women in the support group appear to be bound together by their common life stages, their interest in educational leadership, and their shared experiences as women in that environment.

It is noteworthy that ABC board also has a woman's support group that started, Diane believes, around the same time as did her group. She compares the two groups:

> Now their group was more board-wide, and they used to have breakfast meetings. I think they probably still do. . . . But theirs was more formal, partly because they had an affirmative action coordinator . . . And that woman was involved in some of the planning for those breakfasts, and they were of a professional nature. They got to the core of the matter very quickly since they had major personnel from the board to talk to the women who were there. And they focused a lot on leadership development.

Whether support groups are formal or not, they appear to fulfil a need for women in education, and particularly for women who are entering the male-dominated sphere of educational administration. For example, Grant (1989) and Weiler (1988) mention research subjects who belong to similar support groups. Within such groups, there is potential for women to turn *resistance* into what Weiler calls *"counter-hegemonic"* activity:

> [T]he creation of a self-conscious analysis of a situation and the development of collective practices and organization that can oppose the hegemony of the existing order and begin to build the base for a new understanding and transformation of society. (p. 52)

Implications of the Study

In our interview, Diane raised several important issues. Her experiences of gender relations in the workplace indicate the historical and continuing imbalance in power relations between men and women. In her discussion of employment equity, Diane raised the fundamental question of how change can occur most effectively. Her recognition of the "double-edged" character of employment equity policy makes her ambivalent.

It is apparent that there is a disjuncture between the world experienced by Diane as subject, and the abstract conceptual world of policy statements (Smith, 1987). For example, there is a contradiction between formal employment equity policy and the response of Diane's board to it, as is evidenced by the fact that actual compliance by boards is viewed as revolutionary. This view prevails partly because the discourse of employment equity as programs of "special measures" for women (within a society that promotes a discourse of "merit") encourages the idea that such programs involve reverse discrimination. Clearly this idea results in a backlash from men and feelings of ambivalence for "target group" members like Diane.

It is also clear that existing practices in the workplace – which include male norms in administration and male-preferred career paths – work against employment equity policy since, as Diane suggests, men recognize their power and "see no reason why they should give it up." These practices form the *"invisible policy"* that equity policy interrupts (Lee, 1990). There are also contradictions between the policy and broader social relations in which women are often constrained by the material and ideological conditions of being wives/mothers, with all of the caretaking functions that these roles entail.

This is not to say that we should throw out employment equity policy. Rather, it is important for women to recognize, as does Diane, that there are reasons for their feelings of ambivalence about such policy. It is also important for women to recognize that the implementation of such policy requires their active participation.

For feminist theorists as well as women in education, it is important to name our realities in order to better understand the barriers to equality that continue to exist for women. One way to do this is through women's support groups, which provide a space for women to share their experiences and to explore possible locations for change.

By now, we realize that equality for women in the *public sphere* of the workplace requires material change in the *private sphere* of family life. This change requires women gaining access to the process of defining value (MacKinnon, 1987); not just gaining access to positions within existing patriarchal structures. And it requires us to resist the hegemonic discourses around gender and equality that continue to shape our perceptions of reality.

Notes

[1]Interviews were conducted in November, 1989.

[2]The Principals' Group is made up of all the principals and vice-principals from elementary and secondary schools in the board, and meets monthly.

[3]The Ministry provided voluntary funding to school boards to hire a person to coordinate affirmative action initiatives.

[4]The Ministry has published an annual report since 1986 entitled: "The status of women and affirmative action/employment equity in Ontario school boards." This report presents statistics compiled in an Affirmative Action Data Base.

References

Acker, S. (Ed.). (1989). *Teachers, gender and careers*. Philadelphia: Falmer Press.

Apple, M. (1986). *Teachers and texts*. New York: Routledge and Kegan Paul.

Casey, K., & Apple, M. (1989). Gender and the conditions of teachers' work: The development of understanding in America. In S. Acker (Ed.), *Teachers, gender and careers* (pp. 171-186). Philadelphia, PA: Falmer Press.

Cunnison, S. (1989). Gender joking in the staffroom. In S. Acker (Ed.), *Teachers, gender and careers* (pp. 151-167). Philadelphia, PA: Falmer Press.

Employment Opportunity/Affirmative Action Unit. (1989, January). *Model workshop kit.* (Available from Employment Equity Unit, Mowat Block, Queen's Park, Toronto).

Findlay, S. (1987). Facing the state: The politics of the women's movement reconsidered. In H. Maroney & M. Luxton (Eds.), *Feminism and political economy* (pp. 31-49). Toronto, ON: Methuen.

Grant, R. (1989). Women teachers' career pathways: towards an alternative model of "career." In S. Acker (Ed.), *Teachers, gender and careers* (pp. 35-50). Philadelphia, PA: Falmer Press.

Lee, E. (1990). Anti-racist education: From policy to practice. Public lecture, Queen's University, Ontario.

Lewis, M., & Simon, R. (1986). A discourse not intended for her: Learning and teaching within patriarchy. *Harvard Educational Review, 56*(4), 457-472.

MacKinnon, C. (1982). Feminism, marxism, method and the state: An agenda for theory. In N. Keohane, Z. Rosaldo, & B. Gelpi (Eds.), *Feminist Theory, A Critique of Ideology* (pp. 1-30). Sussex: Harvester Press.

MacKinnon, C. (1987). *Feminism unmodified: Discourses on life and law.* Cambridge, MA: Harvard University Press.

Miles, A., & Finn, G. (Eds.). (1982). *Feminism in Canada: From pressure to politics.* Montreal, PQ: Black Rose Books.

Ministry of Education. (1987). *The status of women and affirmative action/employment equity in Ontario school boards: Report to the legislature.* Toronto, ON: Queen's Printer for Ontario.

Ministry of Education. (1991). *The status of women and employment equity in Ontario school boards: Report to the legislature 1990.* Toronto, ON: Queen's Printer for Ontario.

Ministry of Education. (1993). *The status of women and employment equity in Ontario school boards: Report to the legislature 1992.* Toronto, ON: Queen's Printer for Ontario.

Oram, A. (1989). A master should not serve under a mistress: Women and men teachers 1900-1970. In S. Acker (Ed.), *Teachers, gender and careers* (pp. 21-34). Philadelphia, PA: Falmer Press.

Pascall, G. (1986). *Social policy: A feminist analysis.* London: Tavistock.

Rossiter, A. (1988). *From private to public.* Toronto, ON: Women's Press.

Shakeshaft, C. (1987). *Women in educational administration.* Newbury Park: Sage.

Smith, D. (1987). *The everyday world as problematic: A feminist sociology.* Toronto, ON: University of Toronto Press.

Task Force on Barriers to Women in the Public Service. (1990). *Beneath the veneer* (Vols. 1-4) Ottawa, ON: Supply and Services Canada.

Weiler, K. (1988). *Women teaching for change.* South Hadley, MA: Bergin and Garvey.

8

Women Leaders In Adult Education: Reflections on the Development of Their Leadership Styles

Fay Myers and Vivian Hajnal

Social, economic, and technological changes in Canada impose ever-changing demands upon those who work in public education. In Adult Educational Institutions today, competition for program funding is vigorous, grants are provided on an annual basis, program levels fluctuate, and both local and provincial politics play a role in the operation. Consequently, staff and administration are dealing with constant change. Job insecurity, competition and numerous political agendas are part of daily life. These educational institutions are in need of leaders who are able to empower staff who work in many diverse programs and locations and bind them together through a shared vision of their organization and of the future. A growing number of these leaders are women. This chapter examines the development of the leadership styles of women in Saskatchewan's adult education institution.

The Conceptual Framework: Past, Present and the Future

How women are raised and socialized, how women combine work, family and community, and how women are trained and prepared for the future influence their leadership style. We begin with the past.

Socialization of Women

Gender differences have often been linked to early socialization. Some theorists argue that women have been socialized to be passive, cooperative and caring. Adkison (1981) believes that adult women whose behavior conforms to widely held beliefs about appropriate feminine behavior were "more passive rather than competitive and more conformist and submissive rather than independent and dominant" (p. 312). Porat (1989) believes that women do more "team building, communicate more effectively and prefer contributive, consensual decision-making" due to being socialized to be more cooperative rather than competitive (p. 120). Gelman and Powell (cited in McGrath, 1992) suggest that women are especially good at "blending," a martial-arts term referring to doing everything you can to understand the other person's point of view and match your move to theirs, because in their formative years women "relied on persuasion rather than intimidation" (p. 65).

In a discussion of the role of socialization in the development of feminine leadership, Loden (1985) cites research which suggested that girls excel at verbal tasks due to their cooperative play. This has led women to be effective verbal communicators. Shakeshaft (1987) states, "women tend to use expressive language and intensifiers, tend to use correct speech forms, tend to use questions for a variety of purposes, tend to use more verb than noun forms in description and tend to use language that encourages community building" (p. 181).

In our society, Bass (1981) states, "we are socialized primarily within the nuclear family in a culture that defines sex roles as total roles that define our sense of self and our behavior" (p. 494). Feminine roles are most often associated with submissiveness, passivity, nurturance and an emphasis on giving. However, the role of socialization in the development of the feminine leadership style is best described by Belenky, Clinchy, Goldberger and Tarule (1990):

> Women typically approach adulthood with the understanding that the care and empowerment of others is central to their life's work. Through listening and responding, they draw out the voices and minds of those they help to raise up. In the process they often come to hear, value and strengthen their own voices and minds as well. (p. 18)

Women carry these values they have been socialized to hold – empowering others, listening, responding, caring and nurturing – into their relationships at work, within their families and throughout their communities. We continue with the present.

Combining Work, Family and Community

Women have many roles to fulfil. The strategies and the methods they use and the attitudes they adopt determine their effectiveness in the fulfilment of these multiple roles. The feminine values of responsibility, inclusion and connection have emerged as valuable leadership qualities in the 1990s, particularly to "counteract feelings of alienation prevalent in the workplace, family life and society" (Helgesen, 1990, p. 233). Helgesen (1990) believes that women structure their world around them including family, space and work in the form of a "spider's web" (p. 46). This circle or web creates an interrelated structure built around a central point and is constructed of radials. Implicit within the web structure is the "notion of group affiliation rather than individual achievement as having the highest value" (p. 48). Feminine leadership style based on the web structure promotes free and open communication, where authority comes from connection to the people around rather than distance from those below.

Women have had the capacity to give their attention to many diverse demands without losing the ability to focus on a single item. Seashore (cited in Loden, 1985) has a "hunch that socialization is what causes women to stay alert to their environment because they are still responsible for many diverse family and professional tasks. They see the interrelatedness of things, actions and people more clearly" (p. 204). According to Julia Goggin (cited in Loden, 1985), "Because of the constant demands made on them by their families, their employers and their communities, women tend to be practical and future-oriented" (p. 207).

The boundaries women place around their work and personal lives help to preserve the unique aspects of each and reduced the risk of isolation that came from focusing too much energy on work and too little on personal interests and relationships. Loden (1985) believes that to feminine leaders, a full, diverse life beyond the office is critically important. Today's effective leadership requires more than hard work, ambition and devotion to corporate goals, it means "staying in touch with our own humanity as well" (p. 216).

Helgesen (1990) claims that the integration of workplace and private sphere responsibilities by women makes for a more well-rounded individual with strong psychological and spiritual resources. Due to this integration, women have more of a "process orientation" as their work is cyclical and unending. Therefore, they gain pleasure from actually doing their tasks rather than completing them. They are more focused on the "means rather than the end" (p. 35).

Women appear to be more flexible managers due to their experience and the expectations they bring to the workplace. Helgesen (1990) claimed that "motherhood is being recognized as an excellent school for managers, demanding many of the same skills: organization, pacing, the balancing of conflicting claims, teaching, guiding, leading, monitoring, handling disturbances, imparting information" (p. 31). Women have had to learn how to organize and balance conflicting demands.

Leadership Styles

The 1990s have seen a growth in the number of women in leadership roles. Naisbett and Aburdene (1990) refer to this era as the decade of women in leadership. These leaders developed leadership styles which are reflective of their backgrounds. For example, Naisbett and Aburdene suggest that women lead by empowering others, valuing connections instead of competition and building strength by building up others.

The conceptual framework employed in the study considers women's past socialization, their present multiple roles and their current and future leadership styles. Using this conceptual framework and the context of adult educational institutions, women leaders were asked to share their perceptions concerning their leadership styles.

The Purpose of the Study

This study was designed to investigate women's perceptions of their leadership style. An exploration of the relationship between their socialization, their multiple roles, and their leadership style was considered. Specifically this study sought to identify the personal and professional characteristics these women possessed which enabled them to achieve their present position or career, and to explore the factors in women's past that played an influential role in defining their leadership style. Emphasis was given to the women's perspectives regarding their leadership style, and their reflections on their role within the institutions.

Methodology

The study was carried out in Saskatchewan in 1993. The post-secondary institutions that were employed in this study were the Saskatchewan Regional Colleges and Saskatchewan Institutes of Applied Science and Technology. The Saskatchewan Regional Colleges have a mandate to provide credit and non-credit education to adults throughout their rural region. Their credit program delivery is primarily as a brokering agency with the Saskatchewan Institutes of Applied Science and Technology and the two Saskatchewan universities. The four Saskatchewan Institutes of Applied Science and Technology in Saskatchewan are primarily credit-granting institutions within four major centres of Saskatchewan – Prince Albert, Saskatoon, Regina and Moose Jaw.

These Adult Educational Institutions all have a Principal or Chief Executive Officer who is accountable to a government-appointed Board of Trustees. The Board members are appointed by the Minister of Education in Regina. The Principal or Chief Executive Officer is responsible for developing and maintaining an effective institution. At the present time, there are no women in this leadership role.

One of the major tasks of the Chief Executive Officer has been the recruitment, selection and supervision of staff. In most cases there have been a Director of Finance and Administration and Directors/Deans of Programs who are accountable to the Chief Executive Officer. It is at this level that women have played a larger leadership role. In these positions, they have been accountable for the institute budget, supervision of staff, policy and program development, marketing, needs assessment and development and maintenance of positive working relationships with the community.

The criteria for the selection of personnel for these leadership roles include graduate work, experience in the adult educational field, interpersonal and communication skills, and other personal and professional attributes. Most often these positions are filled from within the system or institute. In 1993, the majority of personnel below the management level of the Institutions were female.

Nine female leaders at upper management levels within the Saskatchewan Adult Educational Institutions of Saskatchewan Regional Colleges and Saskatchewan Institute of Applied Science and Technology were identified. These nine female leaders represented approximately 17% of the possible leadership positions in the Saskatchewan Adult system. They were involved at a management level with program, financial and human resource management.

The data collected emphasized the context and views of women in their leadership role. The questions elicited responses which provided a background profile of the subjects, as well as insights into the individual's experiences, perceptions, opinions and feelings, regarding their leadership style.

The instruments utilized for the data collection were a short questionnaire and an interview schedule. The questionnaire examined personal background information. The interview schedule consisted of open-ended questions concerning the women's leadership role and necessary skills which were common to the role. Questions concerning skills in decision making, communication, delegation, motivation, supervision, goal setting, interpersonal effectiveness, organizational skills, conflict management and visioning were posed. The leaders were asked for their reflections concerning their leadership style. The interview schedule was field tested and was revised as necessary. The aim of the interview process was to create a situation where the subjects responded with specific and concrete information which was self-revealing and personal. Using interviews gave the opportunity for the researcher to probe below the surface. The interviewer listened, interpreted, translated and questioned.

A consent form with a description of the purpose of the study and the short questionnaire were mailed to subjects in October, 1993. During a follow-up phone call, the researcher further briefed subjects, answered questions and established an interview appointment. The subjects were assured of anonymity and of the confidentiality of the information provided. Upon their agreement to participate, the interview schedule was forwarded to the subjects.

Interviews were conducted with subjects on an individual basis in October and November 1993 at their location of employment. In one case an alternative location was selected due to travel distance. Interviews lasted approximately two and one half hours. The interviews followed a semi-structured format as participants were also free to comment on anything they wished to share. There was minimum interruption from the researcher. Interviews were taped. The participants consented to a follow-up inquiry, if needed for purposes of clarification.

The researchers' notes and the recorded interviews provided the data for analysis. The data were analyzed according to recurring themes. While the results primarily provided description, analysis and interpretation were used to make meaning of the data.

Findings

All nine women administrators who were asked agreed to participate. All participants had read the interview schedule beforehand and the majority had prepared notes or jotted down points to bring forward. These women were all Deans or Directors in the Saskatchewan Regional College system or in the Saskatchewan Institute of Science and Technology, although two positions were designated as acting. These administrators ranged in age from 41 to over 50.

One of the women had a Doctorate in post-secondary education, while two had a Master's Degree in adult education. Two other leaders were working on the completion of their Master's program. The highest level of education for three of the nine women was an Education degree. One other leader was currently working on the completion of her Administration degree. Another held a Diploma in Adult Education.

All nine of the women had a wide range of employment experiences. A common thread of teaching and coordination both in the K-12 and adult system was apparent. Additional employment experiences mentioned were nursing, banking, counselling, accounting and health records.

The women's years of experience in the adult education system ranged from 9 to 22 years. Four of the women had 9 to 12 years experience and five had 17 to 22 years of experience. Eight of the women had held their present positions from one to five years with one participant in her present position for 20 years.

Socialization

The majority of the women in this study felt their early years contributed significantly to their leadership style. They were taught early on to take responsibility for their own actions. All nine of the participants described themselves as having a highly developed sense of responsibility and work ethic.

A recurring theme in many of the comments concerned expectations others placed on these women in their early years. Expectations for education, for achievement, and for holding responsible positions were noted. For the most part these high expectations and encouragement came from their parents.

School also played a significant part in the socialization of these women and the development of their leadership style. Two women described their experiences in a convent as being very directive. Education was very important and they were taught to accept responsibility at a young age. One participant described the effect of being an only child in her grade at school; it was a very social education with a lot of oral work. Another participant felt she would have been challenged more in school if she would have been a boy, as she would have been more encouraged to take the sciences and mathematics.

In most cases the women described how they were taught to be independent and to have a high regard for work. Five of the nine participants were from farm backgrounds and attributed their appreciation of the value of working hard to their parents. One participant, however, noted "her inner sense of wanting to be something." This strong sense of achievement and leadership ability was apparent when each of these women described leadership roles they had taken on in their early years – student council, drama, music, church groups. A number of them commented that when they joined a group they invariably found themselves in a leadership role. They had always liked to accept challenges to learn and grow. This approach continued into their adult life and work. In most cases, this willingness to accept challenges was attributed to the influence of a parental role model. One of the women described how she was socialized to pay attention to the needs of others and to avoid "hard" confrontation. Again, this was attributed to the influence of a parental role model.

Combining Work, Family and Community

Eight of the nine women were married and had children. The children ranged in age from 11 to 37 years of age. Eleven out of 19 children were 18 years of age or older. All of the women were involved in other organizations, interest groups and professional organizations. These ranged from adult education associations, Rotary club, Public School Board to Home Care Board. Four out of the nine women held leadership roles in one of these groups. Four of the women were continuing formal education while maintaining a full-time job. The multiple roles these women held were very demanding. How have they managed them effectively? Planning and setting goals, delegating tasks, receiving support from family, mentors and peers, displaying a positive attitude, and keeping a sense of humor were mentioned as key factors.

The interviewees acknowledged that managing multiple roles could be very stressful. One believed it very important for her to compartmentalize and separate work from home. Another believed it important to remember she was not indispensable and that "the place will go on with or without me." Another of the female leaders described parenting as similar to being a leader in the workplace – striving for win/win situations, instilling positive thinking and exploring options.

Diet, exercise and a healthy lifestyle contributed to the women's abilities to manage multiple roles. Examples used to substantiate this were comments such as: "I use the stairs rather than the elevator whenever possible"; "I have a philosophy of life and basic spiritual beliefs which are instrumental in how I approach my life and work"; "I direct myself positively, use herbs in my diet and utilize a method of healing by touching."

Leisure activities described were very diverse. These included reading, writing, walking, jogging, bridge, golf and yoga. Family time was a priority. Two of the women described their leisure time as "Is there time"? and "This area is sadly neglected in my life."

Many women had also changed jobs and careers due to their husband taking a move in his career. One of the participants described how she had moved 14 times in her first 13 years of marriage. This had caused her to be creative, and she continued to use resources within herself to bring creativity to her workplace.

Leadership Styles

The nine women in this study described themselves as workers rather than as leaders. They described their work as encouraging and supporting staff to do new things and look for new opportunities. The challenge one participant felt was to work together in a collaborative manner towards a common goal. She emphasized to her staff that they worked "with" rather than "for" her.

Openness and trust were very important to the research participants. Methods used to encourage and support this philosophy by the leaders included an open-door policy to allow staff access to them whenever required, open recognition of others' strengths and achievements, annual staff retreats and collaborative decision making. One participant felt it very important to look at the person as a whole, to establish relationships in order to be part of the culture of the organization, and to encourage a sense of ownership and belonging throughout the staff.

All nine participants preferred to work on a consultative basis. Two of the women described their style of management as participatory. Others listed their styles as situational, fairly open, collaborative, democratic, eclectic and humanistic. The preference was towards a team approach to management where all players have a sense of ownership towards a common goal.

One participant noted that the challenge for her was to be a positive role model and to share experiences with others. Her goal was to allow others the opportunity to realize their potential within the group and organization. Another participant stated she was "happiest working with a group."

Two of the nine women used the term "empowerment" when describing the self management teams that were set up in their organizations. Task teams were organized to meet objectives and accommodate people's interests. A facilitator and motivator was another participant's description of her management style. Strong team players were created by showing confidence in others' abilities and providing them with a sense of ownership and purpose.

All but one participant used sensing skills in their day to day work and found them to be extremely useful and reliable. They all described these skills as an awareness of outside forces when a person becomes open to others' feelings and needs. Two of the women used their sensing skills when hiring staff. One woman suggested that women were more in tune to feelings. Another woman described herself as very intuitive and knew there was "a time to say things and a time not to." Three leaders described the use of intuitive skills in both verbal and non-verbal interactions. One participant believed this intuition was linked to nurturing within a woman.

All nine participants suggested that good listening skills were essential in their work. One participant felt it very important to be genuine, open and non-judgmental. Another felt that through listening, she was able to pick up on non-verbal communication or what was not being said. Two participants cited Carkhuff (1971) counselling techniques as being particularly useful in perfecting their listening skills.

The nine participants believed the key to effective leadership was effective communication. Eight of the women preferred and used verbal communication over written communication. One administrator found that written communication was too bureaucratic. The women used written communication to provide a paper trail when it was required for clarification, discussion, information, correspondence or agendas. They felt verbal communication allowed for instant feedback and the ability to analyze the non-verbal clues of body language.

Personal sharing was very effective for five of the women in this study. They believed personal disclosure helped motivation, provided for a common ground and allowed people to be more humanistic. One individual used humor concerning herself in order to share. In all cases it was felt there needed to be some caution as to where and when personal sharing was used. It needed to be appropriate and of some value.

Constructive feedback was preferred and adopted by all nine women. Open, honest and gentle suggestions were utilized to provide for positive solutions. Questioning techniques were favored by six of the participants to provide the framework for feedback. Questions such as "have you thought?," "what are you going to do, how can I help you, when will we meet again?" and "how could you have done that differently?" were used by these leaders.

The ability to be consistent and fair to all staff was important to these nine female leaders. In order to develop and maintain credibility they felt fairness needed to be a model for a workplace with no hidden agendas. Clear expectations, constructive feedback, acknowledgement and positive reinforcement were described by the participants as playing a large part in establishing fairness in an organization.

Reflections

All of the nine women leaders were content and happy with where they were in their careers. In their role as adult educational leaders, they felt they were able to develop in many different areas. They gained experience in human resources, financial management, marketing, networking and thinking conceptually. The women enjoyed having a perspective on the broad picture, influencing decisions and meeting new challenges on a day to day basis.

The women were asked to reflect on what they found most rewarding and least satisfying about their role as a leader. There were a number of responses; however, six women referred to the opportunity to share, influence and develop staff as very rewarding. The diversity of the job, independence, knowledge, influence on others and challenging opportunities were other factors women considered rewarding in their role as a leader.

A variety of conditions were discussed as the least satisfying aspects of their role as a leader. One interviewee mentioned that her tasks were often mundane, with issues to be dealt with on an immediate basis, and with little or no time for research. Tasks were often in process and never finished in a neat package. The role of a leader could be very lonely and it was sometimes difficult to be assertive enough to say "no" to tasks. A number of the participants suggested that supervision and dealing with difficult staff were the least satisfying aspects of their leadership role.

The participants were asked to reflect on their leadership skills and what areas they felt they needed to develop in order to be more effective. Four of the participants indicated a need for more academic learning, particularly in the field of adult education. Two of the women felt they needed to improve their communication skills to become more effective. Other responses from the women were the need to better share their vision in order to develop their staff, the need to increase training and development opportunities, the need to better manage by walking around and being more accessible, and the need to better balance their work, family and community commitments in order to avoid the "superwoman" syndrome.

Several women described significant others as leadership role models. Fathers, mothers, co-workers, supervisors, and other leaders were described as influencing the participants' leadership aspirations. What was most interesting was that all of the women described at least one male, either a father, an immediate supervisor, a co-worker, a leader of their organization or a husband who had influenced and encouraged their career aspirations to become a leader. In most cases there was also another female, either mother, grandmother, peer or supervisor, who had acted as a role model at some time during their life.

Summary and Discussion

The nine women in this study highlighted interesting characteristics regarding women's ways of leading and fascinating perspectives regarding their leadership role and style of leadership. Participatory management was their preferred style of leadership. The women perceived their leadership role as a "team member." Cooperation and collaboration were demonstrated through a web model of leadership where the participants acted as a coach and facilitator from the center. These connections allowed for unity in the group and a flatter leadership structure. The women in this study preferred this model for decision making, self-management teams, and accomplishment of goals. They believed this style empowered employees to think for themselves and to meet their individual as well as organizational goals.

The women in this study were effective in their interpersonal skills. They believed in listening, responding to, sharing and empathizing with their colleagues. For the most part, they relied heavily on their intuitive nature and were very astute in observing verbal and non-verbal language. They believed in supporting, encouraging, and motivating staff to higher levels of commitment and creativity.

Family, peer and superior's encouragement and support were factors which influenced the participants' aspirations in becoming a leader. The women described specific role models, male and female, who had inspired them to become leaders in their work, family and community. Because mentors were very significant in the development of each of the participant's careers, each woman was seeking to be a role model for others by being ethical, responsible, flexible, and supportive, and exhibiting interest in lifelong learning.

The nine participants believed one of their most important functions was to assist staff in adapting to the changing environment and learning to work towards a common goal. As Deans and Directors in an information age, it was their role to share information with their staff and to set common goals and directions for the future. Their motivation came from a sense of pride and accomplishment, recognition, meeting challenges and working with positive people.

For the most part, the participants were satisfied with where they were in their careers. The most rewarding aspect of their positions was the opportunity to share, influence and develop staff; the least satisfying aspect was supervision as it is still seen to be control rather than support, performance evaluations rather than coaching.

The primary factor which restricted the participants' leadership aspirations was their own lack of self-confidence. Family responsibilities and lack of formal credentials were also found to restrict their aspirations. Most of the women felt that organizations were changing due to the dynamic paradigm shift within organizations from management by control to leadership through change; from management in the industrial age to leadership in the information age. The women in this study believed they could play an integral part in leading organizations to prepare for the future.

The women performed multiple roles within their work, family and community. All of the participants were highly responsible individuals and held a strong work ethic. This was part of the explanation for their success in achieving leadership roles.

A strong point in each interview with the participants was their sense of accomplishment in meeting new challenges within their roles. The ability to influence and develop staff and their institutes, to gather and disperse knowledge, and to plan and to envision the future was very rewarding to these women. Some were uncomfortable with conflict. Most of the women believed people could solve their own problems given some guidance. Communication skills were key and the majority preferred verbal over non-verbal communications.

The women who described their leadership styles were cognizant of some of the influences from socialization. They attributed components of their leadership style to the experiences they had at home, at work and in the community at large. They recognized the impact of their training or their lack of training. They clearly exhibited the web structure described by Helgesen (1990) in their interactions, and appreciated the merits of collaboration and participatory leadership.

References

Aburdene, P. & Naisbitt, J. (1992). *Megatrends for women*. New York: Random House.

Adkison, J. A. (1981). Women in school administration: A review of the research. *Review of Educational Research, 51*, 311-343.

Bass, M.B. (1981). *Stogdill's handbook of leadership*. (Revised and expanded). New York: The Free Press.

Belenky, M.F., Clinchy, B.Mc., Goldberger, N.R., & Tarule, J.M. (1990). *Women's ways of knowing*. New York: Basic Books.

Carkhuff, R. (1971). *The development of human resources.* New York: Holt Rinehart and Winston.

Helgesen, S. (1990). *The female advantage.* New York: Doubleday.

Loden, M. (1985). *Feminine leadership or how to succeed in business without being one of the boys.* New York: Random House.

McGrath, S.T. (1992). Here come the women. *Educational Leadership, 49*(5), 62-65.

Naisbitt, J., & Aburdene, P. (1990). *Megatrends 2000.* New York: William Morrow.

Porat, K.L. (1989). Women in administration must be women. *The Canadian School Executive, 9*(1), 11-14.

Shakeshaft, C. (1987). *Women in educational administration.* California: Sage.

9

Metaphors for Leadership and Power:
Four Women's Perspectives

Hope-Arlene Fennell

There is a growing literature demonstrating the impact of metaphor on the way we think, on our language, and on systems of scientific and everyday knowledge (Morgan, 1986, pp. 345-6). Discussed in this chapter are metaphors which four women who are school principals have used to conceptualize leadership and power. As part of a long term study, these women are working with the researcher in exploring the ways in which they lead and use power. The development of the metaphors represent attempts by each of the women to gain a fuller understanding of their ways of leading and of their views of and experiences with power.

Language, Metaphor and Power

In many ways we shape our experiences and are, in turn, shaped by the language we use and hear around us as we attempt to bring meaning to lived experiences. The way in which language is used impacts on individuals and the surrounding social systems. Corson (1993) states:

> It is people who have the power to use language in various ways; it is people who give discourse its form and make judgements about the status of various texts; and it is the situations in which people have power and are using language to serve some potent purpose which give language a power that it lacks when it is without such precise contexts. (p. 4)

Those in power frequently use language to extend and maintain their bases of power between themselves and those viewed as less powerful. Language can also be used by opposing groups to critique the activities of the powerful in efforts to bring about changes to the status quo. In the past language has been used in schools and school systems to repress, dominate, and disempower (Corson, 1993). Language has also been used to critique and change school organizations.

In order to truly make a difference, some feminist theorists express the need to "try to reinvent language itself" (Lips, 1991, p. 33). Their need is based on the idea that it is difficult to develop new thoughts and images of women, men or human relationships from ideas which are conceptualized using language grounded in patriarchal assumptions. Lips further notes that in much of current language the "male as the standard or neutral case and the female as special or Other" is maintained so that women "may find it difficult in many contexts not to think of themselves as intruders, people whose presence is often tolerated by dispensation" (p. 34). Those theorists who seek to critique and challenge the current system of language have set themselves an enormous task. However, if they are successful they will begin at last to transform the official knowledge of our culture, including our images for gender, leadership and power.

Lakoff and Johnson (1980) also note that language is an important source of evidence when one is studying the conceptual schemes that govern the ways in which individuals think and act. They contend that "primarily on the basis of linguistic evidence, we have found that most of our ordinary conceptual system is metaphorical in nature" (p. 4). Metaphor has long been used as a way of playing with language and ideas to create new knowledge. Aristotle noted that "midway between the unintelligible and the commonplace, it is metaphor which most produces knowledge" (p. 346). Since the metaphorical expressions used by individuals are tied to their conceptual systems, Lakoff and Johnson (1980) note that metaphoric expressions are very useful for studying individuals' conceptual systems. Metaphors are also helpful in creating new meanings for concepts by highlighting some attributes while suppressing others. Metaphors reorganize our focus on very specific aspects of concepts. They also highlight individuals' experiences, making them coherent in relation to the concept. Because of the coherence, metaphors can be useful in that "they sanction actions, justify inferences, and help us set goals" (p. 142). Finally, the meaning of metaphors is determined partly by culture and partly by the past experiences of individuals. Therefore the same metaphor may be perceived differently by different individuals. Lakoff and Johnson (1980) conclude:

> New metaphors have the power to create a new reality. This can begin to happen when we start to comprehend our experiences in terms of a metaphor, and it becomes a deeper reality when we begin to act in terms of it. (p. 145)

Brunner (1986) indicates that scholars and artists often use metaphors to link folk theories to the world of scholarship. He notes that, while such ideas are more interpretive than positivist, they "provide a richer, yet more abstract interpretation of human theories in action much as the interpretive cultural anthropologist provides an explication de texte of the culture" (p. 49). Morgan (1986) used the creative insights generated by metaphors to create new ways of thinking about organizations. He explored organizations as machines, brains, systems, "psychic prisons," cultures, political systems, and instruments of domination. Earlier, Morgan (1981) used the schismatic metaphor to describe dialectic leadership in which power among organizational members is negotiated and renegotiated as the tensions and contradictions are resolved giving rise to new organizational dynamics. The schismatic metaphor appeared to form the basis for the metaphor of organizations as political systems (Morgan, 1986) which provides a more humanistic way to think about schools than the rationalistic business models which are currently being expressed and acted upon. Language and metaphors provide the main sources of data for the research discussed in this chapter.

Methodology

As part of a longitudinal study of women principals' experiences with leadership, language is both the primary research tool and the primary source of data. Data was collected through in-depth interviews twice yearly over a three-year period with each of the four women principals. Interviews were also conducted during the first year of the study with teachers in each of the four schools. During subsequent visits to the schools, observations and reflective notes were used in addition to the interviews with the principals. The notes focused on the language teachers used to describe their work and the leadership of the principal. The data used for the research on metaphors were collected by asking principals, during a short interval, to think of and discuss some of the metaphors they used for thinking about leadership and power within their current contexts. The short interviews were followed by asking the four principals to write their metaphors giving brief explanations and feelings about each. The written work was followed by an in-depth interview with each principal four months later. During the time between the written metaphors and the in-depth interviews, the principals were asked to link their metaphors to their ongoing leadership experiences. It was interesting to note that, while the four women espoused interest in the development of language in the lives of themselves and their students, each found the written metaphor exercise very challenging.

Each of the four women, whose metaphors form the basis of this discussion, were identified by their school boards as principals who were exceptional leaders. All are elementary principals, two from Northwestern Ontario, and two from the lower mainland of British Columbia. Each has told her story to the researcher.

Eleanor

Eleanor is in her fifth year as principal of Acorn School, a modern K – 8 school in an urban middle-class neighborhood. Eleanor indicated, "I entered administration to see how I could make things better for kids." During the past four years, Eleanor has been working with teachers at Acorn School to implement a whole language program. She believes that her role as leader is to provide support and pressure for the innovation on a continuous basis. Eleanor perceives herself as "an instructional leader rather than just a manager who runs a tight ship." Regarding teachers' involvement, she notes, "Whenever I can involve staff in whatever capacity, I do." One way is to have division chairpersons and divisional meetings for which the teachers determine the agendas and outcomes. Eleanor tries to empower teachers who have expertise in particular areas by supporting them. Eleanor supports professional development by providing adequate resources "to encompass all people on staff." She believes teachers are responsible to take the ownership of their professional development, and she believes that teachers in Acorn School feel "empowered to do these things." Eleanor promotes active communication between teachers and parents through the school's parent advisory council.

Decision-making appears to be both teacher-centred and shared in Acorn School. Eleanor indicates having minor influence on daily classroom decisions and sharing decision-making with teachers about teaching assignments, sharing resources, the school timetable and space. While conflict is inevitable in any group, Eleanor notes that "There is very little conflict between and amongst the teachers," and that any conflict which emerges is "constructive conflict because they work it through." Eleanor states that when issues arise, "they'll come and we'll work it out" by finding solutions which meet everyone's needs. Eleanor indicates that she struggled with finding metaphors for power and leadership. Her first metaphor was this one.

> I was driving to school one day and I started to think of power as being the steering wheel and the ability to direct the vehicle along the intended journey. I could see myself, as school principal, steering the school in the direction of our school vision and mission statement. It means keeping the organization on track and staying out of the ditch as well as finding the best way to travel. It means finding the way that will be the most rewarding and successful.

It was through a discussion with a friend that Eleanor's second metaphor for leadership came. The friend compared Eleanor's arrival at Acorn School with a volcano. While the eruption disrupted the status quo and destroyed many things that had previously been seen as essential, out of the process a whole new situation was created that became very desirable and useful. The eruption involved changes in personnel, teaching strategies, and approaches to curriculum. Although she is somewhat uncomfortable with the volcano metaphor, Eleanor indicates that perhaps there is some truth in it.

Sarah

Sarah is in her ninth year as an administrator and principal of Peacock School, a K – 6 school in an inner-city neighborhood. Many of the children who attend Peacock School are from lower socio-economic levels in the community. A number are also from single-parent, immigrant, or aboriginal families. Sarah entered the principalship to help the work of teachers and students. She tells of her earlier struggles with principals who did not seem to understand her or the children, and who "did mean and hurtful things to children in the name of discipline." She was also influenced by the injustice she experienced during her own school years. Sarah states, "Seeing kids humiliated, that was really difficult. Kids being treated with no dignity; seeing some kids being treated very well and others not." Sarah concludes that, now, when she sees children in school experiencing injustice, she works to help correct and overcome it.

During the past five years, Sarah and the teachers in Peacock School have been developing and implementing a whole language program "to meet the needs of the children. The aboriginal children in particular were not seeing a lot of success with the traditional program." Sarah's beliefs about her role in the implementation process seem to be a strong indicator of her beliefs about leadership generally. She perceives herself as an information sharer, as a supporter, and as a facilitator of the implementation process. She also mentions the leadership of other teachers in the process. "We have a teacher on staff with a great deal of expertise in whole language and the concept is growing on our staff because of her leadership." Sarah indicates that her own leadership in the process involves "the sorts of support I can offer to them in materials, providing opportunities for them to be together to discuss whole language, and to bring in curriculum support people to talk with them about how they are doing in their programs." Sarah values the work and instructional decisions made by the teachers very highly. She states:

> I believe they know what they're doing, they are trained, they can make their own decisions, they are responsible for their own learning, and I sort of provide the structures on which they can make their decisions.

Sarah indicates that there is constant communication between her and the teachers, and that teachers are very much part of the decision-making about their classroom work and their professional development.

There is much collaboration among the teachers in Peacock School and the teachers work together to find their own solutions to issues and problems arising in the school. Sarah notes that "I don't see a lot of conflict. Teachers work pretty cooperatively." When issues arise, she does not 'push' her views about solutions, adding that "I'm very flexible in terms of the way things are done."

Sarah relates two metaphors for leadership and power which she uses to describe and think about her role as principal. The first is that of a shepherd. Sarah states:

> I am a shepherd who moves my flock towards a predetermined destination. I keep my flock moving in the right direction and I keep strays from falling by the wayside or getting lost. I keep a close watch for anything that threatens to

harm the flock. I nurse them back to health when they are ill and correct them when they head astray. I am totally responsible for their safety and wellbeing. While I am in control, I follow behind the flock so it may appear that I am not their leader. Individuals within the flock seem to know the way and lead the others.

The second metaphor is that of a judge. She suggests that she is often called upon to resolve disputes involving children, teachers, parents. She perceives that in order for their wisdom and advice to be sought and considered, and to be revered and respected, judges must be seen as fair, caring, intelligent, knowledgeable, reasonable and consistent. Sarah also perceives that judges are able to empower others by the examples they set and the processes they use to resolve disputes. While she views these qualities as challenging, Sarah is also aware that, many times, she is the only person available to assist with such matters and tries to help as effectively as she can.

Carole

Carole, in the fourth year of her principalship, is principal of Southwind Elementary School in an urban school district on the lower mainland of British Columbia. Many new Canadians are visible in the school. Carole indicates that she was accepted into administration the first time she applied and was sent to a school as a vice-principal. She attributes her success with leadership to her qualities of energy, enthusiasm, organization, and to her passion for her work, and for teaching children. Carole describes herself as an instructional leader whose task is to work with the teaching staff to develop a vision. She states, "I see myself as someone who really wants to be involved with the teachers and the kids on a day to day basis, making a difference for kids, and that's number 1." Carole stresses constant communication with teachers. She talks with teachers about lessons and teaching materials, and about motivating and disciplining students, sometimes even demonstrating alternatives which might be more effective in similar situations on other occasions. Carole works diligently at communicating and working with parents. The parent group at Southwind School has many parents who are new Canadians, so a great deal of encouragement is necessary to get them more involved.

Carole indicates that much of the decision-making in Southwind School is collaborative. Teachers have major influences over decisions regarding classroom teaching. She and the teachers both have major influence in choosing and implementing innovations. Many of the innovations they develop are based on teachers' ideas, and teachers have a major influence in choosing and purchasing teaching resources.

At Southwind there seems to be very little, if any, conflict. In dealing with conflict, Carole tries to be direct and open with people, and to bring people together to analyze situations and search for solutions. She notes that "I just have to keep reminding people to be as direct and forward with one another as they can and to be accepting of one another and their differences." She further notes that, in dealing with conflict situations, she attempts to determine what is motivating people by asking them to describe their feelings, and by working through difficult situations with them to determine how future occurrences can be prevented.

Carole offered to several metaphors for leadership and power. In the first three, she discussed only leadership metaphors. Carole stated:

Some days I'm an orchestral conductor waving my arms, directing, rehearsing, encouraging, and building a unified voice with a variety of sounds, pitches, tones and instruments. Some days I'm a great grandma praising the good, scolding the naughty, and supplying mountains of food to keep everyone well fed and happy. Other days I'm a mother bird, teaching my babies to fly and giving them the skills they need to leave me and live independently of my support.

Carole's fourth metaphor is more complex and appears related to both leadership and power.

She states:

Today, it's raining buckets and I feel like water. I shower people to refresh and invigorate them. I wash everyone equally, ... I urge people to dive deep and explore hidden regions. I try to permeate everywhere to reach hidden nutrients and to stimulate growth. I wash up against everyone, including students, teachers and parents, and I interact with each person in a way which cleanses and supports. I keep flowing without complaint, and never let my resources dry up. I provide honest reflections as I communicate with people. . . . . I can be as simple as a solitary raindrop, or I can be an entire ocean, with the power to buoy up or the power to destroy. I choose a supportive and buoyant method of relating and though I know my own power, I try never to do damage or harm. . . . . I am fluid. I ebb and flow. I am flexible and willing to change, yet I can remain deeply rooted and firm in my convictions. I am trustworthy and reliable, and follow patterns and provide a structure much like the moon and the tides. And in the spring, when the rain has subsided, and little shoots of growth burst from the moist earth, each precious flower will whisper with pride, "I did it myself."

Barbara

Greenville School, of which Barbara is principal, is a bustling kindergarten to grade 8 school in the same division as Southwind School. Greenville School has an enrolment of approximately 450 students, a number of whom are new Canadians. English as a second language is an instructional issue for teachers, students and administrators in this school.

This is Barbara's second term as the principal of Greenville. She served 8 years as a principal and vice-principal with the division prior to her present appointment. Many experiences frame the ways in which Barbara views her work as a principal. Among them are growing up in a large family amid difficult circumstances and developing a strong sense of self, strength, and empathy with injustice and the individual needs of students. Barbara also believes that much of what she has done is because "I've been lucky in having women friends that are genuinely supportive of each other."

As a leader, Barbara believes she is very supportive of the teachers, encouraging them to be continuous learners, interested in professional development. She is working with teachers to implement changes in philosophy and curriculum design in the school. She notes, "I have to be very careful not to be too strong or too enthusiastic, particularly with this staff, or I'll turn them off and I'm not going to get change." Barbara sees her initial role in this situation as one of observing and encouraging what is already happening in the situations. She notes that "I see my role in terms of reflecting to them what they're already doing and encouraging them in their own risk taking." Barbara notes that, while she values the work of teachers, "I always try to bring it back to the students' reality."

Barbara's 'loonie lunch' professional development meetings attest to her concern about developing curriculum to meet the needs of students' realities. The meetings do not have specific agendas, but are a forum for the teachers to 'pick' Barbara's brain about the area of language arts and language teaching. Barbara reiterated that attendance and participation in such meetings is purely voluntary. She added, "that kind of invitational approach seems to be really working" perhaps because teachers feel more powerful and in control.

Barbara also stresses the importance of communication and dialogue to her work. She indicates that she wants on-going dialogue with teachers about bullying, teasing, fighting, and harassing in order "to develop a common response to these things." She also believes that talking with parents about educational policies is important.

Barbara notes that decisions related to classroom instruction, from materials to objectives and concepts, were for teachers to make. She indicates that teachers also have a major influence on allocation of teaching resources, and that the vice principal and the teachers negotiate the school timetables and space allocations without her influence. Barbara reiterates that "I like most of these decisions to be made by teachers."

Barbara states that "if I'm aware there is a conflict I will call the people together and say there appears to be some difficulties here and I really do confront it and talk about it or have them talk about it." Barbara indicates that there is very little conflict among the teachers, and did not note the existence of any cliques or groups. She concludes that because she is new to the context, teachers may not feel as comfortable in challenging her as much as they might, but she encourages them to talk with each other and talk with her about things in order to keep communication levels high.

The metaphor related by Barbara was a metaphor for power. She notes that she views power as influence and not dominance. As principal, Barbara perceives her power as coming from three sources: her position as principal, her expertise and many years of experience as a teacher, and the personal qualities of empathy, and commitment to people and programs. She also believes there is a servant role to being a principal. Barbara stated that "My favorite metaphor for power is that it is a river." In further describing the river, she added:

There is a source – often deep, underground springs.

It is fed by many tributaries that contribute to its strength.

It is dynamic, always moving. It is life-giving and supportive.

It is controlled by its banks (environmental context, I guess).

It can be destructive when out of control.

It can change course when conditions dictate.

Communities grow up beside rivers.

There is usefulness and nurturance there.

Its movement is purposeful.

Metaphors and Meaning

Looking briefly at each of the metaphors, Eleanor's steering wheel metaphor presents an interesting concept in organizational guidance. Stemming from the world of science and technology, this metaphor is also closely related to guiding in a careful, thoughtful manner. The metaphor can also be perceived as being "defensive" as in defensive driving, however the context in which it is derived illustrates a leader who is thoughtfully assertive, very anxious to set a safe and successful course for the journey she is on with all people in the school. If the steering were perceived as "power" steering, the guidance required would be even more careful and sensitive since over-steering a vehicle with power steering often results in "losing control" of the vehicle.

The volcano metaphor presents even more potential for the appearance of a darker side to power. However, while there is a destructive side to a volcanic eruption, it also wipes away and buries that which has grown old and decayed. While Eleanor and others in leadership need to constantly be aware of the darker, destructive side of power, they also need not be afraid of using their power in thoughtful, creative ways. Eleanor's greatest challenge has been to use the volcano metaphor to remove the silence of mediocrity from a teaching staff who have many bright and creative voices which need to be heard (Kenway and Modra, 1992).

Sarah's metaphors, the shepherd and the judge, seem very Biblical in nature, and more closely related to masculine than to feminine images. This is not surprising since many women grow up strongly influenced by male images and surrounded by the expectations of masculine styles of leadership in organizations where they lead and work. The use of such metaphors indicates that Sarah is deeply aware of her own personal power in the lives of others around her, and views such in a relational way as a great responsibility in terms of the lives and work of others (Watkins, 1989). Here power may be viewed by others as a combination of "power with and power over" (Dunlap and Goldman, 1991) which allow her to use power more flexibly, using her voice to advocate for some individuals and to bring out the voices of some others.

Carole's and Barbara's metaphors are both based on water. Carole views water as nurturing and lifegiving, focusing extensively on the facilitative aspects of leadership and power (Dunlap and Goldman, 1991). Her water metaphor also has within it a reflection of "the Tao of leadership" (Heider, 1988) where the water metaphor describes a leader who is fluid and malleable in nature, using power very gently, and only for good. Barbara, in describing her river metaphor, also focuses mainly on the nurturant aspects; however, she does note that rivers, when their power is out of control, can be very destructive. So the water metaphors can have within them dark, murky places as well as refreshing nurturing places.

Conclusions

Three themes were noted among the metaphors for leadership and power that the four women used to describe their experiences. The first is that the metaphors used by each of the women illustrate power and leadership as relational concepts (Watkins, 1989) noting that, particularly for Barbara, leadership is a subset of power. She indicates that her power is multi-faceted, rooted in her personal, professional, and positional experiences. Sarah also perceives her power as multi-faceted when she describes herself as a kindly shepherd leading and guiding on some occasions and as a judge who attempts to empower colleagues and students on other occasions. In describing a critical incident during which she counselled a student having difficulties in his home, she also described the power to speak and to listen. Her description of the great influence which she felt herself exerting as she spoke and listened to the student was filled with concern, but also with a deep humility at the extent to which her influence was felt.

The second theme is the sense of responsibility which each of the four seems to feel and express toward those with whom they work. Carole and Sarah's expressions indicated a profound sense of their own personal responsibility in working with their colleagues. Nested with the responsibility theme is that of servanthood as a kind of modelling for self-giving. These findings are similar to Helgesen's (1990) experiences with the four women she studied and the voices from Gilligan's (1982) study where each expressed an ethic of care and responsibility for others. Their deep sense of concern for others reminds one of Noddings' (1984) description of "one-caring."

The third theme was the sense of nurturance which was expressed through each of the metaphors. Carole spoke of feeling like nurturing water which washed over her colleagues refreshing and replenishing their resources. Eleanor discussed the nurturance of children as a main part of her vision of leadership. Barbara, as a river, nurtured a variety of communities along the banks as she journeyed on toward the sea. Sarah, as the shepherd, expressed a great deal of responsibility for the nurturance and guidance of her flock.

Other themes were expressed by some of the women, but not all. Carole's and Barbara's metaphors linked to water suggest a quiet, constant strength which ebbs and flows throughout situations. The fluidity of the metaphor also attested to their belief in the importance of change and helping others smooth the rough corners and edges of change. Eleanor's volcano metaphor considers change in a different manner. By setting off some minor eruptions, she has been able to help people shake free of the status quo and create the forum for new qualities and programs to begin and grow. These eruptions and their resolution are similar to the tensions and resolutions which Morgan (1981) discusses in his schismatic metaphor. Eleanor's volcanic eruption and subsequent use of hierarchical power are supported by Kenway and Modra's (1992) discussion in which they point out that, sometimes, hierarchical power is required to allow the brightest and best voices to speak up beyond the silencing consensus of a group existing on a false sense of group equality. Such a group, dedicated to the status quo, was reported to exist in Acorn School prior to Eleanor's arrival.

At the outset of this chapter we were introduced to Corson's (1993) claim that language is a powerful shaper of human experience. We are also aware of Lakoff and Johnson's (1980) claim that new metaphors have the power to create new reality. Each of the principals' metaphors appears to be very much part of the realities in each of the four schools. In each situation, the principals' personal metaphors are couched within the overarching structure of holistic language programs which also permeate the processes of constant communication, conflict resolutions, and shared decision-making. There is strong evidence that, rather than controlling the dialectic in the schools, each principal is attempting to empower, facilitate and encourage expressions by teachers, students, parents, and others in the school communities. Similar to Corson's (1993) views that "language is the vehicle for identifying, manipulating and changing power relations between people" (p. 1), each has metaphorically expressed leadership styles which are facilitative, flexible, nurturing and transformative for those they serve within their school communities.

References

Aristotle. (1946). *Rhetoric*. Oxford: Oxford University Press.

Brunner, J. (1986). *Actual minds, possible worlds*. Cambridge, MA: Harvard University Press.

Corson, D. (1993). *Language, minority education and gender*. Toronto, ON: Ontario Institute for Studies in Education.

Dunlap, D., & Goldman, P. (1991). Rethinking power in schools. *Educational Administration Quarterly, 27*(1), 5-29.

Gilligan, C. (1982). In a different voice. Cambridge, MA: Harvard University Press.

Heider, J. (1988). *The Tao of leadership: Leadership strategies for a new age*. New York: Bantam Books.

Helgesen, S. (1990). *The female advantage: Women's ways of leadership*. Toronto, ON: Doubleday Currency.

Kenway, J., & Modra, H. (1992). Feminist pedagogy and emancipatory possibilities. In C. Luke, and J. Gore (Eds.), *Feminisms and critical pedagogy*. New York: Routledge Press.

Lakoff, G., & Johnson, M. (1980). *Metaphors we live by*. Chicago: The University of Chicago Press.

Lips, H. (1991). *Women, men and pwer*. London: Mayfield Publishing Company.

Morgan, G. (1981). The schismatic metaphor and its implications for organisational analysis. *Organizational Studies, 2*(1), 23-44.

Morgan, G. (1986). *Images of Organization*. Newberry Park, CA: Sage Publications.

Noddings, N. (1984). *Caring: A feminine aproach to ethics and moral education*. Berkeley CA: University of California Press.

Watkins, P. (1989). Leadership, power and symbols in educational administration. In J. Smyth (Ed.), *Critical perspectives in educational leadership*. New York: The Falmer Press.

10

Learning From Survivors:
Women Leaders Who Have Stayed the Course
Share Their Stories

Roberta Russell

In a recent interview Betty Friedan, commenting on the direction the feminist movement has taken, said, "What concerns women most is jobs – getting them, keeping them, getting promoted in them" (Wente, 1993). A key determining factor in achieving these goals is a woman's ability to survive and thrive in organizations.

Over the past five years as I conducted research on women and visible minority administrators, I have become increasingly interested in the concept of "survivorship." Why do some people who encounter barriers because of gender or racial discrimination remain positive and proactive while others become bitter, discouraged and paralyzed by the experience? What is it about the first group, the survivors, which enables them to put such experiences behind them and to move on?

This chapter is premised on the belief that the strategies women leaders have used to overcome barriers in their personal paths to leadership positions have much to teach other women. Many of them were pioneers, the first women to move into such positions, and as such they had no maps to follow and few role models to emulate (Betters-Reed, 1994). In many cases they have paid for their efforts, for their "assertiveness," in opportunities and promotions denied. Some developed reputations for being "difficult" or "pushy" and experienced rebuffs and even isolation. The survival strategies which have worked for them are ones which may well help other women trying to navigate the often confusing world of organizations. One of the most exciting aspects of the stories these women have to tell is of their efforts to be accepted on their own terms rather than simply trying to fit in as "men in skirts," as one woman termed it. Their efforts to become change agents on the inside have also opened doors for those women who will come after them. What they offer is not so much a recipe for or road map to one "right way" of succeeding as a range of options to draw from based on what has worked for them.

Whether based on women's diaries and journals or research studies, such as the ones on which this chapter is based, stories through which women share their experiences can serve several purposes. According to Cooper (1987), reading about these experiences serves to "assuage our sense of isolation and validate our perceptions: I'm not crazy. Someone else felt this way before" (p. 98). Milwid (1990) sees a "collective story" which documents the challenges women face in "breaking into all-male fields" as useful because it demonstrates that they face "a remarkably similar set of challenges," despite having unique personalities and positions, as they jump "through the same sets of hoops in an almost identical order" (p. 4). Stokes (1984) argues that it is important to document and quantify women's experiences of exclusion so that they will recognize that the barriers they experience are neither of their own making, nor simply a reflection of their personalities and competence. Such work, she suggests, "provides a focus for institutional change" (p. 1). Their experience is equally important to the next generation of women who will follow them into leadership positions. According to Canadian skier Nancy Greene, the eight Canadian women champions whose victories preceded hers and with whom she had travelled and competed are in part responsible for her gold medal in 1968. She says that "when you stand in the gate, you know it's been done before. And you know that if they can do it, you can do it" (Maclean's, 1994).

These women are survivors in the sense that they have encountered and overcome many of the barriers which numerous studies have documented exist for women. What made the difference for these women? What were the sources of strength and support on which they were able to draw? What kept them going while others gave up? This chapter attempts to answer some of those questions.

Methodology

This chapter is based on two studies of women and men administrators in education and public administration. The participants for one study were randomly selected from school systems in eastern Ontario and middle managers in the public service based in the National Capital Region while participants for the other study of visible minority administrators came from Halifax, Ottawa, Toronto, Winnipeg, and Vancouver. Visible minority participants were identified by colleagues or members of their ethnic community. Sixteen of the forty-three administrators (21 females and 22 males) interviewed were visible minorities. Both studies used a combination of semi-structured individual interviews with the administrators as well as focus groups (N = 5 groups or 38 individuals) and interviews with 26 "elites" (Marshall and Rossman, 1989), people considered to have high levels of valuable insider knowledge on career development and gender and race (employment equity officers, human resource specialists, book editors, union members, task force leaders). Table 1 provides information on the middle managers who were the main focus of the two studies.

Table 1

Interviewees

Secondary School Principals/Vice-Principals*			
Females		Males	
Mary	Dorothy	Dennis	Michael
Connie	Donna	Jeff	Ian
Marianne	Claire	Eric	Matt
Alison	Kathrynn		
Ann			
Middle Managers in the Public Service			
Females		Males	
Nan	Suzanne	Paul	Fred
Joyce	Beth	Richard	Trevor
Maria	Janice	Glen	Ron
Visible Minority Managers in Education**			
Females		Males	
Nelllie	Leslie	Ted	Kelly
Evelyn	Bernice	Ricardo	Jake
Ursula	Sharon	Ned	Will
		Chris	Harry
		Nick	Allan

* school systems in eastern Ontario
** principals, and vice-principals, elementary and secondary schools; superintendents; consultants from school systems in Toronto, Ottawa, Winnipeg, Halifax, and Vancouver

    The individual interviews focused on biographical information and early career experiences; views of mentoring, professionalism, success and opportunities in contemporary organizations; and strategies used for coping with barriers. Focus groups (Krueger, 1988; Morgan, 1988a) and elite interviews were conducted during the design phase to generate insights and vet the interview guide, and after data collection to vet preliminary findings. Standard qualitative methods for the analysis of long interviews (McCracken, 1988) and focus groups (Krueger, 1988) were utilized.

Barriers

Interviewees were asked a number of questions designed to test their awareness of and sensitivity to barriers to career advancement and their ways of dealing with them. Each interviewee was also asked general questions about what it takes to succeed in his or her organization and whether there are special or different barriers for women than for men.

All women educators commented on their feelings of being all alone, being in "a bit of a lonely position" (Mary), of being "on your own" (Ann). Connie illustrates these experiences with a description of the first principals' meeting she attended after her appointment. She was the only woman at the meeting and admits to feeling intimidated by this. Leslie, a visible minority woman principal, says that as the only minority woman principal, "I have no colleagues."

Isolation remains one of the major problems for women middle managers. As one interviewee says, "being a principal is very lonely for a woman." Having fewer people with whom to discuss and work through problems probably limits one's ability to improve problem-solving and decision-making skills. Women interviewees appear to become accustomed to not being included in work-related social events or being included but reminded in various ways that they are really outsiders. This limited participation in the social side of work relations appears to result in more limited access to opportunities to learn aspects of the "presentation of self" as described by Greene (1977). Thus, it appears that in various ways many of the techniques described in the literature for denying access to socialization to organizational norms and values have been experienced to varying degrees by women interviewees in this study.

Women interviewees tend, as a group, to emphasize their credentials, hard work, workaholism in fact, and great attention to detail in meeting all the requirements for the next stage up the ladder. They tend to assume that their superior qualifications and hard work will lead to advancement, while men interviewees tend to stress the importance of visibility and connections. Male careers appear to get more of a head start as the result of contacts with other males who have relevant experiences and information to share, and men tend to be proactive, seeking out such aids to advancement. Women appear eager to please and to fit in and are careful not to be seen as aggressive in pursuing advancement. They may challenge sexist practice, but only indirectly through such things as the use of humor. They appear to try to very systematically accumulate all the required credentials and experience they believe are needed in order to advance. They talk often about the confidence this provides them. Male interviewees appear to be more relaxed about the career advancement process. Only one even uses the word "confidence," using it to say that he was confident he could do a particular job despite not having fulfilled all the experience requirements which most people assumed were prerequisites to promotion. Men see individual contacts and networks as important to the process of advancing a career. Several male interviewees describe skipping steps in the credentials or experience hierarchy and make no apology for doing so.

Marianne describes the negative visibility to which women principals are sometimes subjected, saying that as a "lady principal," as she is sometimes called, one experiences "some fairly heavy duty stress." Like Ann, she has experienced people "taking me on in a very, very demanding way." She clearly feels the performance pressures often experienced by "tokens" (Kanter, 1977). As she describes it, "it's the old Charlotte Whitton thing of having to be better than your male colleagues 'cause there's still a lot of questions about women being competent in this role." Visibility concerns due to performance pressures may account for the fact that women appear to be particularly worried about taking shortcuts if they are offered, while the men interviewed appear to have no such concerns, believing that they could learn what was needed on the way up. While several men described skipping what most people assume are the necessary stages in a career ladder, only one woman did, and several women talked about the need to pay and to be seen to pay one's dues by completing every stage. Despite having a wide range of experience, "you name it, I've now done it. Okay," Janice was still being overlooked or not seriously considered for further advancement.

Several women (Suzanne, Maria, Janice) describe being treated at meetings and when opportunities for promotion come up as if they are invisible to their male colleagues and supervisors. An elite interviewee, a male union representative, describes having observed such a situation. He describes attending a meeting which a female business colleague had with a banker and observing that her ideas and suggestions were ignored by the banker until he repeated them, making him feel, he says, like a "parrot." Nan describes experiencing this invisibility at meetings where she would raise a point early in the discussion which would "go unnoticed until one of them (men) said it and then it's a wonderful idea." Marianne describes the invisibility of the lone female in committees or meetings where her ideas are listened to "respectfully, but her ideas are just dismissed." She says that this happens less than in the past, but that it still happens.

The expression "soft wall of resistance" refers to subtle organizational practices which work against the career advancement of women. Both Janice, a middle manager in the public service, and Eric, a male high school principal, describe this phenomenon at some length, illustrating their views with examples. Janice talks about the "invisible" barriers created for women by the attitudes and assumptions of their supervisors who make judgments about their willingness to relocate, etc. without consulting them directly. Eric provides examples of the preferential treatment accorded male educators in the assignment of development assignments. Members of an all-male focus group also made a number of observations on the phenomenon. The most salient of these subtle practices is a "covert sexism" as expressed by the male focus group:

"while overt sexism is not seen anymore, it is still there. It is just invisible"; "nothing has really changed for women. They may get more computer and scientific training, but they do not get preparation to manage these functions"; and, "only radical means such as a 10 year moratorium on promoting males will bring about change."

Two of the women interviewed (Janice, Maria) commented on the sexism of the system as perhaps being more of a barrier than the sexism of individuals. Some predict that as the numbers of female leaders in organizations increase, models of success and leadership may change since increased numbers will increase the confidence of women managers and they will not feel as pressured to conform to male models. However, one woman focus group member argued that women feel held back by the lack of acceptance of their different style of managing and that, while the system may be gradually integrating some features of that style, it is at the cost of the careers of the women pioneers. Like Janice, Paul talks about the subtle and deep-rooted forms of sexism in organizations. He says that one has to "scratch really deep to become aware of it." Nan talks about the negative result of a "shrill and shrew-like" response to sexism, stressing that women need to deal with it with "as much grace as possible." The barriers one creates by overreacting to sexism, she says, can never be undone.

Ceilings are described not so much in terms of glass as plexiglass, "you can't even scratch it"; concrete, you can't see through it; and quotas or "hiring targets become ceilings." It appears that qualifications and hard work can advance a career to a certain point, perhaps middle manager level, but that who you know and what information you have access to is critical for people who are aspiring to or are functioning at more senior levels of organizational life (Fernandez, 1981).

Overall the women interviewed, while recognizing that there are significant barriers to their building a career, remain optimistic about their personal career prospects. Part of the explanation for this may relate to the fact that these individuals have already experienced some success in having reached middle management.

Thus far, the discussion of barriers to the career advancement of women has focused on the types of barriers women and men describe experiencing or observing. The next section reviews some of the survival strategies and resources women describe using in order to deal with these barriers.

Survival Strategies and Resources

Networks and Support Systems

Like two other women educators interviewed (Mary and Marianne) Ann depends on and receives moral support from a network of friends in the field.

Unlike men's networks, theirs seems to be based more on nurturing support than on professional experience and information sharing. Quina (1990, p. 100) points out that support groups and friendship networks among women workers are serving as models for male workers as well. Several of the men and women interviewed described this as happening in their organizations.

Beth's and Suzanne's first work assignments appear to have been in the kind of nurturing work environment described by Young (1991). Alison describes herself as having a "pretty good network." Like Mary and Ann and Matt, one of the male educators, she says she uses her network now to get a "reflective perspective," as a kind of sounding board. Kathryn identifies one woman colleague as having been very supportive of her career, "because she saw I was competent and just generally, I think, furthering the cause of women." She goes on to point out that "I've had many men who have been extremely supportive of me as a person and as a colleague, absolutely. It's just that the others (ones who tried to hold her back) I remember, they come to mind first."

Several discuss job changes as serving to expand their networks by exposing them to new people and as having the potential for both expanding one's networks and adding to one's bank of skills. Knowing people who hold power and networking with people for what they "do" rather than for who they "are" are important, according to several men. They see managers' information networks and informal networks as more important to their functioning than is training. As older males retire they suggest that networks will open up to women. On the subject of women's networks, men see women's smaller networks as explaining why fewer women are in management, while several women complain that women's networks have a forced and artificial quality as they try to model their networks after those of males, but have so much less information to share.

While the literature suggests that men tend to nurture their networks through socializing after work or shared sports activities, something Matt and Michael describe doing, two women, Joyce and Nan describe networking through personal notes attached to clippings or copies of journal articles they send to contacts who may be interested in that subject. They use mail, telephone, and FAX machines to accomplish this. Joyce suggests that time is a factor; they want to keep up contacts but, because of family responsibilities, lack the time for socializing.

Women perceive themselves as having support systems which are "collegial," not "backstabbing" as they believe the men's tend to be (Mary). Mary says that a very important kind of support, "the kind of support you need," is having someone who calls to see how you are when they know you are in the middle of a crisis. Matt, too, describes that type of support as very important to him. Marianne sees the "very strong women's network" she has been part of as very important to her success. The network seems to have allowed her to vent her frustrations. As she describes it, "we'd get mad all together and talk and rage. You could use bad words and that kind of stuff." These women seem to have discovered the value of support systems later in their careers than their male colleagues. Networks, like mentors, are described by several women as most important for their nurturing function. While acknowledging the importance of women's networks for their nurturant qualities, a number of men and women expressed the view that they do not make up for the fact that women are still excluded from the more powerful male networks where information critical to the organization is shared.

Mentors and Role Models

Mary, like Ann, has a female colleague with whom she prepared for competitions, something male educators have just begun to do. Later in her career she benefited from both mentors and role models, all female it appears. She describes what one of these people, a woman administrator who has served as a role model, has done for her and observed that through that example she has learned to do the same for others. She says of that experience, "but I realized from people helping me how much a little bit is. How little you have to give somebody who just needs that little push."

Connie talks about the difficulty many women have in finding mentors, partly because men in senior positions do not know how to mentor female colleagues. She has benefited from being mentored by someone whom she describes as less than comfortable in the role, but she describes another colleague who was very direct and clear that his was a mentoring role.

Several women allude to the concept of "conditional" mentoring, that is, men who promote "safe" women who will not challenge them. Such women may be seen as controllable and will function as an extension of the mentor, remaining a "loyal lieutenant." Such mentors may be perceived by some as progressive and supportive of affirmative action but may be seen by others as "playing Pygmalion" (Morgan, 1988b). This may relate to a point that men and women make about men who may be extremely supportive of individual women colleagues but may in other ways work against equity for female employees in general.

The advantages of having several mentors was also discussed (Ron). Multiple mentoring was seen as allowing one to be exposed to different styles while at the same time reducing the risk that one's career takes a downturn when one's mentor's career does. Both Beth and Suzanne talk about the nurturing work environment created for them by their mentors, making the work setting a place where they felt they would not be punished for making a mistake. Suzanne says of her mentor that he "created an environment where you could be creative, where you could develop."

Nan talks about the difference between men and women mentors, saying that men make "more show of it" while the women "come through quietly, without fanfare." Glen, who had a mentor for a short period at the very beginning of his career, says that having a mentor "really does help you" and advises people who want to get ahead to "find a mentor, don't wait to be trained." Glen also addresses the issue of timing (Strauss, 1959), saying that he was too young and inexperienced in government at that early stage to benefit as fully as he might have from such an experienced mentor.

Role models are seen by some women as allowing them to take control of their fate rather than waiting for someone to choose to mentor them. Marianne worries that she may be a "negative role model" for some younger women because she is divorced and works eighteen-hour days.

Stretch Assignments and Opportunities to See the Big Picture

The research literature (Hall and Associates, 1987; McCall, Lombardo, and Morrison, 1988; Mintzberg, 1990) stresses the importance of on-the-job learning for those aspiring to be managers as opposed to learning acquired primarily from books or courses. Eric, one of the principals interviewed, talks about the importance of actual exposure to management-like experiences and the fact that women are less likely to get those experiences, particularly early in their careers. He uses the example of the principal who has to be away from his school and asks a member of staff, usually a male teacher, to cover for him. The examples given by Alison and Beth of the ways in which they benefited from being given management-like experiences and responsibilities early in their careers provide support for this view. The all-male focus group stressed that it was more important for leaders to have a broad range of experiences than educational credentials.

Several people talk about the importance of "stretch" assignments, ones which expose them to a wide range of new experiences. These allow neophytes to develop confidence although initially they may generate a lot of stress and anxiety in the individual. Nan describes moving from work with a provincial government to a national organization as "a bit of a stretch," but a valuable experience because the successful transition gave her more confidence and a better overview of her field.

Putting a Positive Spin on Marginality

Marginality was discussed in both positive and negative terms. Although marginal status has tended to be seen as a negative, it may also have positive features which make the boundary spanning capacity of marginal people "functional" (Park, 1967). Women, as relative newcomers to the management world, often unconsciously challenge traditional models of behavior. Marginality can provide people with a wider horizon and a more detached and rational viewpoint, the product of living in two different worlds. Such people can become messengers back and forth between the two worlds – "boundary spanners." Several of the women interviewed clearly believe that they bring valuable new perspectives to the organization. These women take pride in their capacity to see organizational processes in new ways and see their male collegues and supervisors as increasingly more receptive of the differences they bring. Ian, for example, says that he has come to see through observing his women colleagues that someone who is "humane and open" can be more effective than "someone who gains respect through a very cold, autocratic approach." By contrast, the negative perspective on marginalization sees women as tokens who are "ghettoized" in the life of organizations. From that perspective, marginalization contributes to their unequal access to organizational socialization experiences and opportunities.

Positive Visibility

Knowing how powerful visibility is and the kinds of experiences which best provide it enables one to better position oneself for opportunities. Men appear to have recognized early in their careers that visibility is important and are better at "distinguishing themselves from the crowd" (Fernandez, 1991, p. 251). A sports background seems to be related to this capacity. While Kathryn says that it just made sense to her that because "the competition is so extreme you have to do something that makes you noticed more than the others," she was one of only two women who expressed that awareness.

Ann's mathematics degree helped her obtain a position as chair of a "New Math" committee, despite the fact that she was a beginning teacher. Connie had been active in a work group studying child abuse just as the issue was gaining attention. Thus, chance (Bandura, 1982; Young, 1989) played some role in their early career visibility. Routine assignments or ones on which the organization places a low value or priority, such as affirmative action (Ortiz, 1982), were identified as ones to be avoided by those wanting to advance their careers. Such assignments not only keep one invisible, it appears, they may even marginalize one (Ortiz, 1982). Visible minority women interviewed, particularly African Canadians, had numerous stories to tell of being marginalized by the organization's assumption that all visible minorities are interested in, or especially well equipped to be, race relations or multiculturalism specialists, regardless of their academic qualifications or experience. One woman who had been a principal, before a leave of absence, described being offered on her return from leave a position as race relations consultant rather than a principal's position despite her qualifications, which included her superintendent's papers.

Feminism as Commitment to Others

A high proportion of educators and public servants, both male and female, demonstrate a strong service motivation, but there is an added dimension for women. Several (Mary, Connie, Alison), talk about "hanging in" during difficult times because they hope their success will make it easier for their daughters, and others like themselves whose careers will follow theirs. Mary says,

> When I was competing and being rejected there were times when I felt, Who needs this? There are lots of things I could be doing with my time that would make me feel better about myself than having people say, 'No, we don't want you again.' But I thought of (my daughter) and I thought if we (women) don't keep saying 'Yes, we are here, we do want these jobs and we can do them,' it will never be any easier for women behind us, for girls. So it kept me going although I don't think she really appreciates it.

These women acknowledge the debt they owe to the women who preceded them and to those who will follow. Marianne says that one of the "very fortunate happenstances along the way" in her career was the fact that "a woman had been promoted ahead of me, an exceptionally talented woman, so it made it easier, I think. At least in our board we can't afford any female duds yet because there aren't enough of us."

Several women talk about how much their mothers and others like themselves were cheated of a career by the values of earlier times and how they want to succeed for these women. Several saw this as an important component of feminism, breaking down barriers so that others who follow will not have to do so. A number of the older women managers describe themselves as feminists. In fact, a woman elite interviewed commented that "most women don't become feminists until they are 35. I think then they begin to see what's happening."

Fitting In and Taking Control

Men, too, can share the experience of not fitting in. One male says that he is seen as "some kind of Trojan horse." If they let him in, they will have to accept others like him who do not fit the model of the ideal male manager. Dressing for success is still a part of management training in education, according to another who described it as part of the content of a recent superintendent's course. "Dress codes will be the last to go" in education, she said. Those who do not fit the traditional male leadership model are very conscious of the fact that male managers who dominate the senior levels of most organizations tend to select people for special assignments and promotion who fit their own image. They select people with whom they are comfortable, who share a culture and values.

While mentors, role models, and various support systems can be helpful, one female focus group member pointed out that "they're opening up the wrong doors for women." What needs changing, she points out is the culture of organizations to make them more inclusive of different management styles.

Several interviewees describe such "taking control" behaviors as deciding on a career change or redirection (Marianne) against the advice of those "who should know," a change in academic major (Ann), refusing to learn to type (Evelyn), or relocating to get away from a possessive parent (Claire). While Asplund (1988) and others describe women's tendency to overemphasize the value of education and ignore the informal side of organizational life, others see it as an example of their taking control of those aspects of their lives over which they have some control. They make choices, choosing not to be victims of circumstances. Taking control, as illustrated by the examples provided by the women interviewed, may increase one's sense of individual power. It stimulates proactive rather than reactive behaviors.

Playing Games and Playing Roles

Michael describes how sports helps you see your job as a game. He says that women have more difficulty with this because they don't have a team sports background. Many of the men interviewed refer to their work as a game. Marianne, one of the few women to see her work in this way, talked about the need for a manager to "bleed publicly" sometimes, saying that it is just a ritual which makes one's opponent feel satisfied without costing oneself anything in real terms. She attributes her ability to do this to a theatre background. As she says, "I'm a former drama person; I have a range of strategies." Marianne seems to be particularly adroit at tactics (Martin and Sims, 1977), such as self-drama-tization and the art of persuading, which most of the men interviewed describe using or having the capacity to use. Marianne discussed changing and playing roles as part of administrative job expectations and something that involves "not personal compromise but rather, choosing and playing roles purposefully" (Marshall, 1979, p. 176). Women appear to view men as better at this, at "finessing," as Alison terms it.

One female member of a focus group stressed the need for women to learn "how to roll with the punches and not hold a grudge" as well as how "to project themselves in a more confident way." Another female in the same group, however, disagreed with the latter point, saying that women who do not fit the stereotype of passivity expected of them will be punished by finding themselves negatively labeled as pushy or aggressive.

The Importance of a Positive Outlook and a Sense of Humor

Women interviewees remain very optimistic despite some frustrating experiences. Although it has taken some of them a long time to get into management and in spite of having seen others, who were in their opinion less able, promoted past them, they remain optimistic about their future prospects. Most are forward looking and there is little looking back on past decisions with regret. Alison, for example, who had frequent disruptions to her career because of her husband's studies and sabbaticals, made the best of these experiences, adding to her bank of skills by taking courses and doing volunteer work in schools wherever they were living. This eventually paid off for her when she was promoted, perhaps, on the basis of the range of experiences she had to offer.

Evelyn, a black woman school principal, described advising a younger colleague to smile and to avoid complaining if she wanted to get ahead. As she expressed it, "I say, 'Smile. Even if you bitch afterwards or pound the wall, take it'." This does not mean that they do not challenge injustice but, as one said, "you pick your times to go to war." As Evelyn says, "I have learned that fighting is not worth it. I don't lock horns, but I don't give up. I stand firm." If you are unhappy with something at work, Evelyn advises, don't go to your boss with a complaint, take a suggestion for improvement. She believes that nobody wants to be around anybody "with a big chip on their shoulder all the time" because "it drags everybody down because everybody is out there struggling." The difficulty of retaining a positive attitude when one's efforts are not rewarded was reflected in the view of one of the younger black women interviewed. She was clearly feeling frustrated and disappointed that the world in which she is attempting to build her career is not significantly different from that experienced by the generation of Blacks whose careers preceded hers.

Maria says of herself: "I am also an indestructable optimist. I believe that every human success story is a story of optimism. It's also a story of conquered fears. If you fail, you conquer your fear of failure and bounce out of a failure. Because think of it, you've never seen a pessimist be successful."

Most women interviewed provided examples of how they use humor to deal with difficult or frustrating experiences, often ones involving discrimination. A number of writers have talked about the use of humor by victims of discrimination (Allport, 1958), and women (Barreca, 1991). Louch (1992) describe this form of humor as humor of survival. Others have described jokes as being an important part of company culture and describe situations where "having a good sense of humor" was "a requisite for mobility" (Kanter, 1977, p. 41). Women's use of humor is most often self-deprecating and not at the expense of others. Mary says that she was incensed by some of the discrimination she experienced, but stresses that "when you react to them you play into their hands." Instead she advises using such techniques as saying "the things before they say them." For example, in a meeting where only male names are being nominated for a special assignment, she might say, "oh, you don't want to let a girl do that." Using humor in this way, she says, "saves their face" and sometimes stops the behavior. She describes women's humor as more inclusive than men's humor which tends more often to be sarcastic and directed against others. Marianne describes principals of the 1960s as "an interesting funny group," "lots of jokes." The descriptions provided by women interviewees suggest that humor often becomes their way of taking control, of resisting the role of victim.

Making a Difference

In describing what sustains them during stressful periods, women principals talk about what they like about being a manager and tend to focus on such experiences as helping bring out people's talents and helping people develop, of making a difference in peoples' lives. This came out most often in discussions of the way in which they handle conflict. The emphasis was on bringing those involved together to negotiate a solution, and to develop skills in staff and students that will serve them well beyond the current crisis. This point did not come up in focus groups or elite interviews although a couple of men in the all male group talk about women managers as being less likely to be threatened by staff members who make suggestions for change. One man sees male managers as more likely to "squash" ideas and then to revive them later as their own. Marianne describes some of the leaders in the early years of her career as men who had been "outstanding teachers" and who, as leaders, were "lone rangers," non-consultative men "who got on their horse and led their school and the rules be damned." She describes the current group of principals in her system as more efficient, task-oriented, collaborative and having the "ability to diffuse conflicts."

Summary

These themes illustrate some of the special challenges which women face in trying to manage their careers. While female managers in these studies have had some catching up to do, they are developing quickly in their understanding of the need for visibility, the value of stretch assignments, the need to be aware of "the big picture," the value of a variety of work experiences, and the importance of finding mentors and other support systems. At the same time, they are devising alternatives to some of the strategies males have used to advance their careers. In this respect, they report developing networks which focus on the particular needs of women, using marginal status, ingenuity and humor to their advantage, and actively valuing and promoting the different perspectives many women bring to organizational life. Women interviewees describe using a range of techniques for dealing with barriers. Among those they describe most frequently are conflict resolution techniques, negotiated solutions to problems, putting a positive spin on marginality, and feminism as commitment to and investment in others.

References

Asplund, G. (1988). *Women managers: Changing organizational cultures.* New York, NY: John Wiley and Sons.

Allport, G. (1958). *The nature of prejudice.* Garden City, NY: Doubleday Anchor Books.

Bandura, A. (1982). The psychology of chance encounters and life paths. *The American Psychologist, 37*(7), 747-755.

Barreca, R. (1991). *They used to call me Snow White... But I drifted: Women's strategic use of humor.* New York, N.Y: Viking.

Betters-Reed, B. (1994). *Toward transformation of the management curriculum: Visions and voices for inclusion.* Wellesley, MA: Center for Research on Women, Wellesley College.

Cooper, J. (1987). Shaping meaning: Women's diaries, journals, and letters – The old and the new. *Women's Studies International Forum, 10*(1), 95-99.

Fernandez, J.P. (1981). *Racism and sexism in corporate America: Changing values in American business.* Lexington, MA: Lexington Books.

Fernandez, J.P. (1991). *Managing a diverse work force: Regaining the competitive edge.* San Francisco, CA: Jossey-Bass Publishers.

Greene, C.N. (1977). Disenchantment with leadership research: Some causes, recommendations and alternative directions. In J. G. Hunt and L. L. Larsom (Eds.), *Leadership: The cutting edge* (pp. 57-67). London: Feffer and Simon.

Hall, D.T. & Associates (1987). *Career development in organizations.* San Francisco, CA: Jossey-Boss.

Kanter, R.M. (1977). *Men and women of the corporation.* New York, NY: Basic Books, Inc.

Krueger, R.A. (1988). *Focus groups: A practical guide for applied research.* Newbury Park, CA: Sage Publications.

Louch, K. (1992, March 4). Television interview, *On the arts.* Toronto, ON: CBC Newsworld.

Maclean's (1994, February 14). *A ski run paved in gold,* p. 51. Toronto, ON: Author.

Marshall, C. (1979). *The career socialization of women in school administration.* Unpublished doctoral dissertation, University of California, Santa Barbara, California.

Marshall, C., & Rossman, G.B. (1989). *Designing qualitative research.* Newbury Park, CA: SAGE Publications.

Martin, N.H. & Sims, J.H. (1977). The exercise of power in organizations: Power tactics. In J. M. Staw (Ed), *Psychological foundations of organizational behavior* (pp. 272-278). Santa Monica, CA: Goodyear Publishing Co.

McCall, M.W., Jr., Lombardo, M.M., & Morrison, A.M. (1988). *The lessons of experience: How successful executives develop on the job*. Lexington, MA: Lexington Books.

McCracken, G. (1988). *The long interview*. Newbury Park, CA: SAGE Publications.

Milwid, B. (1990). *Working with men: Professional women talk about power, sexuality, and ethics*. Hillsboro, OR: Beyond Words Publishing, Inc.

Mintzberg, H. (1990). The manager's job: Folklore or fact. *Harvard Business Review*, 90(2), 163-176.

Morgan, D.L. (1988a). *Focus groups as qualitative research*. Newbury Park, CA: SAGE Publications.

Morgan, N. (1988b). *The equality game: Women in the federal public service (1908-1987)*. Ottawa, ON: Canadian Advisory Council on the Status of Women.

Ortiz, F.I. (1982). *Career patterns in education: Men, women and minorities in public school administration*. New York, NY: J F Praeger.

Park, R.E. (1967). In R.H. Turner (Ed.), *Robert E. Park on social control and collective behavior*. Chicago, IL: University of Chicago Press.

Quina, K. (1990). The victimization of women. In M. A. Paludi (Ed.), *Ivory power: Sexual harassment on campus* (pp. 93-102). Albany, NY: SUNY Press,.

Stokes, M.J. (1984). *Organizational barriers and their impact on women in higher education*. Washington, DC: National Association for Women Deans, Administrators, and Counselors.

Strauss, A.L. (1959). *Mirrors and masks: The search for identity*. Chicago, IL: The Free Press of Glencoe.

Wente, M. (1993, November 13). "How to be 72: A lesson from Betty Friedan," *The Globe and Mail*, A2.

Young, B. (1989). *Not finished yet: The stories of four women's careers in education*. Unpublished Ph.D. Dissertation, University of Alberta, Edmonton.

Young, B. (1991, June). *On careers: Themes from the lives of four western Canadian women educators*. Paper presented at the annual conference of the Canadian Society for the Study of Education, Queen's University, Kingston, Ontario.

Section Three

Leadership Issues for Teachers and Others

Introduction

Only a relatively few people in any organization will undertake formal administrative roles. This does not mean, however, that only they will be affected by policies and practices surrounding administration. Indeed, the actions and reactions of "followers" are an important part of administration and leadership. Also, leaders often emerge unofficially within groups.

In this section, we look at several studies based on research questions which expand our focus on gender, educational administration and leadership to include the experiences of teachers and others. We find that, in pursuit of their questions, these researchers have used a variety of data gathering and data analysis techniques. Many of these authors add their personal comments and conclude their chapters by considering possibilities for the future. They also illustrate the difficulties which exist when traditional ideas about appropriate masculine and feminine behaviours persist. In this section, essentialist notions are held up for discussion and we continue to consider the contradictions evident when gender is considered within educational leadership research.

In Chapter Eleven, Vivian Hajnal draws on three demographic databases on Canadian teachers to examine differences between the number of children that male teachers have and the number that female teachers have. She considers these differences in relation to full-time and part-time teaching status, marital status and spousal employment. She asks us to consider how current practices and policies regarding teaching and administration discriminate against women due to their childbearing role and how this affects their chances to take on formal leadership. She talks about her own personal experiences and challenges us to reconsider policies which disadvantage women in our schools.

In Chapter Twelve, Tom Gougeon looks at followership as an important part of leadership. Ten male and ten female principals of junior high schools in Alberta agreed to have their male and female teachers surveyed regarding their perceptions of the principal. Using a semantic differential scale, the author illustrates how both male and female teachers in the study held more positive attitudes towards the female principals. He suggests how such attitudes may be related to intrinsic motivations among those who are led by women.

In Chapter Thirteen, Carol Harris presents an ethnographic study of the leadership style of Elizabeth Murray of Nova Scotia. We are encouraged to consider how this charismatic leader shows continuity and commitment in her leadership and how she is able to foster a sense of community amongst those she leads. The author discusses the implications of these observations for women leaders and for all who wish to enhance positive community relationships.

In Chapter Fourteen, Kathie Webb is inspired by a novel by Charlotte Perkins Gilman to develop a fictionalized encounter between Jack and Marly – two people who hold very different views of how schooling might best be organized. Through this innovative approach, the author formulates a feminist utopian vision of what schools without hierarchies might be like.

In Chapter Fifteen, Elizabeth Tucker looks at contradictions which arise when we encourage teachers or administrators to accept without question the value of nurturance and "helping" strategies. Using her study of Educational Assistance Plans (EAPs) in Ontario school boards, she examines biotechnology – a faceless yet intrusive form of power which manipulates individuals by teaching them that they must adjust themselves to the demands of the workplace and the other organizations in which they participate. She discusses how counselling programs, such as the one studied, tend to focus on teachers, a largely female group, and how such programs may operate to stigmatize those who use the help offered. Her analysis helps us see how existing power structures can co-opt well-intentioned attempts to help women and others.

In Chapter Sixteen, Hanne Mawhinney and Linda LaRocque also talk about contradictions with regard to leadership and women in school organizations. They develop a critical ethnography based on interviews with three female educators who have become chairpersons of school boards in Ontario and Alberta. The authors conclude that we need to explore the "ecology" of both public and private domains of women's lives if we are to begin to understand their experiences of leadership.

11

Can I Do A Good Job Of Both Family And Work?
Decisions Regarding Offspring

Vivian Hajnal

I am a female in an administrative position and I want to have children. There seem to be so many barriers that the whole idea is overwhelming. First of all, the issue of time – need I say more. I already have 2-3 night meetings per week and I seldom arrive home before 6:30 pm each day. Then, of course, I'm zonked because I've been enthusiastic, energetic, optimistic, etc. all day and come home to an infant child who desperately needs the same enthusiasm, energy, etc. My husband is quite supportive, but given his traditional home environment I still have my "work" to do with him. The second issue, while related to time, is somewhat different – fairness. Can I do a good job of both – family and work? I think I can, but I'm scared. I am very organized and efficient *and* caring! To be a mother I *must* put my child first. It is a concern. How will my superiors view my roles? (An administrator quoted in Robertson, p. 27)

This chapter examines the differences between the number of offspring that male and female teachers have and relates these differences to demographic variables. Full-time and part-time status, and the number of extra work hours spent away from school are introduced into the examination of the number of offspring of educators.

During recent history, the choice of a teaching career has been viewed as particularly astute for females. It was felt that women were happier with the ease of entry and exit to a career, with the concurrence of teacher's time away from work and children's time away from school and with salaries that, on average, are higher than the mean for other female employees (Sedlak and Schlossman, 1987). The teaching timetable may have provided some of the flexibility that is the first request for working parents (Rodgers, 1992). Rodgers described the need for a great degree of flexibility in the workplace to enable parents to be both productive employees and responsible parents. Not only are there pressing childcare needs, but eldercare is becoming a critical issue for the middle-aged teaching force.

While the first need expressed by employees is for full-time positions with flexible hours (Rodgers, 1992), part-time employment and unpaid family leave are also frequently requested options. For many employees with family responsibilities, a reduced work week with the consequent reduction in pay, is not an option. In the teaching environment, flexible hours, which would conflict with time in the classroom, are not an option that is viewed positively by administrators or parents. Part-time employment is an attractive alternative, with options for a variety of schedules and time commitments and less disruption to students' lives.

The increase in interest in work-family programs has been reflected in the news coverage that it garners. Gonyea and Googins (1992) suggest that

> As corporate work-family programs have moved from the curious to the mainstream, they have also moved from the lifestyle pages to the business section of the newspapers. What was once regarded as a nice gesture by companies is now being examined as a strategic business initiative. (p. 210)

While work-family programs are in their infancy in the corporate sector, they are almost nonexistent in the school culture.

One example of attention to the need of parents is the provision by the Victorian Order of Nurses for child care of mildly ill children, aged 6 months to 12 years (CTF, 1994b). Available in eastern Ontario, this service is frequently paid for by the employer or shared between the employer and the employee. Two hospitals, a university, and a municipality made use of the service in its first year. In Canadian schools where women are the dominant employee group at 65 percent (King & Peart, 1992), it is amazing that no such emphasis has been placed on childcare needs.

Reporting on elementary and secondary teachers' unemployment insurance (UI) claims, Statistics Canada found that in February of 1993, 2 180 women received maternity UI benefits (CTF, 1994a). As well, the additional parental/adoption benefits (10 weeks) which can be taken by either parent or shared between them, were primarily accessed by women. Over 90 percent of these claims were filed by educators who were women. The responsibility for child care remains with mothers.

Research indicates that female teachers have reported greater satisfaction with their jobs than male educators (King & Peart, 1992; Lester, 1988; Chapman & Lowther, 1982; Holdaway, 1978). Even though the school environment is perceived as attractive to women, problematic situations occur. The literature is replete with discussions concerning the glass ceiling, the number of work hours required outside the classroom, and the need to see more females in administration in the school systems. Another issue, mentioned only in passing, is the number of offspring that educators have.

Although several authors in the U.S. and Canada have reported that female educators have fewer children than do male educators (Holmes, 1992; Hajnal, 1991b; Scott and McClellan, 1990), no examination of the patterns of this difference has occurred. One possible reason for this inattention may be the knowledge that the proportion of single women who are teachers is higher than the proportion of single women in the general population (King & Peart, 1992).

There may be a supposition that the difference in the number of offspring is essentially due to the marital status of the educators.

Data Sources and Methodology

Three main sources of data were used in this study: two Saskatchewan databases (Hajnal, 1991a, 1991b) and one Canadian database obtained by King and Peart (1992) in conjunction with the Canadian Teachers' Federation (CTF). In 1990 Hajnal (1991a) investigated job and pay satisfaction of Saskatchewan teachers, while in 1991 Hajnal (1991b) investigated teacher attitudes toward schools. Both research projects employed survey methods and two different random samples of 500 teachers were drawn from a population of approximately 11 000 teachers. In 1990 a snapshot of the work life of Canadian teachers was commissioned by the CTF. Every province and territory participated and responses were obtained from 17 600 teachers across Canada. A detailed description of the questionnaire design, methodologies and the results can be found in King and Peart (1992). This CTF project was an immense undertaking and resulted in a plethora of information about Canadian educators.

Data were collected concerning teachers' responses to questions about number of dependent children, age, gender, marital status, employment status of spouse, full-time status, number of extra hours of work and satisfaction with their job. Techniques employed in the analyses included summary measures such as frequencies and means, correlations, t-tests, and analysis of covariance (ANCOVA).

Results

The study findings that are reported in this chapter fall into three main categories: knowledge concerning the difference in number of offspring between male and female educators, implications for policy, and comments and suggestions for change.

The response rates to the Saskatchewan surveys were 58 and 40 percent for 1990 and 1991 respectively. Significant differences between the job satisfaction of female and male educators were not found. Teachers who were living in husband-wife families or in common law relationships were grouped into the married category. The marital status of the responding teachers indicated that more male than female teachers were married (see Table 1). Comparisons with Census data suggest that more male teachers were married and more female teachers were single than in the general population.

Census data for 1991 reported that the mean number of children for all husband-wife families, including common-law relationships, was 1.1 children for Canadian and 1.2 children for Saskatchewan couples. The Hajnal surveys of educators found the mean number of children for husband-wife families to be 1.71 in 1990 and 1.64 in 1991, while the results of the CTF survey indicated the mean number of children in Saskatchewan was 1.73 and 1.63 in Canada.

Table 1

Percentage Comparison of marital Status Between Female and Male Teachers Across Three Samples and the 1991 Census Data*

Saskatchewan						Marital Status	Canada (including SK)			
Hajnal 1990		Hajnal 1991		Census SK 1991			CTF Canada 1990		Census Canada 1991	
F	M	F	M	F	M		F	M	F	M
73	89	74	82	74	70	Married	71	82	66	65
21	8	16	12	13	21	Single	19	13	18	24
6	3	6	5	10	9	Separated/ divorced	9	5	13	10
		4	1	3	1	Widowed	1	0.4	3	1

*1991 Census: Population aged 25 to 59.

Considering all respondents, results of t-tests suggested (see Table 2) that female educators had significantly fewer children than male educators. In both Hajnal surveys no significant differences in the number of offspring were found for single educators. Significant differences in the numbers of offspring between male and female educators with spouses were discovered. Similar results were found in the CTF data with significant differences both in Saskatchewan and in Canada for all respondents as a group and for husband-wife families.

In both Hajnal (1990 and 1991) data sets, mean age for respondents was 43. Comparison of mean age for female and male respondents indicated there were no significant differences for the respondents as a whole, or when grouped by marital status (see Table 2). The mean age of Canadian respondents for the CTF survey was 40. The average age of the male respondents was 41.6 years while the average age of female respondents was 39.5 years ($t = 15$, $df = 16899$, $p < .001$). The distribution of ages, the larger number of respondents in the Canadian database, and a desire to control for age in the analysis suggested the use of ANCOVA where age could be used as a covariate.

Table 2

Comparison of Mean Number of Dependent Children Between
Females and Males Grouped by Marital Status Across Three Samples

Hajnal 1990		Hajnal 1991		Marital Status	CTF SK 1990		CTF Canada 1990	
F N = 159	M N = 127	F N = 121	M N = 77		F N = 771	M N = 535	F N=7873	M N=5126
1.39	2.03**	1.46	1.84**	Married	1.86	2.27***	1.78	2.10***
0.09	0.00	0.06	0.00	Single	0.15	0.30	0.12	0.18
1.10	1.85*	1.15	1.59*	All	1.57	2.01***	1.49	1.88***

*p < 0.05; **p < 0.01; ***p < 0.001

Respondents were grouped by whether their spouses were employed, and whether spousal employment was as an educator. The mean number of offspring by group was then calculated (see Table 3). The mean number of offspring was highest when the male teacher had a spouse who did not work outside the home. If both spouses were employed as educators, the mean number of children was approximately the same for both male and female respondents. If the spouse was employed, but not as an educator, the 1990 data indicated a significant difference in the number of offspring for male and female educators, and although the 1991 data shows a large difference of .43 (1.67-1.24), this difference was not significant at the .05 level for this sample size.

As the CTF questionnaire did not include a query about whether the spouse was currently working, an exact replication of the previous analysis was not possible. The variable concerning whether or not spouse was an educator was included in the ANCOVA of the CTF data.

Part-time teacher respondents in Saskatchewan were primarily women (92 percent in 1990, and 89 percent in 1991). Examining only the responses of female married/common law teachers (since other categories had too small a number of part-time respondents), large differences in the number of offspring were evident (see Table 4). These results were again supported by the CTF data, where almost all of part-time employees (86 percent in Canada and 90 percent in Saskatchewan) were women. Apparently, female teachers who worked part-time had more children than those who did not.

Table 3

Comparison of Mean Number of Dependent Children Between Females and Males Grouped by Spousal Employment Across Two Samples

Hajnal 1990				Employment status of spouse	Hajnal 1991			
Female		Male			Female		Male	
N	Mean	N	Mean		N	Mean	N	Mean
28	1.61	32	1.59	Employed as an educator	31	1.74	28	1.68
81	1.40	39	1.87*	Employed, not as an educator	55	1.24	21	1.67
6	.33	38	2.58**	Not employed	6	1.67	16	2.25

*p < 0.05; **p < 0.01; ***p < 0.001

Table 4

Comparison of Mean Number of Dependent Children by Full-Time/Part-Time Status for Female Married Respondents

Female married/common-law respondents								
Hajnal 1990		Hajnal 1991		Status	CTF SK 1990		CTF Canada 1990	
N	Mean	N	Mean		N	Mean	N	Mean
31	1.74*	22	1.81*	Part-time	14 4	2.24***	105 8	2.10***
84	1.29	65	1.37	Full-time	62 4	1.77	676 8	1.73

*p < 0.05; **p < 0.01; ***p < 0.001

The CTF survey dealt with the quality of work life and included three questions on the amount of time a teacher spent outside of school in marking, lesson preparation, teachers' federation activities and school-related committee meetings. In the re-analysis of the CTF database, this researcher chose to combine the hours into one variable (extra hours) describing the amount of time spent outside the class working on school-related activities. Additionally, this variable was grouped into four categories defined as 6 hours (20 percent of the respondents), 6-10 hours (30 percent of the respondents), 11-15 hours (24 percent of the respondents), and 15 hours (26 percent of the respondents). The mean number of hours reported was 12. This variable was included in the ANCOVA analysis.

The results of the ANCOVA analysis are presented in Table 5. As expected, the covariate was significant and itself explained 10 percent of the variance. There were significant main effects for marital status, and extra hours. The interaction term of gender and full-time/part-time status was significant as was the interaction term of gender and educator spouse. Marital status explained approximately 1 percent of the variance. The total model explained 32% of the variance in the number of offspring. The number of cases used in this analysis was 15 425.

Table 5
Results of an ANCOVA Analysis
Using the CTF Database for Canadian Teachers

Source of Variation	Sum of Squares	DF	Mean Square	F	Sig of F
Covariates	2810.7	1	2810.7	2243.8	.000
Age	2810.7	1	2810.7	2243.8	.000
Main Effects	349.05	11	31.73	25.33	.000
Sex	.49	1	.49	.39	.530
Full-time/part-time	1.34	1	1.34	1.07	.301
Marital Status	276.28	4	69.07	55.14	.000
Educator Spouse	.13	2	.07	.05	.949
Extra Hours	12.17	3	4.06	3.24	.021
2-Way Interactions	168.47	45	3.74	2.99	.000
Sex Full-time/part-time	22.99	1	22.99	18.35	.000
Sex Marital status	4.92	4	1.23	.98	.416
Sex Educator spouse	47.09	2	23.54	18.79	.000
Sex Extra hours	3.75	3	1.25	1.00	.393
Full-t/pt. Marital status	2.63	4	.66	.53	.717
Full-t/pt Ed spouse	1.07	2	.54	.43	.651
Full-t/pt Extra hours	2.17	3	.72	.58	.630
Marital st Ed spouse	12.59	8	1.57	1.26	.261
Marital st Extra hr	20.93	12	1.74	1.39	.161
Ed spouse Extra hr	.89	6	.15	.12	.004
Explained	9095.61	57	159.57	127.38	.000
Residual	19249.9	15367	1.25		
Total	28345.5	15424	1.84		

One limitation concerning the use of the CTF database must be noted. The Canadian perspective that was determined in the re-analysis is an aggregation of the responses for the provinces and not a weighted average that would be representative of the distribution of teachers across the provinces.

Discussion

While age and marital status were important in the explanation of the variance associated with the number of offspring, other factors provided additional explanation. The relationship between extra hours worked and number of offspring was interesting. A discussion about whether teachers who work many extra hours conscientiously choose to have fewer children or whether those teachers who have more children have less time to do extra work could be fascinating.

The significant interaction between gender and spousal status as an educator is interesting. If women teachers have spouses with credentials as an educator, they have more children than their female colleagues. If male teachers have educator spouses they have fewer children than their male colleagues. An explanation of these phenomena may require an analysis of family income. It is possible that the proportion of the wife's contribution to family income plays a determining role in the number of offspring. In general terms this would be supported by Becker (1991). Further research incorporating family income would be important to the explanation of number of offspring.

Becker (1991), economist and winner of the 1992 Nobel Prize, assured us that parents behave rationally when deciding whether to have children. Consequently, the rational decisions and ensuing actions of the female educators reported in this study have important messages for administrators and other policy makers. Female educators are choosing to have fewer children than male educators. This is a reflection of their reality, where insufficient attention is paid to their needs. These needs may include some flexibility in scheduling and time-off, child care assistance, part-time possibilities, and attention to career planning for female employees.

As reported by King and Peart (1992), the frustration of many female educators was represented by the comments of this grade seven teacher with six years experience:

> From a woman's perspective there are still a lot of stereotypes that have to be dealt with. I think there have to be more opportunities that encourage women to work part time or time share . . . or men. It seems ironic to me that we're in a profession that talks about how poor the family situation is and we have to bear the brunt of it and yet we're also in a profession that does not really encourage women to take five years off and then come back into the profession because they've been at home with their children. You are penalized for doing that and it seems to me that is very, very wrong. (p. 42)

The conflict between the need for adequate care for offspring, its relationship to the social good and the career path of this educator is apparent.

Women may see some solutions. One teacher (Robertson, 1993) suggested:

The solution I see, which is not practised in any of the schools in my district, is the availability of daycare at the workplace. Being close to my son, spending lunchtime together, being near for any emergencies, or just dropping by to say hi and have a hug would solve a lot of concerns and personal conflicts I feel about daycare. On the other hand, the longer hours wouldn't be such a threat having already spent some time with my son, and a relaxed mind would increase productivity. (p. 60)

While women remain a minority in administration in schools and in board offices, and a picayune few in chief executive positions, however, they cannot effect the desired changes.

Although there are no findings to support or to disprove the hypothesis that women are not promoted because they take time off for childbearing or child rearing (Robertson, 1993, p. 28), there is certainly ample anecdotal evidence surrounding this issue. One woman in administration wrote:

I have been working since I was 16 years old. I started teaching at 17. I have been a vice-principal for about eight years. When I was pregnant with my first child there was an opening for a vice-principal at the school I still work at. I was called to the office and told by the principal that I had been marked for the job but couldn't get it now. I thought it was an honor and didn't feel very disappointed. Another female (older and friend of the principal) got the job. When she retired I got it and now have the V.P. position. (p. 23)

Penalizing women for the necessary role they play in procreation and childrearing is abominable. It is often easier to buy back pension credits for educational leave than for family leave. Historically, women have certainly been less likely to obtain an administrative position. To provide for an adequate pension, women are forced to work to an older age than their male counterparts, and they still retire with a pension that is generally much less than their male colleagues (Robertson, 1993).

Calling for an expanded role for educational organizations in this time of fiscal restraint may appear foolhardy, but it is imperative. If school systems and administrators, who daily view the lack of social capital and the consequent effects on children, do not respond to the needs of their female employees, they abrogate their responsibilities and contribute indirectly to the deterioration of children's lives. While at least some business organizations have attempted to increase the availability of child care to employees, the lack of attention by school districts to these concerns has been widespread. The lack of attention to other work-family issues by school districts indicates a disregard for employees that business organizations no longer seem to exhibit.

There will be renewed pressures by younger teachers on school districts to react to these demands. Now is the time to plan for these changes and exhibit the proactive stance that will benefit both male and female teachers and their children. One place to begin is to ensure that women who are interested in teaching and administration are not penalized for their necessary contribution to childbearing.

In many instances we research and write about the things that are important to us. To provide some context for the reader, I want to describe my personal situation. I am the mother of two mature children. I remember being forced two times to resign my job as a teacher because I was pregnant. I remember being devastated when the person responsible for child care didn't show up for work as promised. I remember the times I wanted a part-time teaching position when full-time positions were all that were available. I cannot buy back pension time that I missed for maternity purposes. I am not unhappy about the directions my life and my career have taken. I am delighted at age 50 to be beginning a new career as a university professor. Nevertheless, I do not want my daughter or yours to be penalized throughout her career just because she is a woman.

References

Becker, G.S. (1991). *A treatise on the family*. Cambridge, MA: Harvard University Press.

Chapman, D.W., & Lowther, M.A. (1982). Teachers' satisfaction with teaching. *Journal of Educational Research, 75*(4), 241-247.

Canadian Teachers' Federation (October, 1994a). Most teacher unemployment insurance claims are for regular benefits. *Economic Service Notes.* 1994-9, 10.

Canadian Teachers' Federation (September, 1994b). New VON service lets parents go to work when their kids are sick. *Economic Service Notes.* 1994-8, 16.

Gonyea, J.G., & Googins, B.K. (1992). Linking the worlds of work and family: Beyond the productivity trap. *Human Resource Management, 31*(3), 209-226.

Hajnal, V.J. (1991a). *Teachers' attitudes toward elementary and secondary schools: A Saskatchewan perspective.* (Report No. 91-12). Regina, SK: Saskatchewan Schools Trustees Association.

Hajnal, V.J. (1991b). *The pay satisfaction and efficacy of educators: A multivariate analysis.* Doctoral dissertation, University of Saskatchewan, Saskatoon.

Holdaway, E.A. (1978). Facet and overall satisfaction of teachers. *Educational Administration Quarterly, 14*(1), 30-47.

Holmes, M. (1992). *Educated dissent: The educational opinions of educators, nurses and engineers.* Unpublished manuscript, The Ontario Institute for Studies in Education, Toronto.

King, A.J.C., & Peart, M. J. (1992). *Teachers in Canada: their work and quality of life.* Ottawa: Canadian Teachers' Federation.

Lester, P. (1988). Factors affecting teacher job satisfaction. *National Forum of Educational Administration and Supervision Journal, 4*(3), 202-207.

Robertson, H. (1993). *Progress revisited: The quality of (work)life of women teachers.* Ottawa: Canadian Teachers' Federation.

Rodgers, C.S. (1992). The flexible workplace: What have we learned? *Human Resource Management, 31*(3), 183-199.

Sedlak, M., and Schlossman, S. (1987). Who will teach? Historical perspectives on the changing appeal of teaching as a profession. In E. Z. Rothkopf (Ed.), *Review of research in education, 14*, (pp. 93-131). Washington, DC: AERA.

Scott, K.D., and McClellan, E.L. (1990). Gender differences in absenteeism. *Public Personnel Management, 19*(2), 229-253.

Statistics Canada (1992). *Age, sex and marital status.* (90-91 Census of Canada, Catalogue No. 93-310). Ottawa, ON: Supply and Services.

12

Teacher Perceptions of Principals: A Gender Issue

Thomas D. Gougeon

A basic assumption underlying most research which focuses on gender is that people experience the world about them differently and consequently "see the world through different lenses." Interpretation of people's reality relies upon unique mental constructs. These constructs are inclusive of all that a person has experienced. People will interpret events differently which has an impact upon leadership. For example, when a school principal talks to a group of teachers, each teacher will interpret what was said differently, and will likely respond uniquely to the principal's message. However, because people are socialized into subcultures, commonalties can be assumed by leaders.

People of a common subculture may respond to an event similarly at some levels and differently at other levels. An understanding of this phenomenon is important for school leaders. Since males and females are considered to be different subcultures (Burgoon, 1985; Tannen, 1990; Brown & Gilligan, 1992), it may be argued that females and males may respond to leader communication according to their gender socialization experiences. Thus, school principals are concerned that male and female teachers may perceive the messages they communicate differently. Regardless of whether they are male or female, principals who understand how they are perceived differently by teachers might be able to adapt their communication styles to be perceived more consistently across the gender gap.

This chapter reports on a survey of teacher perceptions of their principals in twenty urban schools in Alberta. These perceptions were analyzed by partitioning variables according to principal and teacher gender.

Theoretical Framework

Lee Thayer (1988) argued that leadership and followership are "things of the mind." He said "That to be seen as a leader is to be seen as a leader by those who see themselves as his or her followers, and things of the mind must necessarily be created and maintained in communication" (pg. 256). This study focuses on follower perceptions of leaders using semantic differential scales. It is a study of the nuance of meaning, things of the mind.

Semantic-differential scales are a unique approach to measuring attitudes (Wolpert, 1984). Even though semantic differential scales are simple in design, they have been tested rigorously over the years and found to be extremely reliable (Osgood, Suci, & Tannenbaum, 1957). Semantics deals with meanings represented by words, sentences, and discourse patterns in a language (Farr, 1986). All people who speak a language have a system of semantics as part of the tacit knowledge of their language, and they use this system both when they are speaking and when writing. While people who live far apart may use distinctly different systems when they communicate, it can be argued that people, who live nearby in the same community and who are socialized into similar subcultures such as teaching, largely use a similar semantic system. This is due to the deep-seated nature of linguistic rules and to the high frequencies of occurrence of the use of these rules within subgroup populations.

A semantic differential scale has three elements: 1. the concept to be evaluated in terms of its semantic or attitudinal properties; 2. the polar adjective pair anchoring the scale; and 3. a series of undefined scale positions which, for practical purposes, is not less than five or more than nine steps, with seven steps as the optimal number according to the originators of the scale (Osgood, et al., 1957; Lopata, 1981).

The use of semantic differential scales with teachers working in the same school system is an appropriate method to measure attitudes. If attitudes toward male and female principals differ by the gender of teachers, semantic differentials can demonstrate these differences. In this study, teachers were asked to characterize their principal by responding appropriately to 42 semantic differentials scales.

Methods

Ordinal data were gathered using a bipolar adjective semantic scale survey instrument originally developed and normed by C. E. Osgood (1957) and used extensively since (De Villis, 1991). The instrument consisted of 42 scales (see appendix). Teachers were asked to think of their principal and respond to the scale by placing an "X" in one of the seven places separating the bipolar adjectives that describe a range of personal characteristics.

Data Source

This study took place in a Canadian school district in Alberta of approximately 94 000 students. Over a hundred elementary and junior high school principals were invited to participate in the study, and ten males and ten females were selected based upon their willingness to commit all teachers in their schools as respondents. In total, 372 teachers from twenty schools were surveyed. Fifty-two teachers were male and 320 were female. Descriptive and non-parametric statistical Kruskal-Wallis One Way ANOVA procedures were used in analysis comparing mean ranks of male and female principal data by male and female teacher groups.

Findings

The findings which are statistically significant at $p < 0.05$, are summarized in Table 1. Only eight significant findings of a possible 42 scales were identified in the male teacher data comparing principals by gender. On the other hand, 24 significant findings were identified in the female teacher data comparing principals by gender. This can be explained in one of two ways: 1. the semantic differential scales were biased to favor female respondents, or 2. the sample of male teachers was not as sensitive to relational dimensions compared to female teachers. In this chapter the author assumes that the data are not particularly biased and that the analysis of the data will possibly provide insights into gender differences.

As semantic differential scales incorporate the concept of opposites, like foolish – wise, and the data characterize male and female principals along the continuum between the opposites, the author will present the data and make comparisons using the positive concept (i.e., wise rather than foolish). In addition, the findings are reported using the perspective of the female principal with an assumption that comparisons are made to male principals.

Male Teacher Perceptions

In reviewing the findings in Table 1 and Figure 1, the first question asked is, "how do male teachers perceive female principals in comparison to male principals?" In this analysis of male teacher data, eight significant findings form the basis for the following comments.

It is demonstrated in Table 1 and Figure 1 that female principals were found to be stronger when measured on the scale "stronger vs. weaker" and harder when measured on the scale "harder vs. softer." These characterizations are teacher attributions of principal leadership. In this respect, being perceived as stronger and harder rather than weaker and softer, may be interpreted as the following through with determination. Thus, male teachers perceived female principals to be more determined than male principals.

Female principals were found to be more lenient when measured on the scale "more lenient vs. more severe" and more feminine on a "more masculine vs. more feminine" scale. Characterized as more lenient and more feminine, it may be said that male teachers perceived female principals to be more considerate of personal needs. These characterizations illustrate the complexity of relationships. When the above four comparisons are combined, female principals are seen as more lenient but not soft or weak, and more feminine but stronger and harder than male principals.

Male teachers perceived female principals to be more structured when measured on the "more structured vs. less structured" scale and more authoritarian when measured on the "more democratic vs. more authoritarian" scale. Thus, male teachers (but not female teachers) perceived female principals to be more classical in the sense of being more structured and authoritarian leaders. In this sense, it may be said that they were perceived to be more top down in communication than male principals.

Table 1

Teacher Perceptions of Principals by Gender
Significant Findings (p < .05 only);
Means on a Seven Point Scale (Weaker = 7, Stronger = 1)

Male Teacher Perceptions		
Differential Scale	Mean of Male Principal	Mean of Female Principal
Weak/Strong	2.640	1.913
Soft/Hard	4.040	3.174
Severe/Lenient	4.760	3.783
Masculine/Feminine	3.880	2.043
Structured/Unstructured	3.600	2.565
Democratic/Authoritarian	5.160	3.700
Stereotypical/Original	3.120	2.261
Effective/Ineffective	2.560	2.044
Female Teacher Perceptions		
Weak/Strong	2.658	1.989
Soft/Hard	4.184	3.644
Dull/Sharp	2.362	2.025
Kind/Cruel	5.447	5.100
Tender/Tough	4.132	3.694
Fun/Work	3.928	3.644
Severe/Lenient	4.678	4.081
Masculine/Feminine	4.026	1.806
Calm/Excitable	4.829	4.463
Passive/Active	2.403	1.969
Slow/Fast	3.197	2.768
Simple/Complex	3.125	2.625
Confusing/Clear	2.842	2.344
Traditional/Progressive	2.335	1.900

Differential Scale	Mean of Male Principal	Mean of Female Principal
Stereotypical/Original	2.947	2.588
Unstructured/Structured	3.651	3.013
Unsystematic/Systematic	2.921	2.563
Informal/Formal	4.401	3.819
Permissive/Restrictive	3.849	3.350
Boring/Interesting	2.303	2.050
Successful/Unsuccessful	2.066	1.784
Ineffective/Effective	2.520	2.081
Unimportant/Important	2.086	1.936
Foolish/Wise	2.336	2.000

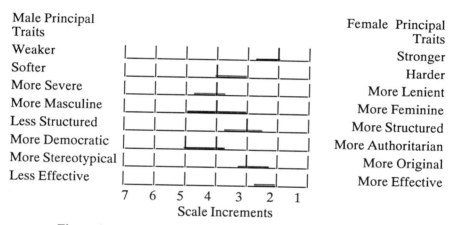

Figure 1. Male Teacher Perceptions of Principals by Gender
Gap Between Mean Scores of Male and Female Principals

Semantic Differential Scales: (Means for Male Principals are indicated by the Left End of the Bold Line; Female Principal Means indicated by the Right End of the Bold Lines)

This finding derived from the responses of male teachers but not female teachers may shed light on differences between female and male teachers as well as on principals. Deborah Tannen, a socio-linguist who studies cross gender communication, asserts that males tend to seek status through independence more than females, who tend to seek intimacy through connection (Tannen, 1990). Tannen characterizes males as constantly scanning their environment for evidence of challenges to their status. Tannen suggests that females, on the other hand, constantly scan their environment for evidence of relational information among people. It follows then that people will not only scan their environments for what they consider most important, but that their communication with others will reflect what they consider most important. Thus male talk will frequently be around status issues often ignoring relational issues, and female talk will frequently be around relational issues, often ignoring status issues.

So In this study, using Tannen's findings, male principals would be more sensitive to status weighted independent/dependent or one-up/one-down alignment talk and less sensitive to relational talk. Female principals would be more sensitive to interdependent relationships where the alignments are more equal and horizontal and not be as sensitive to vertical alignments in talk. Reflecting on the finding that male teachers perceive female principals to be more authoritarian while female principals do not perceive differences between male and female principals on the democratic vs. authoritarian semantic scale, female principals may unconsciously communicate in a manner that males perceive as challenging to their status through one-up/one-down alignments.

Female principals were found to be more original when measured on the "more original vs. more stereotypical" scale and more effective on the "more effective vs. less effective" scale. Being more original may simply be an artifact of the small numbers of females who are principals in schools. It is quite possible that many male teachers were experiencing a female principal for the first time in their careers. However, the survey did not gather information on the number of female principals that teacher respondents worked with, so this point remains unsubstantiated and highly speculative. Regardless of whether male teachers worked with many female principals or not, they rated female principals as being significantly more effective than male principals.

Female Teacher Perceptions

The next question to be considered is, "How do female teachers perceive female principals in comparison to male principals?" As mentioned previously, female teachers perceived many more differences between male and female principals compared to male teachers. In this analysis of female teacher data, twenty-four significant findings are the basis for the following comments (see Table 1, and Figure 2).

Considering the data presented in Figure 2, both male and female principals were characterized as being strong, sharp, kind, neither hard nor soft, tender, and work oriented (i.e., both means for the weaker/stronger continuum were favorably closer to the stronger end of the scale and distant from the weaker end of the scale). But when comparisons are made between them, female and male principals were found to be significantly different. Female principals were found to be stronger when measured on the "stronger vs. weaker" scale, harder on the "harder vs. softer" scale, sharper on the "sharper vs. duller" scale, more cruel on the "more cruel vs. kinder" scale, tougher on the "tougher vs. more tender" scale, and doing more work on the "doing more work vs. having more fun" scale. It may be said that a person who is characterized this way, as strong, hard, sharp, cruel, and doing work, is perceived as being more task oriented than relationship oriented in the workplace.

The data represented in Figure 2 also indicate that neither male nor female principals were lenient or severe. But when compared for significant differences, female principals were found to be significantly more lenient when measured on the scale "more lenient vs. more severe." Female principals were found to be more feminine on the "more feminine vs. more masculine" scale

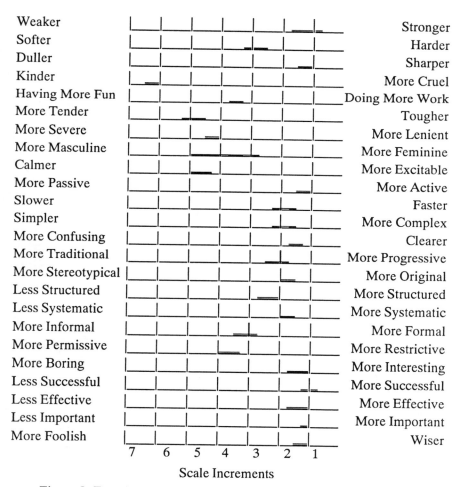

Figure 2: Female Teacher Perceptions of Principals by Gender Gap Between Mean Scores of Male and Female Principals.

Semantic Differential Scales. (Means for Male Principals are indicated by the Left End of the Bold Lines; Female Principal Means indicated by the Right End of the Bold Lines)

while male principals were perceived as being more masculine. It may be said that the characteristics of leniency and femininity infer a sensitivity to others, while the characteristics of severity and masculinity imply goal orientation.

This finding is similar to the male teachers' finding above where female principals were perceived to be more highly relational. Thus, in both cases, male and female teachers perceived female principals to balance high task with high relationship in providing leadership.

Consider how male principals were perceived by female teachers in Figure 2. Compared to female principals, they were perceived to be weaker, softer, duller, kinder, more tender, and fun oriented. This is characterized as being lower task oriented, but in conjunction with perceptions that male principals are more severe and more masculine, which are characterizations of being lower in relational attributes, it may be said that male principals appear to be more goal driven or egocentric in their relationships with teachers.

Female principals were found to be more excitable when measured on the "more excitable vs. calmer" scale, more active on the "more active vs. more passive" scale, and faster on the "faster vs. slower" scale. These characterizations reflect that female principals exhibit higher energy than male principals. Female principals were found to be more complex when measured on the scale "more complex vs. simpler" and clearer on the "clearer vs. more confusing" scale. This combination characterizes female principals as more sophisticated communicators than male principals. Combining the characteristics of higher energy and more sophisticated communicators, it may be said that female principals are more dynamic than do male principals.

Female principals were found to be more progressive when measured on the scale "more progressive vs. more traditional" and more original on the "more original vs. more stereotypical" scale. These perceptions characterize the female principals to be perceived as more active learners than male principals. Combining the above characteristics, it may be said that female principals who are perceived to be more dynamic and to be more active learners are portrayed as more typical of leaders of learning organizations (Senge, 1990) compared to male principals.

Female principals were found to be more structured when measured on the "more structured vs. less structured" scale, more systematic on the "more systematic vs. less systematic" scale, more formal on the "more formal vs. more informal" scale, and more restrictive on the "more restrictive vs. more permissive" scale. Combining these characterizations, it may be said that female principals seek stability more than do male principals.

Female principals were found to be more interesting when measured on the scale "more interesting vs. more boring," more successful on the "more successful vs. less successful" scale, and more effective on the "more effective vs. less effective" scale. These perceptions indicate that female teachers admire female principals more than male principals. In addition, female principals were found to be more important when measured on the scale "more important vs. less important" and wiser on the "wiser vs. more foolish" scale. It may be said that female teachers value female principals more than they value male principals.

In summary, male teachers characterized female principals to be relationally oriented, more principled, more effective, and to seek stability through the use of power more than male principals. Female teachers characterized female principals to be task oriented, relational oriented, and stability seeking. Female principals were also seen by female teachers as having higher energy and being more active learners, more inclined to seek improvement, more sophisticated presenters, and more admired and valued than male principals.

Analysis

A conceptualization that adequately explains the differences presented in Figures 1 and 2 was developed by Mitchell and Spady (1977). They proposed a theory of social control for teachers in the classroom involving the concept of authority. Gougeon (1989) applied this concept to better understand communication between teachers and principals. The concept of "authority" used by Mitchell and Spady is different than that normally used in the current literature. Mitchell and Spady argued that the concept of authority originally referred to a follower's response to the inner character of a leader (*ex ousia* means out of character) whereas today, authority generally refers to a delegated power to which followers respond. In the original conceptualization, the inner character of a leader, that which motivates a follower, is intrinsic, whereas in the current conceptualization, the delegated power which motivates a follower is extrinsic. The 42 semantic scales used in the study are more descriptors of the inner character of leaders than resources extrinsic to them. In applying Mitchell and Spady's conceptualization, people are predicted to respond to four types of intrinsic characteristics or motivations: traditional, charismatic, legal, and expertise (see Figure 3).

Mitchell and Spady (1983) described these four types as fundamental to all methods of social control and influence as follows. Traditional motivation arises from

> the importance and innate attractiveness of experiences that confirm (people's) self worth. Traditions (are) embodied in norms, celebrations, customs, mores, rituals, etiquette, and other behavioral systems expressing respect, dignity, and the confirmation of full membership in a social group . . . (and) enable us to define social values and let other people know how we evaluate them and their actions. (p. 17)

Charismatic motivation arises from

> innately attractive experiences of interpersonal intimacy . . . both involving friendship and those involving leadership . . . from the creation of authentic

encounters and spontaneous, frequently somewhat mystical, interpersonal bonds between individuals . . . (and) enable individuals to overcome social distance and enter into communal relationships. (p. 18)

Legal motivation is grounded on the capacity to

provide experiences of security and orderliness for others . . . in the form of rules for social behavior . . . (which) clarify role expectations for individuals . . . (and) serve as a vehicle for defending each individual's rights against arbitrary or capricious interference from others. (pp. 18-19)

Expert motivation arises from

those experiences in which one person enables others to feel greater personal adequacy, efficacy, or potency. (Experts) reveal . . . new ways of understanding or new skills in performing tasks that permit them to achieve immediate goals more effectively. (p. 19)

Figure 3: Model of Follower Experiences in Leader Communication; Representing Mitchell & Spady's Social Control Theory (1977). Adapted from Armstrong (1994).

The data presented in Table 1 and Figures 1 and 2 are consistent with these four conditions that characterize authority. In addition, they are consistent with gender differences described by Tannen (1990) in the previous section, and the following analysis is guided by both Mitchell and Spady's and Tannen's frameworks.

As presented in Table 1, female teachers described more differences between male and female principals than did male teachers. Therefore, generally, female teachers were able to conceptualize motivational communication in a more complex, multifaceted way than male teachers. Both male and female teachers experienced traditional motivation with female principals more than male principals. Male teachers perceived female principals to be more structured and more authoritarian[1]. Female teachers perceived female principals to be more structured, more systematic, more formal, and more restrictive, that is, embodying the norms, customs, and rituals that define social values. In Mitchell and Spady's terms, these characteristics would enable teachers to define social values and to understand how their actions were being evaluated by the principal. Understanding the social values and how they were to be evaluated would provide teachers with experiences that confirm their self worth. Female principals were perceived to communicate more with teachers using traditional motivation than were male principals.

Both male and female teachers experienced more charismatic motivation with female principals than with male principals. Male teachers perceived female principals to be more lenient and more feminine, while female teachers perceived female principals to be more lenient, more feminine, more interesting, more successful, more important, more excitable, more active, faster, and wiser. In Mitchell and Spady's terms, teachers experience interpersonal intimacy through leadership from the creation of authentic encounters and enter into communal relationships. Thus, female principals were perceived to communicate using charismatic motivation more than male principals.

Since female teachers experienced traditional and charismatic authority from female principals more than male principals, it follows from Figure 3 that female teachers will experience a greater sense of identity within the organization when they are led by a female principal.

Both male and female teachers experienced more legal motivation with female principals than with male principals. Male teachers perceived female principals to be stronger and harder than male principals, while female teachers perceived female principals to be stronger, harder, sharper, more cruel, tougher, and more work oriented. In Mitchell and Spady's terms, these characterizations indicate that female principals provide a clearer delineation of rules for social behavior for both male and female teachers, thus clarifying role expectations more than male principals. Female principals were perceived to communicate using more legal motivation and providing more diverse experiences of security and orderliness for all teachers.

Since female teachers experienced legal authority from female principals more than male principals, it follows from Mitchell and Spady (Figure 3) that female teachers will experience a greater sense of status within the organization when they are led by a female principal.

Both male and female teachers experienced more expert motivation with female principals than with male principals. Male teachers experienced female principals to be more original and more effective, while female teachers experienced female principals to be more original, more effective, more progressive, more complex, and clearer. In Mitchell and Spady's terms, female principals provide a greater sense of personal adequacy, efficacy, and potency for all teachers, although these experiences are more diverse for female teachers than males. Thus teachers experience more expert motivation from female principals than from male principals.

Since female teachers experienced more expert authority from female principals than from male principals, it follows from Figure 3 that female teachers will experience a greater sense of adventure within the organization when they are led by a female principal. In addition, since female teachers experienced more expert and legal authority from female principals than from male principals, it follows from Figure 3 that female teachers will experience a greater sense of opportunity within the organization when they are led by a female principal.

In summary, female teachers, more than male teachers, are sensitive to and motivated by intrinsic experiences with female principals. In addition, female principals provide significantly more intrinsic motivational experiences to all teachers than do male principals.

Conclusions

The attitudes measured for female principals on the whole are more positive than those measured for male principals. Since it did not matter which way comparisons were stated, this paper focused on female principal characterizations because they could be stated more positively. It followed that an intrinsic motivation framework could be used to explain the results. The more negative characterizations of male principals presented in Table 1 portray them to be significantly less effective leaders using the concepts of Osgood's 42 semantic differential scales. Analysis of data from the perspective of the male principal might best use Mitchell and Spady's power or extrinsic motivation framework (1983), which was not introduced in this paper. In this case a different instrument would be used, one that would focus on dipolar adjectives referencing Mitchell and Spady's (1983) power or Gougeon's (1989) extrinsic motivation framework including moral standards, psychological manipulations, contractual force, and technical knowledge as resources for motivation.

More work needs to be done in this area by both male and female researchers using a variety of methodologies. For example, a study presently in progress[2] is using an elegant case study methodology testing these findings (Allison, in progress).

The findings and analysis in this paper may enable principals to be more self-aware, to reflect upon their own practice, and to discover differences in interpersonal relationships with teachers of their own sex and teachers of the opposite sex. Principals who learn to be more self-aware will become more effective communicators with both male and female teachers. In the next millennium, schools that lead the way to meet the diverse demands of interest groups in their communities will have principals who are capable of deeply and authentically understanding the needs of others.

Notes

[1]Here the term is used by Osgood in a more current sense of the top down influence rather than the "inner character" of a leader.

[2] Allison, P. (in progress). A case study designed to be read and reacted to by male and female teachers. The case study is in two forms, one using all female pronouns and names and the other using all male pronouns and names. The forms were randomly assigned to respondents. London ON: University of Western Ontario.

Appendix

Semantic Differential Scales
from Osgood, C.E., G.J. Suci,& Tannenbaum, P.H., (1957)

Active / Passive
Strong / Weak
Sharp / Dull
Rugged / Delicate
Social / Unsocial
Kind / Cruel
Graceful / Awkward
Successful / Unsuccessful
Important / Unimportant
True / False
Positive / Negative
Wise / Foolish
Effective / Ineffective
Interesting / Boring
Hard / Soft
Lenient / Severe
Constrained / Free
Serious / Humorous
Masculine / Feminine
Excitable / Calm
Complex / Simple
Predictable / Unpredictable
Clear / Confusing
Traditional / Progressive
Permissive / Restrictive
Authoritarian / Democratic
Structured / Unstructured
Formal / Informal
Accepting / Rejecting
Flexible / Rigid

Original / Stereotyped
Systematic / Unsystematic
Responsive / Unresponsive
Happy / Sad
Work / Fun
Open / Closed
Relaxed / Tense
Genuine / False
Tender / Tough
Approach / Avoid
Pain / Pleasure

References

Allison, P. (in progress). Untitled research in progress. London ON: University of Western Ontario.

Armstrong, R.L. (1994). Faculty job satisfaction as a function of the social control methods of college leadership. Unpublished Ph.D. dissertation, University of Calgary, Calgary, AB.

Brown, L.M., & Gilligan, C. (1992). *Meeting at the crossroads: Women's psychology and girl's development.* Cambridge MA: Harvard University Press.

Burgoon, J.K. (1985). Noverbal signals. In M.L. Knapp and G.R. Miller (Eds.), *Handbook of interpersonal communication.* Newbury Park CA: Sage.

DeVillis, R.F. (1991). *Scale development: Theory and Applications.* Newbury Park CA: Sage.

Farr, M. (1986). *Language, culture, and writing: Socioliguistic foundations of research on writing. Review of Research in Education.* Washington D.C.: American Education Research Association.

Gougeon, T.D. (1989, October). *Assessing principal leader qualities: Using a comprehensive research strategy.* Unpublished manuscript presented at the University Council for Educational Administration (UCEA) Convention.

Lopata, H.Z. (1981, May). Widowhood and husband sanctification. *Journal of Marriage and the Family,* 439-450.

Mitchell, D.E., & Spady W.G. (1977). *Authority and the functional structuring of social action in the schools.* Unpublished paper. Revised version of an AERA Symposium presentation submitted for review to the *American Educational Research Journal.*

Mitchell, D.E., & Spady, W.G. (1983, Winter). Authority, power, and the legitimation of social control. *Educational Administration Quarterly, 19*(1), 5-33.

Osgood, C.E., Suci, G.J., & Tannenbaum, P.H. (1957). *The measurement of meaning.* Urbana IL: University of Illinois Press.

Senge, P.M. (1990). *The fifth discipline: The art and practice of the learning organization.* San Francisco CA: Jossey-Bass.

Tannen, D. (1990). *You just don't understand: Women and men in conversation.* New York: William Morrow and Company.

Thayer, L. (1988). *Leadership/communication: A critical review and modest proposal. Handbook of organizational communication.* In G. M. Goldhaber and G. A. Barnett (Eds.), *Handbook of organizational communication* (pp. 231-263). Norwood NJ: Ablex Publishing Corporation.

Wolpert, E.M. (1984). *Understanding research in education.* Dubuque Iowa: Kendall Hunt.

13

Innovative Leadership In A Community Context: Elizabeth Murray And The History Plays Of Tatamagouche[1]

Carol Harris

In every action what is primarily intended by the doer . . . is the disclosure of his [or her] own image. Hence it comes about that every doer, in so far as [s]he does, takes delight in doing; since everything that is, desires its own being, and since in action the being of the doer is somehow intensified, delight necessarily follows. . . . Thus, nothing acts unless [by acting] it makes patent its latent self. (Dante, trans. in Arendt, 1958, p.175)

On an evening in mid-June, I drive from the Halifax International Airport to Truro and over the Cobequid Hills, past Earltown, to Tatamagouche, Nova Scotia.[2] As I approach this North Shore village, I glance through the maples, elms, and lilac bushes upon the serenity of the Waugh River's glassy, full-tide surface. This summer will mark my second visit to Tatamagouche to take part in the July 1st "play."

I drive straight to the elementary school where 25 cars are parked in the yard, hurry inside, aware of my late arrival, and catch my breath on the sidelines as Elizabeth (Betty) Murray directs a chorus of 60 men, women, and children. Five minutes pass before I am noticed; then I am greeted warmly, given my personal score, and seated among the sopranos. Several singers, without missing a beat, acknowledge me with smiles and signals of welcome; however, there is little time for pleasantries until "the break" an hour later. For the moment, I am in harness, part of a team whose responsibility is to produce the most beautiful music of which, individually and collectively, we are capable.

In this chapter I trace the leadership of Betty Murray, now 77, as she prepares and directs the annual play-with-music in which the people of Tatamagouche and the surrounding area re-create a significant moment in their village's history. This artistic event provides the setting for my own purposes, which are to focus on the educational and personal values of Betty Murray, to describe her interactions with the people who work with her, and to interpret her beliefs, attitudes, and actions in the light of what others have found to be the nature of leadership.

This "ethnographic" phase of my study is part of a larger life-history in which I am examining four periods of Murray's educational activities as a rural teacher, a pioneer in the development of the Province of Nova Scotia's Adult Education Division, a teacher in an inner-city school in Halifax and, latterly, as an innovative leader in the cultural life of her community. While these categories serve a heuristic purpose for analysis, themes of rural education, community coherence, lifelong learning, and creative action permeate each phase of Murray's life. Here can be traced the story of a woman who has chosen to be a "doer," in terms of the opening quotation, at the grassroots of community development. She has received much recognition for her work, including an honorary Doctorate in Education and honorary memberships in various national organizations; yet she finds her greatest pleasure and reward in working to accomplish, with members of her community, social, cultural, and educational projects.

In the continuities, commitments, and connections exemplified during Murray's project of producing two history plays, we see a leader who directs from *within* her group rather than from some hierarchical position. A highly affective and innovative leadership style demonstrates her attitudes towards "truth," justice, and community action. The affective component indicates leadership by charisma, a term which, in this chapter, receives careful examination in its artistic context.

Conceptual Point of Departure

Each researcher brings to her study a set of theoretical and methodological beliefs that bear on the selection, evaluation, and criticism of evidence (Kuhn, 1962, pp. 16, 17). My first theoretical assumption acknowledges the significance of historical review – that there is value in the "collective memory" which develops from the accumulated knowledge of past generations (Arendt, 1968; Bowers, 1987, p. 22), I also acknowledge that "understanding" is approached best by combining past wisdom with present insights. For the past to yield its strengths to the present, however, the viewer must reflect critically upon such elements as essences and appearances, alienation and belonging, and individualism and societal coherence. I look both ways, between social interaction's potential to liberate and to bind, to find a balance and to show that both the individual and society may grow by integrating the new with the positive aspects of the past.

A second assumption concerns balance. Several feminist educators have challenged the validity of traditional accounts of leadership (e.g., Blackmore, 1989; Shakeshaft & Nowell, 1984) by maintaining that the questions, approaches to research, and determinations of significance have been profoundly androcentric in context. In noting their criticism, I assume that a detailed examination of the leadership of women, and the inclusion of women's "voice" in educational theorizing, will introduce a revitalized language that eventually may tip the scales toward a more balanced view of curriculum and the practice of pedagogy, evaluation, and the administration of schools.

My reasons for choosing this particular biography for study parallel the interests and assumptions outlined above. Watching two of her history plays in the late 1980s, I noted Murray's evident respect for traditional values balanced by a critical examination of those values. I suspected that her approach to the strengths and weaknesses of traditional life might relate to contemporary situations of "disenchantment" wherein individuals, set adrift from family, religion, and community, experience alienation (or anomie, fragmentation, or estrangement). This condition was forecast by early philosophers and sociologists[3] and is recognized widely today (e.g., Bowers, 1987, pp. 4-28; Rizvi, 1986, p. 31; Jameson, 1992, pp. 14, 15). I anticipated that the people of Tatamagouche could provide important insights into both the nature of leadership and the unifying force of historically based community action.

An interest in modelling and mentoring provides a further reason for this study. The example of Murray's teaching had influenced directly the career choice of at least six educators. As one of the six, I was intensely curious to learn about influence on a more extensive scale – in particular, whether the influence of this leader on others went beyond the areas of career choice and the task at hand. How extensive is the scope, and what is the nature, of the leadership of one who leads by strength of character rather than by authority of position?

I take as my point of departure the advice of Greenfield (1984, p. 143), who urges researchers of leadership to abandon the traditional search for the most effective and efficient *characteristics* of the leader and to concentrate, instead, on his or her *character*. I assume, therefore, the primacy of character and, further, that character may be thought of as that complex of beliefs, attitudes, and values, and the actions that flow from these; that is, as philosophy-in-action. A methodological assumption is, thus, that the words and actions of people involved as leader and followers offer the best opportunities for understanding. Hodgkinson (1983, p. 201, 202) suggests that the proper concerns of leadership studies focus on such guideposts as affect, motives, attitudes, beliefs, values, ethics, morals, will, commitment, preferences, expectations, and responsibilities. Not all of these features are reported upon in the present section of my study, but it was with these in mind that I entered the field.

Methodology

During my time in Tatamagouche, I lived in Betty's home, observed her daily routine, sang with her choir, and attended meetings of the Play Committee. As a participant, more than as observer, I helped out whenever possible, at times with household chores and, at other times, by "running errands" in the village. Occasionally I taught songs or dances to the children of the cast. My assumption was that leadership, as expressed by one's character-in-action, is not restricted to the committee meeting, the rehearsal, or the administrative office but is enacted in all aspects of the leader's existence.

In order to understand the meanings held by Betty Murray and those who work with her, perform under her direction, and share with her their lives, a wide range of qualitative data was gathered. The most important evidence came from interviews with cast members and other villagers. These were in fragmentary conversations recorded either in my journal or as semi-structured events tape-recorded in people's homes, in restaurants, on schoolhouse steps, in shops (between customers) and, on one occasion, in a pick-up truck. For this phase of the work, I interviewed approximately 25 men and women, and a dozen children. Other information was gleaned from newspaper reviews, documents of local history, and from my own direct observations.

In the first interviews, I asked about participants' educational and experiential backgrounds, their reasons for joining the choir and/or the cast, and what participation meant to them. Why did they give so much of their time to this project? How did they understand Betty's direction, her leadership style, and her underlying values? What had they gained personally from taking part in the play(s)? How important were these events to their sense of family and community? With Murray, these questions were directed toward her own perceptions of purpose. Betty's voice, analysed in conjunction with the words of the village children, men, and women provided a rich source of "triangulation" or cross-referencing of meaning. As an important verification, I asked Murray and her associates to confirm or correct their descriptions of events and conversations. I assume full responsibility, however, for my interpretation of Murray's leadership.

Betty Murray, the Person

When Betty Murray enters a room, everybody notices. Although slightly stooped at 77, she is tall and strongly built, and she carries herself with great presence. This presence seems to emanate from her unusual public voice and her tendency to encompass within her span of observation everyone in the room. As noted by her nephew Bruce, Betty commands attention "without placing the focus on herself. It's obvious that you are going to focus on her but, at the same time, you know people are important to her and they all recognize this. She has a way of making everyone feel special." She attends outwardly to the interests and concerns of others.

Betty has two voices, both punctuated regularly by warm chuckles as though surprised constantly by the vagaries of human nature. One voice, the private one, is soft-spoken and conversational while the other, her public or "megaphone voice," projects to the far reaches of any hall. She uses this projected voice for hours at a time to call dances, direct rehearsals, or to greet friends, all with no evident signs of tiring.

Dressed usually in a comfortable jogging suit and sneakers, Betty can be found reading in her sunroom, working about the grounds, swimming in the river below her home, chatting with neighbors, or gathering waste paper from the sidewalk on her way to some committee meeting or bridge game. She does not move quickly, but she has immense reserves of energy. She works steadily, balancing domestic chores with planning and writing her play. Her leisurely pace convinces others that she has "all the time in the world for [their] problems."

Betty lives in the gabled house that her father, Dr. Dan Murray, bought in 1906. The house, located in the centre of the village, remains structurally true to its mid-19th century period of origin. The furnishings fit as well; there are many wooden surfaces, hooked runners on the stairs, and papered walls. While Betty has never married, she enjoys a large family. Numerous Murray relatives call Tatamagouche "home," as do many others who were at one time in her classrooms or choral groups. During the summers of my visit, the family varied in size from three during the week to six or more at weekends. Somehow, there was a room for everyone. Though she did not stipulate that any of us would be part of the play, invariably we became involved.

The Singers and Their Play

The choir of the Tatamagouche and Area Singers was first formed 14 years ago when Betty Murray retired from teaching in Halifax and came back to her old home. Betty, had, everyone knew, a talent for music and "getting things done." Years ago, as the young teacher in "Tarbet school across the river," she and her students had painted the school, renovated rooms, and landscaped the yard. In a most unconventional approach to education for the 1940s, the students "learned by doing." As well, and with outstanding results, Betty entered her entire school, Grades III to IX, in music festivals. A few years later, as an adult educator, she was instrumental in locating the Provincial Adult Education Division's folkschools in the village and, after that, helped place the Nova Scotia Festival of the Arts and the School of Community Arts in Tatamagouche. Still later, in the 1960s, she directed summer camps where young people from all over the Province staged operas, from both abridged and full scores. It was fitting therefore that Betty be asked to organize a choir. Today, the history plays represent one focal point in the Singers' annual schedule, which includes a Christmas concert, carol singing for the community, invitational concerts, and cooperative ventures with other provincial choirs.

The plays started modestly, primarily as a vehicle for choral singing enhanced by costume and a "thin story line" about the early "settlers" of Scottish descent. Over the years, emphasis moved away from choir singing and towards the historical re-creation of specific events. Music is now servant to the play in that, within certain artistic boundaries, it represents the musical content and performance appropriate to the period. Today's plays adhere, moreover, more closely to historical record; for example, the first inhabitants are shown to be the Mi'kmaq people, followed by the French, then by the Scots, and, latterly, by other European and Asian families.

Betty Murray begins writing the story of each play in late January. Betty, who is a "community resource on family and area history," decides on an appropriate historical period, usually one that has some connection with current interests. When the trains were "taken" from the North Shore, for example, her play centred on the coming of the "Short [the local] Line." As Creighton's Creamery, one of the village's main industries closed, she re-created the advent of electricity and the opening of the Creamery in Tatamagouche. The war years, which tend to stand on their own interest value, provided yet another setting. Last year, local ship building and the loss of a ship bound for Japan with its village crew, provided the story-line.

One visitor that I interviewed described Betty Murray as the "Grandma Moses of drama." Elaborating on this, he pointed out that "while she's obviously not a playwright, she presents all the natural ingredients that the people love. We have laughter and sorrow, beauty and ugliness, and all those vignettes of everyday village life." Betty seems, indeed, to bring historical moments to life through events predictable in almost any rural village. We have conversations between town "gossips," meetings of the Women's Institute, children at play discussing adult affairs and, for the larger social gatherings, village picnics and church services. Historical props – hay wagons, antique cars, covered buggies, pump organs, and other furniture – add to the recreation of historical events.

There is about her plays a sense of festivity. A band of local fiddlers entertains the audience before curtain time. Affording the people a view of "their town," the stage set extends the full length of the Community Recreation Centre. Animal sounds emanate from behind the sets and the audience knows that, before the night is out, they will see a marvellous assortment of domestic and farm animals join the human cast of about 140 persons: horses, cows, goats, puppies and cats, pigs and rabbits. One year, the story goes, Betty wanted to introduce a boa constrictor. She was thwarted, however, only by a senior cast member who declared emphatically that he was "*not* taking part with any bo-er constricter." As Joanne points out, Betty does "things I don't think anyone else would do, and it's all in her desire to make it as natural and as real as possible. So many things happening . . . of course there are grumblings and growlings backstage. Yet, sitting in the audience, it's very effective and it's very real."

The "players," ranging in age from three months to 90 years, extend this sense of reality. Although the Singers provide a nucleus of 40 for the cast, "Betty pulls in another 100 or so a month before the play." Each year the play has a baby who is presented to the villagers during the July 1st picnic. Betty may stop a newcomer on the street and ask her to "bring her child along to the play." This is but one example of how the play acts as a social mixer for newcomers and locals.

The village children love the play; they meet new people, learn new songs and dances and, best of all, "get to stay up real late." Several young girls give other reasons. One loves "going back in time. It's neat." "It's such fun," explains another, "that you don't get embarrassed with all those people looking at you." Still another girl notes that, as part of the cast, you "get to have different parents and more brothers and sisters than at home." All agree that, although the play takes "hours and hours, it's not boring."

Teenage boys and girls bring other perspectives. They appreciate the "new social contacts made in setting up the stage" and the "chance to learn about acting." These young people recognize that "Betty knows what she's talking about." Although "she's a hard task-master, [they] pay attention and let the ragging go by; you have to, because she's so totally committed." One theme that resonates with all the young people concerns the social aspect of "getting to know people you wouldn't know otherwise." This reference is to the social and economic heterogeneity among the cast members and the 20 additional people who "work the lights," shovel the horse manure that falls on stage (to the immense amusement of the audience), design costumes and makeup, "look after the children" and, following the show, serve punch and cookies to the audience.

During the month leading up to production, rehearsals are held on Monday evenings. Although these begin officially at 8 o'clock, Betty starts calling out the square sets as early as 7:40. We begin with one and, during the dancing, another set of eight people form a second square. While she takes in the moves of all dancers from her spot by the record player, Betty directs her comments to "those who know her best, who can take it." Using her megaphone voice, she focuses on me, for I have missed the four beats of the "forward and back" introduction, "Carol, can't you count to four? Let's start again and this time *listen* to the music – 1, 2, 3, bow." Within five minutes the floor is full, some men partnering young girls and ten-year old boys leading their mothers through.

Then, at 8:00 sharp, the singing begins and the lines are reviewed. Betty, conscious of the time given by the farmers, shopkeepers, and other workers, considers that a tight schedule provides the "only fair way to treat people who have sacrificed their time" to attend rehearsals. This consideration is not missed by the cast for, as Jeremy notes, "you start promptly and you work and don't chitchat. The miracle of the whole thing is that Betty is very pointed."

I observed some of the planning that resulted in this "pointed" approach. Betty spends much time in reflection, in writing and re-writing lines, in consulting with others, and in studying the musical score and dialogue. Her planning is detailed and, after "a decade at this game," she can gauge quite accurately the last stages of production.

Five days before opening night, the pace quickens. On Saturday morning, several of the young men gather at Byer's barn to load the sets for the Recreation Centre. Guided by Bill, these floor-to-ceiling structures go up; they span the length of the hall/rink, and depict Tatamagouche in the appropriate period. People come and go all day, doing what they can between regular jobs and family duties. A high school student takes care of the taped music, selecting a wide assortment of popular music, opera, hits from the shows, and folk. Jean, the costume mistress, approves and supplements costumes, while her husband Paul works on sound and lighting and her children run errands and help with the staging. As indicated earlier, important community and family bonds are formed here as the set takes shape.

The next day, lines are rehearsed and choreography tightened. Here Betty "knows what each person can do and she constantly urges each on to the next level" of performance. "Chad, put your book, i.e., the score, down. Anyone who can make 95 in school subjects can learn a few lines." Chad grins and does as he is bidden, obviously pleased with the reference to his scholastic success and newly confident in his ability to memorize his part. Ira, always a lead actor and one who admits readily to leaving the mastery of his lines until the last minute, takes the full brunt of Betty's admonition. Both Betty and Ira know that he could do better, a source of conflict as inevitable as the play itself. On the other hand, Betty pushes the novice actor or the young child just so far. She acknowledges that "in this game, you win some and lose some. You should see how good his performance is, compared with last year."

The next three nights of rehearsal, including the dress rehearsal, are long. During each practice, lasting about four hours, Betty exercises her megaphone voice to direct lighting, stage hands, and cast. She entreats, cajoles, and bullies us all in our advance towards a naturalistic re-creation of historical events. But again, she seems to sense how far she may push us before relieving the tension by some amusing action, for instance, by demonstrating the ragtime dance of last year's 1889 theme. One night, she summed up our progress with these words, "You're 100 times better than you were last year." Then, in reference to both the long history of the plays and her own perennial output, she adds, "If I live to be 95, you'll be something."

By opening night we are ready, more or less, to go. The makeup team swings into action at 6:30 and, at 7:40, Betty assembles the cast. All day she has been fretting that the cast, especially its younger members, have missed her social message in including two "characters about town." Over lunch that day, she mused that "there are so many good things about modern life that we take for granted." Now she climbs on a chair, greets "my fellow Thespians" and continues:

> The short meeting tonight will take the form of a quiz. Some people have asked me why I included old Dave Kent and Archie McIvor.[4] I thought everyone would know. Anyway, it's essential that you do. Why do we have Dave and Archie there?

Someone replies joshingly: To fill a space?

But Betty is not to be deflected: "No, I mean this seriously." There are several more tries before she informs us that these two characters are "to contrast those days with today":

> I suppose Dave had what we'd call Alzheimers today. In those days, he'd have to go to the Poor Farm and no one from his family would be able to see him again. Today, what happens? You go to the Hills of Annan and then to the Willow Lodge. From there it's to the hospital and, then, across the road to the cemetery [laughter all round]. And it's all free! Now Archie, why is he there?

A young boy answers, "There was no divorce." "That's right," Betty responds.

> If a marriage wasn't working, there was no way out but to leave. You'd never see your children again. Today, as you know, people find other ways to work out their differences. Better arrangements, isn't that so? [Pause for reflection] Now, let's go.

We play to a house of about 300 people that night and for the next four evenings. The people come from the village, from other parts of Nova Scotia, and from beyond. There are always friends from Prince Edward Island and from Ontario, and tourists visiting the province.

Betty buys a scribbler on the way to the play, and puts this "guest book" on the ticket desk for members of the audience to sign. For days after the play, she pours over the names of friends, never complaining about those who couldn't make it and delighting always in reading of those who did. Another reward comes from meeting old friends after each show, as local women serve homemade cookies and punch.

We return to her house by 11:00 but, still, Betty has much to do before retiring for the night. With some families of the cast, she examines the video of the night's performance. Betty notes the changes to be made: choral lines that must be emphasized, entrances and exits that need to be adjusted, dialogue to be tightened and, even, new material to be inserted into the script in order to clarify the action.

Last year, after the second night "post-mortem," Betty sent me to Lloyd Baillie's house to fetch Dr. Patterson's *History of Tatamagouche*. I was intrigued that Betty, at that late stage, intended to add an entire scene explaining the details of a shipwreck. I was reassured by Lloyd's wife Jackie, however, that this action was not unusual for Betty. Indeed, at the cast party, I overheard this exchange:

> Voice (politely): Betty, how long did it take you to write the Play?
>
> Betty: Oh, it's not done yet. If I had another two weeks, it might be quite different.

Again, I had the impression that writing and producing a play with a cast of 150 for an audience of 1 500 was perfectly natural, the sort of thing that one does as long as time permits. Betty certainly does not regard the play as a finished work of art; its production, rather, represents an innovative *process* and one that may help reveal to people their present identities and their links to the past.

Discussion

Themes of continuity, commitment, and connections permeate the story of these history plays. Continuity is seen in Betty Murray's underlying motivation for action, her vision of education through community projects, and in the medium by which she conveys her message – the Arts. Her commitments are to "truth" as embodied in history and music and to the unique needs of each person. The connections she forges are those between children and adults, past and present, and her own personal and public life.

Continuity

Members of the cast offered various conjectures about Betty's motivation in undertaking such a mammoth task. One person suggested that Betty needs people in her life and that this may even serve as substitute for a conventional family. Another person noted her delight in seeing the old friends who "turn up regular as clockwork each year." Yet another says that "Betty simply takes pleasure in bringing people of the community together." While each of these opinions show contributing motivators, Betty herself maintains that

> there is something innate within people that makes them long to create. When this urge ceases, they begin to die. Notice this in the elderly who are so beset by troubles that they resign themselves to inactivity, to waiting.

As indicated in my opening quotation, Betty views creative action as "bringing out the individual"; through expression, the person reveals himself to himself or herself to herself. This action, for Betty Murray, usually has taken place in rural settings where she has witnessed dramatic "changes in the way people assume leadership roles within their own communities" after "their little brush with acting or other mediums of expression."

With the plays, for example, Betty notes the cast's changing attitudes. In the beginning, people were "reluctant to take part, to have lines. Now, it's the opposite and everyone wants a role!" As much as she appreciates this fervor for the stage, Betty finds her job becoming increasingly difficult. She must find a role for each of the eager "actors while keeping a lid on the length of the play." The confidence gained by cast members, she notes with satisfaction, continues into their leadership in cultural committees, church affairs, and other areas of community life.

This outcome is similar to her experience in the residential folkschools conducted by the Adult Education Division in the 1950s or her work in community development with graduate students at Acadia University in the 1940s. In both of these settings, too, following opportunities for extended and meaningful dialogue among neighbors, people were seen to emerge as community leaders. From today's educational perspective, we might think of this as personal empowerment through the finding of "voice" or, in Bower's (1987) words, as the "communicative competence" of defining oneself in relation to the social constructions of the past and present (pp. 40-42). Bowers and others (e.g., Collingwood, 1958, pp. 235-238; Eisner, 1991, p. 2), of course, refer to modes of expression apart from or in addition to discourse.

For Betty Murray, the major motif of communication has been music and the social arrangements surrounding musical activities. This dominating interest emerged through her official roles as a generalist teacher and as a community organizer of cooperatives, credit unions, farm forums, Women's Institutes, and so on, where "this sort of thing just evolved."[5] Of the early days, she recalls "feeling so guilty about getting into all this music. It was no problem at all, getting people turned on." I remind her, though, that she was supported in her musical endeavors by Guy Henson, Director of the Adult Education Division.

> Yes! And I suppose that is the thing about leadership, to find out what people's interests are and let them go to it.[Chuckles] There was never anything laid down, really, about what you were supposed to do. [As for my involvement in the schools], I shouldn't have been there at all. I just did it because I was interested.

While continuity is reflected in music as Betty's means of expression, we see also a continuous pattern in the way she carves out her own experiences independently of other people's expectations. As Ira points out today,

> she has the courage to live her life as she sees fit and not be dictated to by what the neighbors might think. To be a driving force in the community such as she is, and organize and generate volunteers and support for unusual things, that takes courage – not to be a 'yes' man. So, she's a bit of a maverick and that right in her own community surrounded by relatives and people she has grown up with.

Using an analogy of Heilbrun (1989), it can be said that Betty Murray possesses the strength of conviction to write her own story line or, to borrow Chatwin's (1987) appropriate image, her own *songline*.

184 Leadership Issues for Teachers and Others

Commitment

The action that illuminates a particular songline may be examined according to commitments of will. Murray is committed both to the task and to the individual. In discussing performances under Betty's direction, people spoke of her "great passion," "compulsion," and "perfectionist tendencies," as well as her "commitment." Details of the history play had to be "right," as did the music. Concerning the *music*, I asked Betty why some of us are so obsessed by the need for in-tune singing. She replied without hesitation, "Well, it's a form of truth, I suppose. It's like anything else; we work to make things fit." To Betty, music either fits or fails to fit, as does a rational argument or an historical detail. Discussing the ongoing conflict surrounding the play's church scene, Betty talks about "getting it right" in terms of her audience and of historical accuracy.

> I try to think about what the majority of people want. And what best represents what I'm trying to do. In the case of the church service, for example, there's no way you can portray the village historically without a church in it. Even if [the play is] too long, I think something else would have to be cut out rather than that. I've had a lot of complaints, like [this fellow] who said, "it would be a good play if you'd leave all that churchy stuff out." I say to him, "If you leave out all the churchy stuff, it's not real." That's all there was here, even in my childhood, everything revolved around the church. The younger people now don't realize how strong this was.

In bending others to her will on this issue,[6] she brings a laugh from the cast by juxtaposing the traditional importance of religion with today's dominant theme of materialism: "I know this isn't of burning importance to *you*. You've got the Chamber of Commerce. But it was to people then."

Then, too, there is Murray's tenacity in working on the *performance* until the last curtain falls. During the meeting of the cast on the second night of the play, she reviews all the problems of the previous night that she picked up during the performance or in viewing the video. She urges the cast yet again to "arrange themselves aesthetically during the garden party." She mentions that the three little girls at her feet weren't "all agreeing with the notes that well." Could they curb their excitement a little and listen more? Then, in the church service [following the death by drowning of the hero and his brother] "let your bodies echo your grief." She tells us all to "watch George [who is one of the most senior cast members]. His body tells everything. We can all take a lesson from George; he's a natural actor."

Murray's commitment to the development of the individual surpasses, however, her need for musical, dramatic, and historical "truth." Ross, who took a leading role in the play several years ago, noticed that, "in many instances, she was [dealing with] more than a member of the choir. It was a *particular* individual, with a particular background and we have to consider that person's needs." Joanne's observation that "her incredible ability to pick somebody off the street in a small town and develop talent" was borne out by those who had experienced that individualized attention. Debbie tells how this takes place:

> The first person on my doorstep in Tata was Betty Murray. Somehow, she knew I loved singing. That was just after the Pope had been here and she knew that I had gone to sing in the papal choir. I knew as soon as I walked into that room that I was going to learn something.

Others spoke not only of social and general educational benefits but also of acquiring the particular skills of reading music, singing harmonies, and acting.

Not all performers, however, are skilled. When I ask Betty about a particular weak performer, she assesses it in relative terms, pointing out how he or she has "come along." Each year Betty ensures that a few novices join those cast members "who have arrived." In her selection of actors, as well as in her admonitions of cast members according to their experience and degree of self-assurance, Betty applies a sliding scale of requirements. Despite the common belief that "Betty treats everybody the same," this does not appear to be the case; rather, she discriminates in favor of those who need extra help and encouragement.

Young, Staszenski, McIntyre, and Joly (1993) and Watkinson (1993) point, in their studies, to fresh interpretations of justice as exemplified by women leaders whereby "one rule for all" is replaced by a "fair" emphasis on situation and relationship. This finding supports Bourdieu's (1974, pp. 37, 38) contention that, as individuals bring to an educational experience vastly different cultural advantages, equality of treatment merely assures inequality of outcome. Betty, in her emphasis on the individual person, builds on the "natural talents" or private training of some, while creating the space in which others can develop talent. As well, she holds differing expectations for people, according to their opportunities; then she demands the "most that you can give." As Beth, a long-standing cast member, notes with humor, "if you have been with her a long time, she feels freer. So Barbara [another cast member who first sang with Betty Murray 40 years ago] and I, during the year, get more negative attention paid to us than almost anyone else." Through such "negativity" do newcomers gain the necessary information, time, and experience to improve their own performances.

Making Connections

A recurring theme in the study of women leaders points to the importance that they place on making connections among people, either within organizations and communities or between their private and public lives (Bepko & Krestan, 1993; Helgesen, 1990). For Betty Murray, one of the most significant connections takes place when children and adults come together for a special purpose. Although she considers that all people gain from the mixing of age groups, she thinks that it is particularly important for the older ones. For them,

> it's really more invigorating to be with younger people. Not segregating them, for there are so many ailments . . . to be talking about. I know they range from 8 to 80, in this little choir. It seems to me it's like a family reunion, you're just all milling around and talking to one another.

> Carol: And the young ones, I'm sure, gain immeasurably from it. I wonder if there was more of that years ago or if we, as a society, have always organized ourselves more into homogeneous groups.

> Betty: No, there *was* more [mixing]. But there was more of an authoritarian approach from the older people. The kids weren't supposed to talk much. They were more subservient. Today the kids are just as important as anybody else. They contribute to everything.

Betty acknowledges that she herself does not particularly enjoy segregated activities. "It's so much more fun to sit down at a bridge table and have words with [people of all ages] than to talk exclusively about health problems."

We noted earlier that the children appreciate this blending of age groups. Parents speak, as well, of the richness of family participation within the context of community. Ann, whose three daughters have taken part in the plays, feels that "it's something of great value that they will remember always."

Vivian, who participates in the play along with her husband Jeremy and their three children, finds similar rewards although she recognizes that there are prices to pay.

> Absolutely no housework gets done. We just have to focus on [the play]. We have to sleep in late, or let the children sleep in so that they have enough energy to get through the evening. Yet, for all of us, it has been a wonderful experience. [The children] have this opportunity which they wouldn't have in another community.

Vivian and Jeremy must balance the disruption to their family routine against the educational and social benefits.

Joanne explains that her daughter Jane, and Jane's friend Gillian, were under two years old when they first joined the cast. These girls "have always used their dancing experience in some little way." Joanne's ten-year old son Gordie joined the regular choir about two months ago and "he's driving us crazy at home because he's singing all the time. The training is unique really, for it combines choir, theatre, and dancing."

> C: I understand that Gordie was an actor prenatally. Was he in it the next year, as a baby?

> Joanne: Yes, he was the baby in the play. The whole family takes part. Alan [Joanne's husband] acts as an escort and he helps move some props around. Now that [Jane] has become a teenager – and there are so many teenagers in trouble – we have things like this to do together and things we can learn together. Generally speaking, [now referring to several families in the Play] when the play is on, the whole family is there. So you don't mind giving up your time

then. In the other things I do – such as attending board meetings of the hospital in Halifax – I would be taking time away from the children and Alan.

Not all families fit the traditional nuclear pattern as do Joanne, Vivian, and Ann's. We had at least six single-parent families last year, with equal gender representation among the parents, and several "blended families." Regardless of the family type, however, each appears to be part of the "Betty's extended family" with its "social identification of 'oh, you're in the play with Betty'."

The second link in Betty Murray's activities connects past with present, whereby the present provides a vantage point from which to reconstruct the past. While the past is portrayed according to documented evidence, the idiosyncratic moment is held up for inspection. As Vivian notes, Betty Murray "uses her plays to make current political statements" about various kinds of intolerance. When I ask if the children understand these messages, Jeremy suggests that they "are influenced by the medium rather than the message. They realize that others can think on this broader plane. By osmosis, they learn."

Vivian and Jeremy, who come from England, find the history fascinating because "it's a story we're not aware of. [Betty's] taking it from the human level and making it come to life." Jeremy adds that it is even more important for the people whose ancestors are in the plays, for they "discover a sense of who they are."

On a personal level, Betty's own past and present are interwoven within the play. It provides opportunities to meet with old friends and colleagues as well as to work both with students of long standing and with newcomers. As Helgesen (1990) found with her women leaders, we see a continuum between Betty Murray's "private and public" personae. It was impossible for me to determine the boundaries between her research and writing and the little chores of domestic life that provide, apparently, the needed space for reflection. The extensive lawn mowing and the long drives to fetch friends, relatives, and cast members or props were solitary chores, at the end of which often she jotted down another line or scene. The shipwreck scene, mentioned earlier, was one example. Another scene took shape on day three of the play as she tidied the house for her sister's arrival. In her cleaning, she happened upon educational records from the Public Archives of Nova Scotia. Reading of a policy indicating clearly sexist assumptions regarding women in 1879, she decided to incorporate it into the play. She scratched out the dialogue in longhand, I typed the lines, and both of us knew that Debbie and Beth would have them in place by the evening.

Innovative Leadership

Bepko and Krestan (1993), working under the assumption that women face an ongoing tension between the importance in their lives of relationship and creative action, delineate four ideal life patterns by which women find resolution as "lovers, artists, leaders, and innovators." Betty Murray, for whom both relationship and creative action are highly significant, exemplifies leadership and innovation in equal measure. We see with this type of leader the overriding importance of relationships enacted in the public sphere (p. 123). While the lover or the artist may "find fulfillment in the private sphere of home and family, at least for some part of her life," the innovative leader acts on a more expansive and generative level. She enjoys the collaboration, affiliation, and interaction of a strong social network, and she moves people to connect and to change (p. 126). This leader spots potential for growth and possesses the will, the energy, and the talent to foster this growth. Betty Murray exemplifies both will and energy in attempting the mammoth task of writing and producing a play every year. Harcus, now a musician with the Toronto Symphony Orchestra, comments on Murray's talent, recalling the opera camps in the 1960s and Betty's "terrific ear, her ability to spot any mistake, and to sing any part." Bruce, who sang with Harcus in those days and is now an experienced performer and music teacher, speaks of Betty's "amazing knowledge of the score" combined with a "will for perfection."

Perhaps even more important than Betty Murray's talent for music is her talent for drawing others into various projects. There are many people in the village, apart from those associated with the play, who speak of this influence. Cathy, a local news reporter, tells how this happens.

> She has a nose for potential. Lots of people complain that there are no volunteers but Betty goes out and asks. I do the same now, ask a person who isn't involved if she'd like to be.

And, as the Rev.Russell Elliott recalls from his folkschool days, "She has a special way of getting people involved. There is no possible way to say 'no' to Betty." According to Jeremy, though, Betty Murray remains an integral part of each project. She "leads from *within*. She sits with the choir. You know, it's a group."

Such social and innovative leadership can result, however, in a rejection of authoritative positions. Betty has been unwilling to accept hierarchical arrangements if, by these, she would be removed from the kind of interaction that leads to creative expression (Bepko and Krestan, 1993, p. 142). The function of the school administrator, with its bureaucratic structures (Bates, 1983; Rizvi, 1986), holds absolutely no appeal for Murray. Though her leadership involves influence (and "power" in that sense), it need not be associated with an authoritative position. As Jeremy notes apropos Betty's leadership, "It is *stature* [that we see] and not *status*. You can work toward status, but stature is given to you. By being dedicated to what she does, and by doing it with all her heart, she doesn't need to have any 'upward mobility'." Murray, like the Innovators of Bepko and Krestan's study, seems to seek a kind of leadership-in-action rather than one of position.

Although there appears to be an overwhelming component of charisma in such leadership, this concept calls for elaboration in the context of the Arts. There may well be, in that mystical phenomenon known as "aesthetic experience," a tendency for people to combine their regard for the leader with the affective moment itself. In the creation of beauty, the force of aesthetic feeling may be transferred to everything and everyone within the sphere of experience – to place, to drama and music (the media of expression), to friends and co-actors, and to the leader. This is not to deny the strength of such charisma but, rather, to suggest that its complexity deserves examination beyond the scope of this chapter. I mention it here, both to introduce and to delimit the word "charisma" for Betty Murray is considered charismatic by many who have studied, worked, and played with her. Part of this charisma may be attributable to the depth of musical experience that she provides for others. A significant part inheres, undoubtedly, in the character of this particular leader.

A feature of Betty Murray's leadership is that she convinces others of the worth of her projects. She is, in this sense, truly an entrepreneur of values who, through the words and music of this artistic venture, shapes language and thought and, to that degree, shapes herself and others (Greenfield, 1984, p. 154). Those who sing in her choirs, act in her history plays, and meet her daily on Main Street, Tatamagouche, are enriched in their spirit and own determination to contribute to her community projects. On many fronts, Betty Murray's personal project, the story of her life, continues to unite the realities of community and the larger society and enable people to reflect upon the best of traditional values in order to choose more wisely from among those of modernity. Murray's project is, above all, one of educational leadership.

Implications and Conclusions

In tracing Murray's leadership in the grand theory of Weberian typologies, we see a closer fit with charisma than with either traditional or authoritative models. This is not surprising in a postmodern era where traditional values have been much eclipsed and where authority (government, church, and the professions) is under fire. If we think of "charisma" in a Weberian sense as a natural endowment and an idiosyncratic control over people, it becomes almost synonymous with strength of character.

Leadership based on character or charisma tends to be ever-present, however, rather than solely situational. In this study, we see a woman "lead from within" in all aspects of her life. This form of leadership supports the dominant theme in other studies of women's leadership. Women lead from the heart (Young et al., 1993); they seek connections (Burge, 1993); they create webs of leadership (Keller, 1986); and they seek to be with their co-workers, rather than "above" them. Betty Murray, too, leads in all aspects of her life but always from among her people.

Murray's leadership taps into a wide range of intelligences (Gardner, 1985) in order to provide her followers with "other ways of seeing" (Berger, 1977). In addition to widening the possibilities of discourse, people in the Tatamagouche plays develop ways of seeing through dance, music, art, and dramatic speech and movement. If, indeed, "in action the being of the doer is intensified," Murray extends greatly the means for such self-revelation.

This comprehensive approach to education extends into Murray's commitment to community. She sees community as including people of all ages and of every racial, social, and economic background. For her, it is inconceivable that a successful teacher would be divorced from the community in which she or he teaches. This attitude toward school and community introduces a fresh perspective on the well-worn concept of integration. The term "integration" has been rationalized in educational parlance to signify largely the interweaving of subject content. Murray's approach, however, returns the word to its larger context, prevalent at mid-century, of "home and school."

The messages that Murray's voice and actions convey may not be popular within all of today's educational circles. In many geographical areas, teachers have assumed private lives totally apart from their communities of work. Ease of transportation and a desire for respite from the pressures of parents and students may be two contributing and understandable factors. A third divisive factor is, surely, the dualistic assumptions of contemporary living whereby child is separated from adult, working adult from senior citizen, private life from public action, and so on.[7] We hear today a call from parents for their own inclusion in the educational decision-making affecting their children. While much of the momentum for inclusion may be fuelled by conservative reactions to what is perceived as excessive progressivism, part, as well, may indicate a committed interest in finding connections between the communities of home and school. In the search for such connections, all of us would do well to include the voices of leaders such as Betty Murray.

Notes

[1]The researcher gratefully acknowledges support for this study from the Social Sciences and Humanities Research Council of Canada and the University of Calgary.

[2]The village takes its name from a Mi'kmaq word signifying the "meeting of the waters" for, at Tatamagouche, the Rivers Waugh and French converge and flow into the Northumberland Strait.

[3]See Giddens (1985) for a discussion of this condition stated with varying emphases by Hegel, Durkheim, Marx, and Weber.

[4]Historical figures, now deceased.

[5]From the inception of Nova Scotia's Adult Education Division in 1946, until 1952, Murray was a Regional Representative, first in the Annapolis Valley and then in Colchester County. The position of Music Supervisor was created in 1951 and Murray

served in that position until 1960. Both posts involved extensive community develop-ment and the use of drama, dancing, music, and discussion groups as means for teaching and learning.

[6]I use William James's definition of "will" here, as the combination of a desired end and the confidence that one can achieve this end. James explains that "if with the desire there goes a sense that attainment is not possible, we simply *wish*; but if we believe that the end is in our power, we "will" that the desired feeling, having, or doing shall be real; and real it presently becomes, either immediately upon the willing or after certain preliminaries have been fulfilled" (Hunt, 1993, p. 158).

[7]For a comprehensive discussion of the effects of rationalism on organizational and community life, see Hodgkinson, 1983, pp. 95-101. For a critical discussion apropos schools today, see Barlow and Robertson, 1994.

References

Arendt, H. (1968). *Between past and present: Eight exercises in political thought.* Markham, ON: Penguin.

Arendt, H. (1958). *The human condition.* Chicago: University of Chicago Press.

Barlow, M., & Robertson, H.J. (1994). *Class warfare: The assault on Canada's schools.* Toronto: Key Porter Books.

Bates, R. (1983). *Educational administration and the management of knowledge.* Monograph: Theory and practice in educational administration. Geelong: Deakin University Press.

Bepko, C., & Krestan, J. (1993). *Singing at the top of our lungs: Women, love, and creativity.* New York: Harper Collins.

Berger, J. (1977). *Ways of seeing.* London: BBC/Penguin.

Blackmore, J. (1989). Educational leadership: A feminist critique and reconstruction. In J. Smith (Ed.), *Critical perspective on educational leadership* (pp. 93-129). New York: Falmer Press.

Bourdieu, P. (1974). The school as a conservative force: Scholastic and cultural inequalities. In J. Eggleston (Ed.), *Contemporary research in the sociology of education* (pp. 32-46). London: Methuen.

Bowers, C.A. (1987). *The promise of theory: Education and the politics of cultural change.* New York: Teachers College Press.

Burge, E.J. (1993, June). *Connectiveness and responsiveness.* Paper presented for the Feminist Pedagogy and Women-Friendly Perspectives in Distance Education International Working Conference, Umea, Sweden.

Chatwin, B. (1987). *The songlines.* Markham, ON: Viking Press.

Collingwood, R.G. (1958). *The principles of art.* Oxford: Oxford University Press.

Eisner, E.W. (1991). *The enlightened eye: Qualitative inquiry and the enchantment of educational practice.* New York: Macmillan.

Gardner, H. (1985). *Frames of mind: The theory of multiple intelligences.* New York: Basic Books.

Giddens, A. (1985). *Capitalism and modern social theory: An analysis of the writings of Marx, Durkheim, and Max Weber.* Cambridge: Cambridge University Press.

Greenfield, T.B. (1984). Leaders and schools: Willfulness and nonnatural order in organizations. In T.J. Sergiovanni and J.E. Corbally (Eds.), *Leadership and organizational culture* (pp. 142-169). Urbana: University of Illinois Press.

Heilbrun, C.G. (1989). *Writing a woman's life.* New York: Ballantine Books.

Helgesen, S. (1990). *The female advantage: Women's ways of leadership.* Toronto: Doubleday.

Hodgkinson, C. (1983). *The philosophy of leadership.* New York: St.Martin's Press.

Hunt, M. (1993). *The story of psychology.* Toronto: Doubleday.

Jameson, F. (1992). *Postmodernism or the cultural logic of late capitalism.* Durham: Duke University Press.

Keller, C. (1986). *From a broken web: Separation, sexism, and self.* Boston: Beacon Press.

Kuhn, T. (1962). *The structure of scientific revolutions.* Chicago: University of Chicago Press.

Rizvi, F. (1986). *Administrative leadership and the democratic community as a social ideal.* Monograph, Deakin University Press.

Shakeshaft, C., & Nowell, I. (1984). Research on theories, concepts, and models of organizational behavior: The influence of gender. *Issues in Education, 2*(3), 186-203.

Watkinson, A.M. (1993, June). *Inequality and/or hormones.* Paper presented at the Annual Meeting of the Canadian Society for Studies in Education, Carlton University.

Young, B., Staszenski, D., McIntyre, S., & Joly, L. (1993). Care and justice in educational leadership. *The Canadian Administrator, 33*(2), 1-8.

14

"Ourschool": Reclaiming Teaching As Leading

Kathie Webb

Introduction

Inspired by the wisdom of *Herland*, Charlotte Perkins Gilman's 1915 utopian novel, this chapter presents *Ourschool*, a fictional Canadian school community. In this chapter the philosophical assumptions of educational administration as constructed in western nations are questioned and a new structure for schooling which honors the work of teachers and students is described. Whereas Gilman raised motherhood to its highest power in her fictional society of Herland, *Ourschool* uses a twist on her plot raising good teaching to its highest power. *Ourschool* portrays what schools might be like without hierarchy – without administrators. In this view of schooling, good teaching is regarded as the highest achievement: Good teachers are recognized as those who care for their students.

Ourschool presents teaching as leading. Attention is drawn to relationships and community in teaching and leading. The emphasis on caring in this educational community emerges from an understanding that what the teacher knows from caring and being "in-relation" (Hollingsworth et al., 1994) affects her pedagogy and the curriculum that is lived out with students. All aspects of schooling in this community focus on supporting the development of caring and trusting relationships between teachers and students. Teachers and students are positioned at the centre – as the focus of education. There is no promotion system for educators, no career ladders, no market place ideology underpinning educational policy, no competition, and no standardized tests. Learning is valued for what is in a child's mind and what a child can do. There is no belief that learning can be measured by numbers.

Ourschool assumes that hierarchical school systems are founded on a lack of trust of teachers and suggests a view of schooling which trusts teachers to determine their own professional development and to know the best interests of their students.

The Scene and the Characters

It is the year 1999. Let us imagine a conversation between two people, Marly and Jack, who live and work in entirely different educational worlds. Marly is a grade 3-6 teacher in the *Ourschool* school community. The use of the term "community" to refer to the school is deliberate, purposefully focusing on the relationships between students, teachers, families, and others involved in the dynamics of learning. The *Ourschool* community is situated within the larger district of *Herschool*, on a densely populated, but isolated island off the coast of British Columbia. Marly's is a community in which teachers are valued and prized. For more than forty years the schools on this island have been led by teachers with the help of parents, families and students. In status and importance the teachers are second only to the students. This community views teaching as the most important job in education, and students, the next generation, as precious – the possibility for the future.

For more than 15 years Jack has been a superintendent in a wealthy school system in a large mid-western Canadian city. His school system is arranged hierarchically and Jack has conceptualized all his beliefs about education in terms of this structure for schooling. He is, however, deeply concerned by the findings of recent North American research that shows that a significant proportion of the students selected for entry to university on the basis of SAT scores have done very poorly in courses that require problem-based learning, fieldwork or a practicum. Universities and the media in the United States and Canada are laying the blame on schools. Jack wants to find out why 100 percent of the students allowed to enter the University of Mid-Western Canada (UMWC) from *Ourschool* (a K-12 school in the Herschool district), have done so well, receiving some of the highest awards and scholarships. A recent publication has reported that a high proportion of students from *Ourschool*, have become successful educators, musicians, painters, architects, chemists, and writers. Jack arranges to visit *Ourschool* to find out what is happening there.

The Conversation

Jack and Marly meet in the staff room at *Ourschool*. Marly welcomes Jack and introduces herself as a grade 3-6 teacher. She explains that in response to Jack's letter requesting that he visit with a view to gaining insight into the reasons for the academic success of *Ourschool* students, she has been requested by the community of students, teachers and families to explain the history, philosophy and workings of the school community. She was chosen for this task because it was her turn. The school practices rotating responsibility among teachers and other members of the school community, including students, for such tasks. Marly leads Jack to some comfortable seats and a sofa near a window. She has already ordered coffee and muffins so they can start work immediately in comfort and with refreshments.

At first, Jack seems disconcerted that he has been met by a classroom teacher – a grade three teacher. He has come to talk about achievement levels and performance of students entering university. This is not at all what he had expected. Jack spreads his ample portions on the sofa and announces, "Well, young lady, I AM impressed by the academic record of students from your school system and I'm keen to do an analysis of the policies your administrators are implementing. I'm surprised though (tugs at his lapels) that none of your administrators have time to meet with me. Just who is in charge around here?"

Marly is thrown for a moment by his language and his expectations. "*Administrators?*... I, I'm not sure ... We have no administrators. *Ourschool* is a community ..."

Jack doesn't hear her. Cutting her off, he says, "I've not met any administrators from this school district at the TQM in Education conferences I've attended in the last few years."

"TQM?"

"You know," he scoffs, "*Total Quality Management!* It's made a power of difference to how we manage schools!"

Marly is not sure where to begin but decides she should stay with her original plan to outline the philosophy and origins of *Ourschool*. "We have no 'administrators'. *Ourschool* is an educational community. There's no one person 'in charge'. We are all educators. We – teachers, students, parents, and family members – are all responsible. The district of Herschool, in which *Ourschool* is only one school community, was founded more than 40 years ago. The founders of our community concept for schooling drew on Gilman's (1915) ideas as the inspiration for a different way of thinking about education. In her book, Gilman constructed a society in which the care and education of children was regarded as the highest achievement."

"Yes, the care and education of children is a priority in our school system too."

Marly continues: "*Ourschool* was created with students and their learning as the central focus. Our founders realized that the people who teach children play the most important role in education and that all aspects of education have to be supportive of the relationship between student and teacher. We have developed our concepts of educational leadership around this philosophy so that students, their family members and teachers were all recognized as playing important roles in learning. The status of teaching was elevated to meet this expectation. We have no positions more senior than teacher."

Jack intervenes, "But who decided this? How did ... ?"

"Community meetings, continuous involvement of all partners in our educational community is the norm for us and has provided the major way in which we develop our vision and practices for schooling. Our students and their families have always had input into planning with teachers – the curricula, assessment strategies, and reporting of student progress. A community approach to school planning has also caused us to rethink teacher development. Our teachers are commonly engaged in collaborative work: meeting, talking, researching and writing about their practice. Our teachers help each other. Teacher development time is included in the school timetable. Our teachers conduct professional development activities in their classrooms where university professors, members of the community, people from business, students and parents or other family members are engaged in workshops; where teaching and learning is constructed and deconstructed. Often the students will take on a teacher role in these activities."

"Yes – quite a radical concept. But, what about the school system? What about central control? What are your accountability measures? *Where's your three year plan?*"

"I'm not familiar with some of the terms you are using Jack. Why don't *you* tell me about your school 'system', . . . is that what you called it?"

Jack jumps in, keen to outline the strengths of his system. "In the last 20 years we have been using the business model to address what is wrong with education. We realized that if we came to look at the school as a factory and student learning as the product, then we could really begin to control the process of education. The first step was to decide what we wanted our product to look like at the end of the manufacturing (teaching) process. Our business is knowledge, so by deciding what's worth knowing, and mandating this fixed knowledge at the beginning of the process then we were able to eliminate any unnecessary learning. We also need to measure outcomes to ensure quality control. It is a worry that the teachers might be changing some of the teacher-proof materials we have supplied, or that the product might not be turning out as we intended. Hence, we spend about $10 million per year on standardized tests to ensure that we are getting a quality product. Of course we employ outside experts to design these tests."

Marly is more than a little concerned. She asks, "Why do you see it as necessary to implement all of these controls over the learning process?"

"The economic crisis of course!" Jack, slams his hands together, his whole body emphasizing his words. "Canada is in the midst of economic crisis and schools have to lift their game so that the country can compete in the global market!"

"The global market, do you consider that it is something that teachers and children are likely to benefit from?" inquires Marly.

"Well of course if the corporate sector is doing well, the rest of the country benefits," Jack replies confidently.

"This is very surprising," says Marly. "Our teachers would never accept a factory model for learning as such a view is in conflict with what our teachers know and why they are teachers. Who are your teachers? Who does the work of teaching? I find it difficult to understand why your teachers would support this view? How *are* teachers positioned in your schools?"

Jack begins to outline the demographics of schooling in his province. "We have administrators and teachers," he responds enthusiastically. "More than sixty percent of all teachers are women, but the administrators are mainly men. In the elementary schools about 40 percent of principals are women; however, at the junior high and high school levels women occupy less than 15 percent of the administrative positions."

"Is this the same throughout your education system . . . this distribution of men and women?" asks Marly.

"Hmmm. I haven't given this a lot of thought . . . (He pauses.) At the universities I guess it is more or less the same picture. I'm not sure, let me just check in some of my papers here. (He flicks through some files in his briefcase.) "Yes here it is." He reads: "Figures released last year showed 89.7 percent of the full professors are men, with women making up about 34% of associate professorships and about 37 percent of assistant professorships."

"And what about teacher education education?" asks Marly.

Jack replies, "Our teacher education courses are mostly filled by women students, about 21 students out of every 28. Most of the teacher educators, and those in the most senior positions, however, are men. More than nine out of ten of the decision maker positions, . . . *the administrators*, such as the president, vice presidents, deans, chairs of departments . . . yes they are usually men."

"These administrators . . . Could you explain the need for *administrators* in your educational system? What do these people do?"

Jack becomes serious. "In our school system, administrators are paid much more than teachers – about 40-60 percent more." Almost as an off-side he says, "I earned $136 000 last year, though I could probably earn more in private industry." His voice deepens as he moves back to more relevant issues. "Educational administrators do not teach of course. They make the policy decisions and decide how the money will be spent. Basically they have all the power. Oh, and yes, each administrator usually has a secretary or two to do the typing, answer the phone, make appointments for meetings and so on."

"It is not this way with us. Teachers are honored and valued here," says Marly; the reality of the difference between the two educational worlds in which they each work is beginning to dawn on her. Marly looks directly at Jack as she explains: "Women make up 70 percent of our teachers, and constitute the same proportion of our most highly regarded instructors. Some of the tasks you have described that your administrators do we consider managerial and of much less importance than teaching. We have hired accountants to manage the money, of course at much lower salaries than the teachers. It is very unusual in our community for an assistant, secretarial or otherwise, to be allocated to persons who do not teach. Policies which directly affect instruction can only be decided by teachers, though parents/guardians and students also have input. How can you be sure that these *administrators* will make decisions that are in the best interests of students and teachers?"

Suddenly Jack makes the connection and is disturbed by the lack of apparent administration at Marly's school and within the larger district of Herschool. "Okay, you're kidding me," he says. "There must be administrators. We all know that teachers cannot organize themselves."

"Ours do," replies Marly firmly.

"And all these women," remarks Jack. "That doesn't seem right. Women don't want the responsibility or the work where I come from. They seem to accept that leadership needs a certain toughness, a ruthlessness, a vision, to make it to the top."

"But we are all leaders in this school," explains Marly patiently. "The students can be leaders, as well as members of the support staff. We do not see leadership as the role of one person – there is no 'top'. Also, we do not see a leader as having power over others, more as an excellent example to others – a way for us all to strive to be. We take turns at leadership and have many leaders at one and the same time."

"What about your promotions system?" asks Jack. "Don't you promote the best people?"

"What is promotion? How does this work?" responds Marly, her brows knitting together. Jack looks shocked. He shakes his head. "You mean, . . . you don't have promotion?"

"No."

"You know, a move up and out of the classroom."

Marly cannot fathom what he means. It is inconceivable to her that to move a teacher out of the classroom can be thought of as a career improvement. The classroom is the site of the most important work in education, working with children, helping them to learn. In *Ourschool* to be allowed to teach, to work with students, is considered the highest honor. The best and most skillful teachers are allowed the most contact with children. Only those persons who can be trusted to respect students, to honor their creativity, and who will not abuse their authority, are allowed to be teachers. A careful screening process has been used for more than forty years to ensure that persons, male or female, seeking entry into teaching for the purposes of wanting or striving for power are selected out. Such persons, if they still want to work in the field of education, and if they are qualified, are assigned managerial tasks such as monitoring the school resources – tasks which do not require one to relate to other persons. Being able to form positive relationships with other people, being able to care for and to nurture the learning and development of others takes precedence at *Ourschool*.

"Tell me some more about this process of *promotion*," Marly asks as she leans forward to pour herself another coffee.

"Let's see," says Jack, "if it is being done by interview, then the teacher sends in a curriculum vitae or C.V., as we like to call it, and several candidates are short-listed on the basis of the information therein. "

"Oh, and I expect that this 'CV' would have samples of the work done by students of each teacher," chirps Marly, pleased that she is beginning to make sense of this strange procedure. Jack coughs and squirms a little as if uncomfortable in his seat: "No, that is not required at all. The CV is a list, like a shopping list, of the teacher's achievements: courses taken at university to upgrade qualifications (an MBA is good), inservices attended (especially anything to do with effective management, supervision of teachers, or budget preparation), articles published in administrative journals, and most importantly, leadership initiatives taken."

"Leadership initiatives?" Marly wonders out loud. Jack brightens, thrilled to be asked to explain one of the most central aspects of promotion in his school system. "We are looking for persons with the potential to make good leaders, people who can attack a problem, plan strategy, implement bold manoeuvers, manage the troops, and all with maximum effectiveness and cost efficiency. Potential leaders reveal themselves through their CV by indicating their experience of school level management – organization of the school professional development day and the like."

"Is it really normal for only one person to decide how all the teachers in a school might spend their professional development time?" Marly asks in amazement.

"Why yes, this is most common," replies Jack. "Our principals usually nominate someone they are 'grooming' for a leadership role. I'm impressed that you've zeroed in on one of our leadership training practices."

"And the interview for promotion, I presume that is conducted by the teacher's peers, some of the students, and the parents of the students, those who would know the teacher's work best?" she queries.

"Actually no, . . . the interview would be conducted by one, or possibly two, senior administrators."

"And these *administrators*, they are usually men, whilst the teachers are usually women?" she asks again.

"Yes, well that is the way it is," Jack shrugs. "Most of the women don't bother applying for promotion. It is mainly the younger men we see in interviews."

"So your process of *promotion* has little to do with a teacher's caring for students or with the quality of students' learning," Marly responds.

"I wouldn't put it exactly that way," says Jack. "We do admit caring is important, but it's one of those touchy-feely things that is just too difficult for us to measure."

Marly thinks for a moment and then she says, "And what are your criteria for *promotion?*" Jack answers, "Well of course, to be promoted one has to be seen to be implementing policy. You have to have attended, or organized, several inservice courses for teachers. Documentation is important as well – all the paperwork needs to be in place. And then of course there's the dress code."

"Are you saying that there is some consensus about appropriate dress for teachers?" Marly queries. Jack looks a little embarrassed at this question.

"No," he pauses, "there's no consensus of course. But everyone knows that when you are being evaluated you dress up. The men wear a suit and tie and the women wear the female version of executive dress, without the trousers. Administrators, of course, are always expected to look like executive material."

"So the students and the teachers are given strong messages about who is more important through dress?" she questions.

"I haven't given this much thought. But yes, that's how it works."

"What did you mean by 'evaluated'?" asks Marly. Jack brightens. "Another way of checking up on what teachers are doing in classrooms is teacher evaluation. This allows administrators to see teachers at work and to rate a teacher's performance. A real consideration in teacher evaluation is the kind of teaching that goes on in the classroom. We are very much into group work – student-centred teaching, you know – just as long as the teacher maintains control." Marly's eyebrows lift.

"How long does an evaluator spend in a teacher's classroom?" she asks.

"Oh usually no more than a day, two at the most, sometimes only an hour. We really cannot spare the time."

"Tell me about the paperwork for *teacher evaluation*? Do your teachers have to put a lot of time into writing things on paper that they might do in their classrooms, to satisfy administrators?"

"Oh yes," replies Jack leaping in. "The programs of content, teaching strategies and evaluative measures a teacher intends to use with each class." Marly's practitioner experience causes her to question such a policy. She asks, "But what if what really happens in the classroom is totally different from the original plan? What about the students? Don't they change things? What about the impact of things happening in the media, in the daily lives of the teachers and the students? Don't these create a curriculum in the classroom?"

"Yes, I suppose all of that happens." Jack adopts a more authoritative tone, and adds: "But our main concern as administrators is whether the teacher is following the mandated curriculum and whether the teacher has provided evidence that she has. It's the evidence that we are really concerned with. We have to cover our own backs in case there are ever any questions about what teachers are doing in their classrooms. We have got to be accountable! It's the number one priority."

"How will these, *administrators*, know what to look for in evaluating a teacher's work?" asks Marly, quite perplexed at the prospect.

"Oh that's easy," says Jack relaxing back in his seat. "The guidelines as to what the teacher should be doing are sent out in advance. There's a set of criteria that the teacher's work will be measured against. We call it 'performance evaluation'. It's all decided before the administrator arrives in the school and sees the teacher at work. There's a set procedure. It's the same for every teacher."

"How could this be? Are you saying that 'good teaching' can be measured, that it can be decided externally of the teacher's work? . . . Let me see if I'm understanding this. A few people, mainly men, get 'promoted' out of the classroom and no longer teach. They get to decide what good teaching looks like and then come back and judge whether people who do teach are 'good' teachers."

"It doesn't sound quite right when you put it like that (then he brightens), but it works quite well. Our administrators are paid more than teachers because of all the responsibility they have to carry. Teachers might have to take flak from students, but that's a pretty small stick compared to what we administrators have to face. We have to be answerable to politicians you know. And the media people are always after us for interviews. And then there are all of those secretaries to keep in line. It's a difficult job."

"It is very different within our community," says Marly with emphasis. "Everyone wants to be a teacher, but not everyone can be. The academic requirements for those wishing to teach are the highest of all professions except perhaps, for health care of infants and young children. The second most important job next to teaching is health care of children. Education has been recognized by the people as the single most important factor in building and maintaining our society. We have a long waiting list of qualified doctors and lawyers who would like to be teachers. Careers such as engineering, chemistry, and the law – none of these is perceived as having as high a status as teaching." Jack seems very surprised that this could be possible.

"But why," he asks. "What rewards are there in teaching?"

Marly is quick to respond. "Firstly, our teachers are highly paid for their work, which sends a message that it is important and valued work. Our teachers, however, are motivated more by intrinsic rewards – the pleasure of being with learners and helping them. Response is an important part of this. We implement a number of means by which teachers, students and other partners in the learning process, might respond to good teaching. Our students are encouraged to respond to their teachers orally and in writing about their experiences as learners in our classrooms. We have found that our teachers value time rather than money, as a form of recognition of good teaching: time to reflect, to visit other teachers or schools, time to read or to write about their teaching, time to collaborate with other teachers or teacher-researchers."

Jack whips out his notepad and starts writing furiously. Excited by the accounts of teacher collaboration that he is hearing from Marly, he makes substantial notes to himself about how he might mandate some of these strategies on return to his school district. One of the things that he cannot figure out though is how this system sorts out the more successful academic students from the least successful. From what Marly has said there is no record keeping system that uses numbers anywhere in the school or in the district. Marly has shown him several bulky student portfolios and he has read several of the narratives of student progress, written by students, their parents and their teachers. He is discreet, however, in not revealing his lack of interest in either of these measures to Marly as she continues enthusiastically in her explanations as to how these are compiled and how students find these meaningful and validating. To Jack, the obvious time and cost involved immediately rules out any interest on his part. He is looking for a means of sorting students by their ability, quickly and cheaply. As an administrator, accountability and efficiency are his main priorities.

Uncomfortable with the idea that narratives and portfolios of student work are being used at the grade 12 level for university entrance, Jack insists that other measures are needed to compare students in order to decide which are the best.

"But all of our students are considered to be working at their best," replies Marly.

"How can you decide who to send to university without comparative measures?" he asks.

"One of our criteria is really 'vanting to study – the desire to learn, and more importantly the desire to share one's knowledge with others. We only allow those who have demonstrated their ability to help others as learners to attend institutions of higher learning," she responds.

Sensing that the rationale for assessment of students' work is different in Jack's school district from her own, Marly tries to explain the underlying philosophy at *Ourschool*. She begins, "The idea that putting a number on a student's work is a useful practice has long since been abandoned. Notions of grades, tests and the ideology of competition have been rejected as it has been recognized that only a few students benefited from such practices. We have worked hard to eliminate testing and competition. We know that an overwhelming majority of students are disadvantaged by the implied deficit when only 10 percent can achieve the highest grades. It is well known among the parents and teachers, that in their own generation some of the students who had scored the highest grades in a competitive environment lost faith in what education was all about. Some of these paid a high price for their 'success'. The growth of children is considered the most important goal for teachers in our educational community. Good teaching is reflected in the work of the students. It is the quality and creativity of children's poems, writing, art work, constructions, problem solving, questions, and discussions, that reveals their learning. What is in their mind and what they can do with their mind and their hands. Memorization of facts is considered a minor indication of learning and not necessarily indicative of understanding. Scores on written tests constitute a minor mode of assessment for most of the teachers in *Ourschool*."

"But all this sounds so, so subjective," winces Jack. "Your assessment measures are all influenced by what the teacher thinks is important."

"Oh, I see," says Marly. "When your teachers put a number on a child's work you believe that is objective."

"Yes, and it is a much more truthful way – not influenced by emotions, values and feelings."

Marly merely nods.

Day 2

Marly has a lot of questions for Jack on their second day of meeting. There are a number of things that bother her. As soon as they have finished their first cup of coffee and settled into their seats, she asks, "Tell me Jack, where does 'freedom' fit in your management orientation for education?"

"Freedom?"

"Yes," she continues, "how are the students in your schools free to do things differently, free to change the status quo?"

"Oh, so that's what you mean." He shrugs. "The same kind of democracy exists in schools as in the population at large. Our schools are very democratic. Each school has an elected student leader and usually there is a student council which puts forward suggestions to the school administrators. We believe strongly in equality and freedom."

"But do the students, or for that matter the teachers, have input into the curriculum that is taught or the assessment measures that are used? Do your students have choices about what is assessed, when, why and on what basis as ours do?" asks Marly.

"Not usually," mumbles Jack.

"Mmmm," Marly begins, "I get a sense that what you mean by 'freedom' and what we mean by 'freedom' are profoundly different. At *Ourschool* the basic freedom for teachers and students, is freedom of mind and whatever degree of freedom of action and experience is necessary to produce freedom of intelligence. Freedom is the capacity to take initiatives. We do not conceive of freedom as distinct from critical thinking, hypothetical inquiry, or the open exchange of ideas. For us, freedom represents the sense of possibility for every child. We celebrate the child who says, 'I am in the world to change the world'. The pivotal issue here is the nurture of intelligence, the encouragement of creativity, fostering the instinct to question and to re-create the world. As teachers, we work from the perspective that we are also learners, we do not know best, we do not know all there is to know. We do not believe that we have got the world right and that our students need only to follow our instructions. It is our belief that children who have been challenged to reach beyond themselves, to wonder, to imagine, to pose their own questions are the ones most likely to learn. We know that arousing a search for freedom in young people requires special teachers, teachers who also are in search of their own freedom."

Jack leans forward in his seat and pulls a face. Tugging at his chin and frowning, he thinks for a minute or so before responding to what Marly has said. "Are you saying that you trust teachers to teach students what is best?" he asks looking very uncomfortable.

"Yes, but more than that, we trust our students to make wise choices about what they want to know, about what they want to learn. We respect the learner, the learner's experience, the knowledge the learner already has, and we try to foster an education that will help the learner, whether child or teacher, to make sense of her/his experience. We encourage our students to take responsibility, to make choices, to author a way of being in the world, to grow. A sense of community, of being in a caring relationship with others, is essential to this growth. The *Ourschool* community represents a smaller version of the larger community, a society if you wish. In our society, difference is embraced. Our students do not work in competition with each other, but with care and concern for each other."

Marly's last comment causes alarm bells to ring for Jack. He swings his body around to face her, sitting bolt upright. "You can't be serious! No student will work well unless he has to!" declares Jack.

"He?" inquires Marly.

"No, I mean no boy *or* girl is going to work without incentive. There has to be competition for kids to do their best. Competition is the motivation to work. We know this from business and sport."

"Mmmm," ponders Marly, "so when a child paints a beautiful picture or writes an emotive poem, he or she only does that to be better than another student?" Jack admits that is not what he means. There are some things like beautiful works of art that are just too hard to explain. These do not fit into the world of work that he is referring to – the world that requires the competitive element. Jack tries to put in a good word for competition, but Marly remains unconvinced. She picks up the thread of her earlier comment and continues her explanation of how caring, concern, and community are essential to the educational philosophy and practice of *Ourschool*. She begins to speak of morality and mutuality, and the ways in which a sense of community is created.

Jack interrupts and continues his argument for competition in education. "We encourage our students to strive to be the best! Individualism and autonomy are perceived as the highest personal attributes," he emphasizes, drawing himself up then exhaling loudly.

"But I thought Carol Gilligan's work revealed that such views were predominantly male views and that women's values and morality differed. Don't you consider that her research has implications for education?" queries Marly.

"I'm not familiar with that study," snorts Jack. "Is she a feminist? I suppose it was done on a lot of girls!"

Still somewhat confused, Jack tries to make sense of Marly's rationale for *Ourschool* with what he believes about 'effective education'. The lack of administrative controls within the Herschool district and within *Ourschool* in particular fly in the face of what he knows about quality education. He frames the question that has been bugging him all along.

"How is it that your students are doing so well at university?"

"And, more importantly, in the world," adds Marly with pride. "But it all depends on what you construe as success. In order to prepare our students adequately for the future we believe that we need to move them to perceive alternatives, to look at things as if they could be otherwise. Our students are encouraged right from kindergarten to be inquirers, to be researchers. It is the most basic part of our philosophy to encourage our students to grapple with and to construct hypothetical alternatives to what is – to construct alternative ways of being in the world."

"What about technology and the information highway?" asks Jack, taking a new turn. "How are you assisting your students to deal with the technological changes that will be required of them in the future?"

"Firstly," responds Marly, "we expect our students to question the assumption that technology is good for us. Clearly all technology is not good for us and there is a need to think critically and constructively about the uses and abuses of technology. The amount of useless information that we are able to store using computers is a good example of an aspect of technology worth questioning. Are we wasting our lives accumulating information that is useful to no-one? Instead of equating technology with progress and worshipping machines, we are more concerned with a humanizing education, one which values human creativity: the power of a written or oral story, the passion in a work of art, the beauty of a musical composition, the drape of an elegantly designed costume, the fluidity and magic of an expertly choreographed ballet. We have rejected uniformity, the mechanical idea of 'one curriculum fits all' education."

Jack shakes his head in disbelief. This is a philosophy that contradicts all he believes. It is very difficult for him to comprehend that the students of *Ourschool* are making their way into the 21st century, so confidently, so expertly, so successfully.

Day 3

After three days of talking and sharing philosophies, Marly and Jack begin to draw their meetings to a close. Many issues remain unresolved between the two of them. The greatest difference between Jack's hierarchical view of education and the philosophy of *Ourschool* lies in how teachers and students are being perceived.

"I still don't get it," says Jack. "Why is it that you see teachers as so central to education? Our policymakers take the view that we have only to get the curriculum right and then all we have to do is to pay the teachers to deliver instruction in keeping with our mandate. It is not quite as simple as this, but we are working towards this. The standardization of testing is really helping us control the curriculum and limit the extent to which teachers can change what happens in the classroom. We are also hopeful of saving a large amount of money through the use of computer assisted instruction. This should eliminate the need for a teacher in some instances. Salaries are 90 percent of our costs you know. Also, your emphasis on the place of children and teenagers in education is interesting, yet puzzling. You speak of students as if they are already knowledgeable, yet we all know that students come to school to learn because they do not know anything. I find it rather ludicrous to expect that the input of children could be productive in educational policymaking."

"Yes, I think you are right to focus the differences in our thinking on how we see teachers and students," says Marly. "I think we also answer the question, 'Who, or what, is education for?' very differently." Carefully choosing her words in order not to offend Jack, she adds: "The need for administrators in your system belies a lack of trust of teachers." Jack nods in agreement. She continues, "At *Ourschool*, we are all teachers. We became teachers because we believe that children are special, precious, and their learning about the world is of extraordinary importance, but a fragile process. It is a privilege to be allowed to spend time with children, to share in their wonder and their questions. To enter into the world of a child and to be a part of their learning is a very special honor. It is also very risky, because sometimes we make mistakes. Sometimes a student is hurt in the process of learning and we have to carry the responsibility for that. We care. That means we wish to do something meaningful with our lives that will help other people. The students are the center and focus of our work. Everything we do is considered in terms of its effect on them. You see, *we are teachers*," she repeated, as if she had said it all.

Epilogue

For many years I struggled with the meanings and contradictions inherent in "promotion" – promotion out of the classroom – and views of educational leadership that did not include teachers. At first, I thought I could do it my way and believed that I could be successful by caring and being a wonderful teacher. Also, that as an administrator I would be able to hang on to all that I had learned and valued as a classroom teacher. Whenever a harsh lesson taught me otherwise, I internalized the problem with the rationalization that it was "just me," and I interpreted myself through the deficit model of not being "male enough." When I eventually admitted to myself that this was a gender issue, and when I could stop crying, I became angry. More recently, I have come to understand and name *community* as central to my philosophy for schooling. In doing so, I have realized that students and their parents/guardians have also been ignored in leadership theories that are entrenched in hierarchical structures for schooling.

This is my 21st year of being a teacher and this chapter is part of my more constructive response to what I call "systemic violence" in education. It is about making a difference. The ideas represented here are not new. I have borrowed heavily from Charlotte Perkins Gilman's thesis that as women we would do the world differently if we had the opportunity. I have interpreted her ideas through my own filter. I believe that teachers, in particular women teachers, would do the world of education differently if we had the opportunity.

Maxine Greene has said that we need to open the windows in education and allow some startling winds to blow through the classrooms of the nation. She suggests that we:

attend to those who struggle for fresh air. . . . seek a vision of education that brings together the need for wide-awakeness with the hunger for community, the desire to know with the wish to understand, the desire to feel with the passion to see. . . . to empower the young to create and recreate a common world – and in cherishing it, in renewing it, discover what it signifies to be free. (1988, p. 23)

This chapter is all about that struggle for fresh air.

References

Gilman, C.P. (1915). *Herland*. New York: Pantheon Books.

Gilligan, C.J. (1982). *In a different voice*. Cambridge, MA: Harvard University Press.

Greene, M. (1988). *The dialectic of freedom*. New York: Teachers College Press.

Hollingsworth, S., Cody, A., Davis-Smallwood, J., Dybdahl, M., Gallagher, P., Gallego, M., Maestre, T., Minarik, L. T., Raffel, L., Standerford, N.S., & Teel, K.M. (1994). *Teacher research and urban literacy education: Lessons and conversations in a feminist key*. New York: Teachers College Press.

15

Nurturing Teachers Through Workplace Help: Some Contradictions

Elizabeth Tucker

I too believe that humanity will win in the long run; I am only afraid that at the same time the world will have turned into one huge hospital where everyone is everyone else's humane nurse (Goethe, Italienische Reise, 1862)[1].

My purpose in this chapter is to explore the gender implications inherent in workplace helping strategies known as Employee Assistance Programs (EAPs). Data are drawn from an analysis of these programs in Ontario school boards[2]. Study findings suggest that while formal and preferred objectives of EAPs seek to reconcile and indeed maximize both individual and organizational needs, the programs may actually serve to undermine the social and political interests of educators, particularly teachers – a largely female population.

Underlying the study is a theory about society that holds social structures to be created, maintained and/or modified through human agency, human intention and human will for specific human purposes (Berman, 1984; Greenfield, 1984; 1993; Weber, 1964). Rationalized knowledge, educational administration, bureaucratic hierarchy, as well as EAP programs, policies and practices are perceived, therefore, to be expressly designed structures which help individuals integrate more harmoniously into workplaces of particular kinds and into a given society. Another assumption is that these structures possess a peculiar recursive quality, which, over time, can lead even their creators to perceive them as part of the natural order – the way things are done. A third assumption is that these structures combine in a unitary but dynamic fashion with each other and with everyday activity to produce the empirical situation under study (Foucault, 1984; Giddens, 1979; Mills, 1959).

My focus on contradiction and ambiguity is grounded in the diverse views expressed by teachers, principals, superintendents, federation representatives and EAP providers. Interviews with these participants reveal that while helping others is widely perceived as a nurturing, moral endeavor beyond reproach, the nature, meaning and intended outcome of helping change when the giving and receiving occur within the hierarchical educational workplace. In this setting the help tends to become co-opted into the existing power structures and to therefore negate the process of reciprocity which inheres in more equitable exchanges of help. Consequently, what is happening and what is supposed to be happening are quite different.

Three changes occur during the cooptation process which may lead to unanticipated consequences for both teachers and administrators.

First, school board counselling tends to be perceived as mainly for teachers – a largely female population;

Second, those perceived as needing help tend to become devalued or stigmatized whether or not they actually avail themselves of the help; and

Third, discomfort and distress associated with social, structural and situational problems tend to be treated in the same way as personal and dispositional problems and transferred to medical or therapeutic professionals.

Before presenting the data which led to these findings, I explore the changing nature of power in our society and its significance for the emergence of teachers and other individuals as pathological workers.

Rationalization, Power and Pathology

Cooptation and stigmatization are complex social processes which involve a loss or curtailment of individual freedom. Yet in the school boards studied, both proceeded in the manner of an "unformulated power struggle" as described by Gramsci and Bordieu (Risseeuw, 1988, p. 5) – one step always appearing to be no more than a logical and even desirable result of the preceding one. My contention is that these processes are facilitated by the rationalized, calculable social relationships which dominate educational administration and the larger society. These relationships contain a number of subtleties and complexities which need to be more fully explored and reflected upon for their immediate and long term threats to personal and individual autonomy.

On the one hand, the progressive rationalization of society has led to a power reversal of some significance and to widespread improvements in material and social well-being. It has allowed us to rid ourselves of superstitious notions and beliefs, such as the divine right of kings, to devise new structures for governance, and to develop more humane practices for the education and social integration of individuals. But as Goethe, in the opening quotation warned, the imperative of efficiency which accompanies rational logic may give rise to more subtle and seductive forms of oppression. A century and a half later, post-modern authors such as Bartky (1990), Foucault (1984), Greenfield (1993) and Saul (1992) echo these concerns.

These authors argue that in a rationalized society power no longer wears an identifying crown but instead appears to be anonymous – a faceless yet centralized and pervasive force which becomes ensconced within knowledge, expertise, bureaucratic roles and within the language used to disseminate these socio-cultural artifacts. These structures "feed upon expertise and expertise upon complexity" (Saul, 1992, p. 7) so that power appears to be wielded by everyone and yet by no one in particular. Citizens, on the other hand, become objects of intense scrutiny in what Foucault (1984, pp. 3-50) refers to as a system of bio power – a regime in which knowledge and power become a joint technology while the human body becomes an object to be improved, manipulated, controlled, strengthened and transformed to meet the demands of the situation.

Systems that rely on bio power or bio technology become deceptive and unjust means of controlling human behavior, Foucault explains that this is mainly because measures of what is "normal" or most widely accepted replace values of what is right or wrong in social encounters. The result is a disproportionate focus on individual competence and improvement which is assessed through methods of measurement, gradation and distribution of people around norms – methods which mask human agency, devalue individual differences and lead to a gradual erosion of individual autonomy. The illusion of autonomy is maintained, however, through what Foucault refers to as the *isomorphic fantasy* – the notion that the helpers or change agents will disappear when recipients of their services become competent enough to manage themselves. But as the norms and standards of measurement become internalized and accepted as the central ways of thinking and knowing, they induce feelings of inadequacy, guilt and shame in those individuals who fail to "measure up." Those who deviate often become subjects in a dual sense – subject to self-disciplinary practices such as rigid time management, dieting for weight and image control, or running around the track to alleviate symptoms of stress; they also become subject to pressures by the larger society and its various institutions concerned with their personal welfare.

Both Szasz (1973) and Zola (1972) have pointed out how swiftly a reliance on therapeutic or biological solutions can depoliticize important social issues and transfer power from individuals to those perceived or certified as more expert or more knowledgeable. Within an individualized or medical frame of reference, they explain, problems formerly solved through public and political debate are often diagnosed as symptoms of illness, physical, mental or emotional. Workplace problems such as alcoholism, poor work performance, and low motivation are cases in point. A medical diagnosis locates the problem within the individual, redefines the individual as sick, and legitimises intervention on behalf of the "helpless" patient. As a patient, the individual has little right to appeal the diagnosis. The debate shifts instead to the degree of sickness and the treatment required while issues of individual choice or freedom and situational factors that may be impacting on the problems are often shunted aside. The resultant power shift goes unchallenged as both individuals and organizations come to rely on therapeutic and medical experts as an immediate source of relief from personal and workplace conflict.

Educational institutions, because of the central role they play in assessing, certifying and disseminating knowledge and skills, also play a crucial role in perpetuating systems of bio power. As Saul (1992, p. 26) writes, education is one place in which "lofty ideals and misty mythology cannot avoid meeting the realities of crude self-interest." For more than two decades, Greenfield (1993) sought to draw attention to the delusionary aspects of rationalized educational administration practices. He argued that the value-free claims of rationalized or scientific knowledge could only be upheld by eliminating from social investigation "all human passion, weakness, strength, conviction, hope, will, pity, frailty, altruism, courage, vice and virtue" (p. 139). In order to achieve a more accurate picture of the social world, Greenfield urged researchers to transcend the scientifically rational and explore the realm of the subjective where values, meaning, understanding, emotions and feeling – "all that people do in fact as they make choices and strive to transform their values into reality" (p. 139) count as valid knowledge of the social world.

Weber (1949), one of the earliest proponents of this type of investigation, argues that it is only by juxtaposing and comparing one image or set of images against another that we come to understand the full reality of a social situation, with all its paradoxes and contradictions. Following this same logic, feminist scholars such as Bartky (1990) and Blackmore (1989) point out that rationalized social relationships and bio technology work against women's sociopolitical interests more so than those of men because, throughout history, males have dominated the social world. Consequently, their bodies and their particular ways of thinking and acting have been perceived as the norm while female characteristics and traits have been viewed as deviant and tabooed[3]. Moral virtue is also assigned in a gendered manner – reason, principle and justice for males; benevolence, modesty, charm and compassion for women – a practice that assures that women will not only experience and internalize more intense feelings of inferiority and "ethical incompleteness" (Miller, 1993) but that they will be judged by significant and powerful others as less rational and less moral than the "great men" whose characteristics and traits provided the norms.

Bartky (1990) insists that women's inferior status cannot be understood in isolation from theories of oppression. This oppression, she writes, pervades every aspect of our culture, engenders humiliation, deprives women of self-esteem and fills them with anguish as they internalize their inferior status and engage in behavior that makes them accomplices in their own oppression. The only way for women to break the cycle of oppression, she says, is to recognize the contradictions in their social milieu as contradictions – not as natural, inevitable and inescapable facets of life. They must recognize them as morally unjust – as inequalities between what is and what ought to be.

I turn now to the data that prompted my focus on contradictions and led to the conclusions that the therapeutic help of EAPs tends to become coopted into the educational hierarchy, to devalue teachers and to depoliticize important systemic and structural problems.

The Focus on Teachers and Personal Problems

In the Dellarton board[4], the EAP was considered a completely voluntary, self-referral program for all board employees. Part of the policy reads as follows:

> Personal problems are viewed as a normal part of everyone's life and an EAP is regarded as a resource to help individuals . . . The board and all employee groups wish to include preventative and educational activities in the EAP, in recognition that many problems may be averted or at least minimized by this approach. *However, identification and referral to appropriate community resources or short-term counselling will also be required* for employees whose problems are more acute [italics added].

The policy does not make explicit who will identify and refer those with acute problems but study respondents clarified that these referrals follow hierarchical lines of authority. Nearly all interviewees expressed a strong moral conviction about providing help and empathy for those who might need it. However, both the policy and many of the comments below contain the judgment that it is mainly teachers who have problems and that these problems, no matter where they originate, are due mainly to personal deficiencies that must be corrected. Also evident is a definite separation between teachers as "employees" and administrators as moral entrepreneurs – a separation that reflects Berman's (1985, p. 28) observation that, within purposeful rational knowledge, control over and manipulation of others appear to be the very touchstone of truth.

A male principal, in the Dellarton Board, for example, describes the advantages of an EAP this way:

> What I've discovered is that most of *my* teachers are suffering from some sort of crisis at one time or another. They go through an awful lot . . . If you can show individuals, who are *the teachers, the employees,* that it (the EAP) is a safe house, that they don't have to feel that it is going to be disclosed. . . . that it is confidential, that it is accessible then they will be helped.

A superintendent clarifies very early in the interview that his association with the EAP is strictly managerial:

> My department looks after the reports, putting them in the files, brochures for new hirees and things like that. Strictly from an individual point of view, I have not been involved at all . . .

A superintendent in the Jamestown Board[5], which has an explicit mandatory referral clause in its EAP, observes that personal difficulties can't help but find an outlet in the "classrooms and corridors" of the school. The EAP in his board, he claims, acts as "a tool to correct those difficulties and ensure that performance will return to its previously high level." Later, however, he describes the EAP in both moral and instrumental terms:

> There's also a moral obligation I believe, to provide that kind of service (EAP) for employees in the organization. . . . If we're confident in what our objectives are, in providing moral teaching for children, then it follows that we have to provide the best possible environment for our teachers so that they can be achieving those objectives.

For this Jamestown consultant, the EAP provides a much needed "safety net" and creates an

> ambience that permeates the whole system when people know that they can reach out for confidential help . . . Teachers can use the EAP to solve personal problems. They are able to bounce back into the straight and narrow, that is, improve their work performance. The system gets more value for its money and the students are better off because they don't have a spaced-out teacher.

Although most respondents recognize that teachers' problems come from a variety of sources, they believe counselling to be an appropriate way to help teachers cope with the many social issues that have become part of the school curriculum. A female principal speaking of the advantages of an EAP, says:

> I see teachers trying to meet the needs of all the kids all the time. You have some kids hungry, some that have learning difficulties, some kids are going through family breakdowns. You have this multitude of needs . . . The better the teachers, the more stressed they are going to be . . . One of the major stresses is that teachers have no control and it makes them feel so helpless.

Ms. Bowles, a personnel administrator, believes teachers are continually faced with problems such as,

> What do I do if I am aware that AIDS is present in my classroom? . . . How do I deal with the fact that many children these days are not living in a family unit? . . . who can actually come into the school to see the child? There is a lot of violence too. We have native students in the system who are rebelling because of their situation and teachers don't know how to deal with that. How do they provide support and understanding or even the discipline necessary to control the classroom situation for learning? . . . And there are also the developmentally delayed students and the differently abled – those with special needs.

Teachers' first encounter with many of these problems, Ms Bowles tells me, is often in the form of policies they are required to implement, whether or not they agree with them. Ms. Bowles also draws attention to the gendered nature of the teaching profession and the double bind that the constantly changing educational workload may create for female teachers, even when their "home lives are going smoothly."

> Sometimes they are in a position that almost everyone in their life is drawing in some fashion from them. There is an acceptance that you don't complain. You just do your best. You stifle yourself. A coping strategy is just to keep on working. Sometimes the solution seems to be to work harder at home and work harder at school, but that is not the solution either.

Despite an awareness that many of teachers' problems are not personal, interviewees like Ms. Bowles are convinced that counselling helps teachers relieve their mental stress by allowing teachers to bring their problems "out into the open" without fear of recriminations that is, without fear of being evaluated as "unable to handle their job requirements."

A counsellor in one of the programs explains the mutual benefits to be derived from an EAP. If a person in the community is suffering, she says,

> ... it's going to have an effect on their working performance for a period of time until they can get some counselling. And that is going to cost the employer more in absenteeism and reduced productivity and staff morale. . . . So it [the EAP] meshes quite well.

Regardless of the origin of their problems, counselling helps individuals, she explains, because it teaches them to help themselves. Individuals learn

> how to minimize stress or how to cope better with the stress; taking a good lunch break, doing some exercise, getting proper nutrition, some better time management skills, so that even though the stressors are still there, the person is going to be stronger, to be able to cope with the stress.

This argument is a valid one in several respects. Through counselling, individuals learn to assess how much of a problem is theirs and how much is due to the system, what individuals can do to advocate for change within the system and what they can do to cope with stress that is unavoidable. Disseminating assistance of this nature could be extremely helpful in reciprocal, non-threatening, problem solving situations. In the comments above, however, it becomes quite clear that counselling help takes its meaning from the structural system in which it occurs. In school boards, this includes hierarchical organization which draws upon a highly rationalized knowledge base for its decision-making criteria. Although the counselling assistance is formally intended to help all employees who experience personal problems, it comes to be seen as a method for helping teachers adjust and adapt to workplace conditions that are discussed in ways that make them appear anonymous, unchangeable and unavoidable.

The Lack of Reciprocity or Who Will Bell the Cat?[6]

A tacit understanding in much of the interview data above is that EAP counselling has a unidirectional, top-down flow. In order to test this understanding, I asked whether a secretary, a teacher or a principal would recommend counselling to a superordinate who appeared distressed. A female federation representative tells me that it would be far too risky to suggest that her principal get help:

> I'd be afraid he'd strike back at me . . . you might get fired. He might just start finding little things and documenting them. You can get away with a lot more when you are at the top level.

Mrs. Rideout, an elementary teacher, explains that teachers often feel a great sense of powerlessness in schools where principals are not carrying out their responsibilities for whatever reason:

> Teachers are in a bit of a sticky situation. There's only so much one can say or do before getting into trouble. If there is no discipline policy, supplies are not ordered on time, major events are not planned until two weeks before, e.g. putting together a Christmas concert, it's difficult for teachers to go up and say, "Look, I'm sorry. I can't work under circumstances like this." It gets really tricky. You find yourself with extra lunch duties to struggle with. At meetings, something you want on the agenda is forgotten. There are ways to make you buckle under. Like shooting down your ideas at a staff meeting. Lots of little ways . . .

The ridicule you may have to endure, Mrs. Rideout states, can make you feel more miserable than just putting up and remaining silent until the next one (principal) comes along.

In one school, a consultant recounts, the principal appeared to be distressed and neglected staff meetings and other responsibilities. One or two teachers first approached the principal privately but when he did nothing after four months

> some of the teachers expressed their concern downtown (at the Board office). They were just told that they were out of line and acting very unprofessionally.

Several interviewees said that they would not or could not suggest that a principal or superintendent get help, no matter how far the situation deteriorated because "confronting superiors is just not done in our society." They'd just "wait until administration downtown caught on or transfer." A male teacher says:

> That's what I did last year. You have to recognize the situation is one you cannot change so you have to learn to deal with it the best way you can. Stay out of the person's way. Try to ride along throughout the year without getting into too many conflicts with this person. Find someone you can blow steam off to, just enough to get through the year and then transfer.

These data indicate that although the counselling is intended as a humanistic resource for all members of the school board, the right to extend help to others does not cross lines of power and authority. This restriction supports an observation made by Fisher, Nadler and DePaulo (1983; 1984) that the very act of extending help, particularly psychological help, may communicate to recipients that they are less responsible, less reliable and less competent than others.

Although there is little doubt that therapeutic counselling is appropriate in a certain number of individual cases, interviewees in the next section reveal that it can also be a belittling and threatening experience. Moreover, as the dialogue in the next section lets us see, even those who do not avail themselves of the help proffered appear to be affected simply by being a member of the group targeted as most in need of help.

Stigmatization Through Nurturing

A Canadian Union of Public Employees (CUPE) representative, below, emphasizes that in his board it is mainly teachers who are in need of EAP help:

> As I sat on the committee, it was related mostly to teachers. . . . Teachers required help. Some teachers were having emotional instabilities and there was some counselling for that and they were free to call. Basically, that was the gist of what I got from it. . . . For us it's a voluntary thing. For teachers it's mandatory.

Mandatory, as he has used it, means that the elementary teachers negotiated the EAP as a partially paid benefit in their contract so that now all teachers are obliged to pay their share of this benefit. CUPE members

> are standing in the background letting the teachers feel out the system first because my people are not paid anywhere near the level of teachers and cannot afford to donate a portion of their paycheck towards something that may be of no use to them . . . custodians don't blow an elastic[7].

When I ask if he can think of any advantages of having an EAP for his group, he responds:

> Over and above the bent string part[8]? . . . Most custodians don't have that much stress unless a principal or teacher is riding them. If somebody steps out of line, that's what the union is for. The union takes over in severe cases.

His use of derisive metaphors for what he perceives as "emotional instabilities," while humorous in intent, serves to devalue teachers and to emphasize the perception that they are less able than his group of workers to cope with their problems. A female teacher, describing the advantages of an EAP, particularly its confidential aspects, says that when teachers encounter problems,

> there is a stigma and a great shame. People very seldom want their employers to know, and I think in the teaching profession, if someone has a problem, especially an emotional problem, if they are going through a difficult period in their own lives, they don't want the community to know that. They don't want the employer to know . . . It somehow reflects on their job. And they don't want somebody peeking over their shoulder. They don't need the added pressure.

Constant evaluation and demands for change in the workplace, another female teacher explains, repress diversity and undermine teachers' confidence in themselves and in their own experiential knowledge. Even with excellent teachers, she says,

> There is a fear of not measuring up, of having somebody think that they're not doing a good job. Teachers are the hardest professionals on themselves. We do not want anybody in the classroom watching us because we might be doing something that we shouldn't be doing. We've been so programmed that there are right ways of doing things. . . . Our ways may be old fashioned, not up to the latest methods. We are very insecure as a profession. . . . we think we cannot

make a mistake. You must have no difficulties whatever, and if you do have difficulties in your home life then those never can reflect in the classroom.

When Ms. Gold, a teacher with about ten years experience, received a brochure outlining the EAP service she put it in the garbage immediately. She says:

When our federation rep spoke to us about this confidential benefit, everyone listened but no one asked questions . . . No one wants to be seen as having problems.

Teachers less interested in acquiring positions of responsibility, she believes, might see the programs differently. But if she were to encounter stress-inducing problems, she would seek help through a doctor or therapist of her own choice and not through a board-sponsored program because:

you don't know how some principals and administrators view it. They may see it as a personality flaw, a sign that you can't handle responsibility, too much on your plate . . . You're supposed to be an example to those beneath you. You might be overlooked for a promotion if your flaws become known.

Counsellors may keep your particular problems confidential but the teaching profession, Ms Gold says, is very "gossipy."[9] If someone were to see you going in or coming out, word would get around:

and you can't change schools to lose a reputation. Principals talk among themselves, trade information. You know, (in a derisive tone and rolls her eyes), 'That one's a real wing nut. Good luck'. That sort of thing.

Although they are encouraged to make use of the EAP at no cost to themselves, some teachers in this board prefer to avoid the services, just as a precaution.

A male teacher, who did use the EAP, tells me that asking for help of almost any kind in the educational workplace is traumatic and risky. And one of the problems with accepting EAP strategies, he points out, is that

nothing ever changes in the workplace. You know, if you can't stand the heat get out of the kitchen. If you do end up with a stress problem, then you're a poor example, not strong, not steady. Nobody wants to be associated with people with problems. There's such a stigma.

A female teacher who used the EAP says it's good to have that support,

but it really takes the heat off the administration. EAP becomes a bandaid and the system never gets fixed. They just ship off the individuals into a never-never land and they hire somebody else, put them into the same situation and wonder why things aren't improving.

According to these interviewees, the attribution of inferiority to those perceived as needing help comes mainly from cultural expectations about individuals and their levels of competence. The stigmatization associated with needing help, however, appears to be facilitated when the help is distributed in a paternalistic[8] manner, with principals and other administrators, who have achieved more "success" in education, enacting a morally aggressive role toward "less successful" subordinates.

It is mainly for these reasons, Mr. Griffin, president of his local federation (the Ontario Secondary School Teachers' Federation), seldom recommends the EAP to his constituents. Like the interviewees above, he believes that EAP strategies often amount to little more than a "quick fix," and do little if anything, to address or change underlying issues – "the root causes." This is particularly true, he believes, in relation to gender issues. Despite employment equity and other legal safeguards, he says, a recently conducted study shows that teaching at the elementary level in particular, remains a largely female profession dominated by male principals and superintendents:

> It's a very paternalistic fiefdom in most of our elementary schools. Not all of them, but in most of them. Many of these teachers are intimidated by the *bossism,* if you will, of these people. We've got an 85 percent male population of principals over an 85 percent female population of teachers...There is intimidation in so many ways.

Very few female teachers, he finds, are assertive enough to put federation business at the top of the school agenda. The ones that do report that they are continuously acting alone in the school situation. Many of their colleagues do not support them when it comes to standing up for workplace rights.

The federation is running leadership courses and is encouraging female teachers to take more responsibility and leadership, but progress, Mr. Griffin says, is extremely slow and discouraging. Many teachers, he says, are still reluctant to air their views even at the school level because "principals can crimp career moves too."

Conclusions and Implications

In the school boards studied, two different perspectives of EAP intervention prevail, the intended and the actual. In the first, these helping strategies appear to be caring and compassionate methods of helping individuals overcome either personal or workplace problems that interfere with their happiness or their work performance. Within the second, they appear to be designed in such a way as to help align human needs, interests and concerns more perfectly with demands and requirements of the workplace. What is supposed to happen varies from what actually occurs.

The empirical findings indicate that school board EAP programs tend to focus mainly on teachers, a largely female group of workers. Teachers were generally perceived, and in some instances perceived themselves, as being overwhelmed by personal, systemic and social problems and in need of help in meeting the demands of their jobs. Regardless of where their problems originated – within the system, in the larger environment, or within themselves – counselling was perceived to be an appropriate means of resolving educational workplace problems.

In theory, therapists offer teachers opportunities to overcome their weaknesses and failings privately and confidentially, and thus prevent job loss and organizational failure. But the very diagnosis of a workplace problem as therapeutic changes both the nature of the problem and the attribution of blame. A therapeutic or medical diagnosis locates problems within teachers and makes them responsible for solutions, regardless of the systemic and environmental issues that may contribute to both the occurrence and magnitude of problems. The guarantee of privacy and confidentiality, paradoxically, serves to buttress political silence over educational issues that may need to be publicly discussed or negotiated within the context of the educational workplace or the wider public arena.

While the therapeutic assistance offered through EAP's sometimes brought immediate psychological relief to certain individuals, both male and female respondents spoke of being devalued or stigmatized by this form of help. Stigma is a response *to and from* those whose social status empowers them to create standards of success and to demand that others meet these standards. But when the criteria of success are expressed in terms of individual control, there are many – for example, women, the physically challenged and members of minority groups – who, because of the system itself, may have difficulty realizing such control. Moreover, stigma serves to confirm the superiority of those in positions of power and reproduce existing structures and unjust social practices (Foucault, 1980; Gilligan, 1982; Goffman, 1963; Miller, 1976).

The tendency to lump teachers' work and personal problems together may be construed as a form of institutionalized stigmatization that devalues women and others in educational organizations. The definition of certain conflicts as "personal," solely because they manifest themselves as stress or discomfort, means the subsequent removal of these problems from the political arena of debate and requires that they be solved by members of the medical profession.

As noted earlier, cultural bias or cultural blindness may arise from a reliance on scientific or instrumental social knowledge and forms of organization that are "based on the domination of some humans over others and of humans over nature" (Kauffman, 1987). Within patriarchal organizations, for example, Kauffman notes, individuals tend to become differentiated on the basis of physical, national, religious, or sexual differences that are completely unrelated to their work competence. When this occurs, difficulties related to gender differences, which are linked to entrenched cultural attitudes about family and household responsibilities, and to inadequate formal laws and social protection for women, tend to be treated as nothing more than personal problems for which women themselves must seek solutions.

Therapeutic counselling within the educational workplace may be as threatening to women teachers and others as the impersonal, calculated relationships of bureaucracy and other forms of instrumental reasoning these nurturing programs seek to oppose. The unidirectional flow of therapeutic help may be intended to be a temporary strategy for fostering teacher development that will eventually remove disparity; however, when these forms of help become melded with the non-reciprocal hierarchical order of the educational workplace, the inferior status of women teachers and others may become more permanent. Such inferiority may come to be perceived in much the same way as the structures themselves, as part of the natural order. The dominant/subservient order may then continue to be accounted for by theories that explain it in terms of superior/inferior traits or characteristics, statistical norms and averages (Foucault, 1980; 1984; Gilligan, 1982; Miller, 1976).

What is at issue is not merely a difference of opinion about the locus of control over individual action in organizations, but a philosophical difference about the purpose, dignity and meaning of human life itself. In hierarchical workplaces, helping transactions can and do encourage increased instrumentality. That instrumentality contradicts broad educational purposes and values which are aimed at developing individual potential so that all members of society become purposeful human beings capable of managing their own lives with dignity and respect and affording others the same right and privilege.

Notes

[1]Quoted in Reiff (1966:24), *The Triumph of the Therapeutic.*

[2]Tucker, 1993. Doctoral Thesis. Ontario Institute for Studies in Educattion, Toronto, Ontario.

[3]Gerth and Mills (1953: 177) distinguish between tabooed traits and premium traits, the former being negatively evaluated by significant or powerful others and repressed through formal or informal sanctions.

[4]A pseudonym.

[5]A pseudonym.

[6]A question from one mouse to several others in an old folk tale.

[7]Translation: Custodians don't have emotional instabilities.

[8]Translation: Over and above the nervous breakdown part?

[9]Ball (1987: 216-221) points out that gossip is a powerful informal means of decision-making which can undermine people and their reputations. Through gossip, Ball claims, the formal and public image of an organization can be maintained while any threats to the existing social and moral order can be stifled.

References

Ball, S. (1987). *Micropolitics of the school.* London: Methuen/Routledge & Kegan Paul.

Bartly, S.L. (1990). *Femininity and domination: Studies in the phenomenology of oppression.* New York: Routledge.

Berman, M. (1985). *The reenchantment of the world.* Toronto: Bantam Books.

Blackmore, J. (1989). Educational leadership: A feminist critique and reconstruction. In J. Smyth (Ed.), *Critical perspectives on educational leadership.* New York: Falmer Press.

Fisher, J.D., Nadler, A. & DePaulo, B.M. (1983; 1984). *New directions in helping.* New York: Academic Press.

Foucault, M. (1980). *Discipline and punish.* Translated by Alan Sheridan. New York: Pantheon Press.

Foucault, M. (1984). *The Foucault reader.* P. Rabinow (Ed.). New York: Pantheon Books.

Gerth, H., & Mills, C.W. (1953). *Character and social structure.* New York: Harcourt Brace Jovanovich.

Giddens, A. (1979). *Central problems in social theory: Action, structure and contradiction in social analysis.* Berkeley: University of California Press.

Gilligan, C. (1982). *In a different voice: Psychological theory and women's development.* Cambridge, MA:Harvard University Press.

Goffman, E. (1963). *Stigma: Notes on the management of spoiled identity.* Englewood Cliffs, N.J.:Prentice Hall.

Greenfield, T. (1984). Leaders and schools: Wilfulness and nonnatural order in organizations. In T. Sergiovanni and J. Corbally (Eds.), *Leadership and organizational culture.* Urbanna, Ill., University of Illinois.

Greenfield, T. (1993). The decline and fall of science in educational administration. In T. Greenfield & P. Ribbins (Eds.), *Greenfield on educational administration: Towards a humane science.* London: Routledge and Kegan Paul.

Kauffman, M. (Ed.). (1987). *Beyond patriarchy: Essays by men on pleasure, power and change.* Toronto: Oxford University Press.

Miller, J.B. (1976). *Toward a new psychology of women.* London: Beacon Press.

Miller, T. (1993). *The well tempered self: Formation of the cultural subject.* Baltimore: Johns Hopkins University Press.

Mills, C.W. (1959). *The sociological imagination.* London: Oxford University Press.

Reiff, P. (1966). *The triumph of the therapeutic.* New York: Harper Torchbooks.

Risseeuw, C. (1988). *The fish don't talk about the water: Gender transformation, power and resistance among women in Sri Lanka.* Leiden: E.J. Brill.

Saul, J.R. (1992). *Voltaire's bastards: The dictatorship of reason in the west.* Toronto: Penguin Books.

Szasz, T. (1973). *Ideology and insanity.* London: Calder and Boyars.

Tucker, E. (1993). *Employee assistance programs: Improving work performance in Ontario school boards.* An unpublished doctoral thesis. University of Toronto, Canada.

Weber, M. (1964). *The theory of social and economic organization.* New York: Oxford University Press.

Weber, M. (1949). *The methodology of social sciences.* E. A. Shils, and H. A. Finch (Eds.). New York: Free Press.

Zola, I.K. (1972). Medicine as an institution of social control. *Sociological Review. 20,* 487-504.

16

Women Educators as School Board Chairpersons: Problematizing the Public/Private Dimensions of Leadership

Hanne Mawhinney and Linda LaRocque

Reflecting on the state of research on educational leadership in the 1980s, Immegart (1988) concluded that "the number of aspects, dynamics, and variables" that have commonly been examined must be increased in order to regenerate a domain of inquiry in educational administration that "has not recently appeared to enjoy a very high priority" (p. 274). Typically, studies in this domain have focused on the highly visible and specific roles of the principal and superintendent, ignoring the leadership of other members of the educational community such as teachers and school trustees who may "in certain situations and at certain times become what might be termed a leader" (Smyth, 1989, p. 11). Casting the net to capture such leadership behavior requires that the domain of inquiry be broadened to reach into "a variety of rich arenas," such as school boards (Immegart, 1988).

School trustees, for example, are commonly ignored in the traditional leadership research, despite the fact that they are the authorities responsible for the final policy direction of a school board (Townsend, 1988). In this chapter we address the need to expand the traditional focus of inquiry into the nature of educational leadership by drawing from the experiences of three female school board trustee-chairpersons who were viewed by their fellow trustees as influential educational leaders, and who were also practicing teachers.

Our focus on female educators in the "non-traditional" leadership role of chairpersons of school boards is purposeful. It reflects the need for a broader view of leadership roles in education. Most important it is also a response to the feminist critique of current leadership research. Following this critique we examine the implications for an expanded understanding of one of the core dimensions of leadership: the gender patterning evident in the separation of public and private domains of social life.

The conceptual issues raised in feminist theorizing on women's career development form the basis for problematizing the traditional separation of public and private dimensions of the social life of educators. Our approach is framed by the assumption of feminist inquiry that "gender is a basic organizing principle which profoundly shapes/mediates the concrete conditions of our lives" (Lather, 1991, p. 71). Our intention is to correct the invisibility of gender as a frame of analysis in most research on school boards by giving voice to the experiences of female teachers leading school boards. Through our exploration of the narratives of three women educator trustees, we seek to give deeper expression to the experiences in the context of the educational leadership they practice as chairpersons of school boards.

Methodology

We use the methods of critical ethnography which integrate the "methods of cultural anthropology and fieldwork sociology with an activist critical theory" (LeCompte & Preissle, 1994, p. 26). Critical ethnography is "concerned with political dimensions of both public and private lives [and it] focuses on how these play out differently by gender" (p. 27). The feminist frame for inquiry adopted puts "the social construction of gender at the center of inquiry" (Lather, 1991, p. 71). We recognize that although there is no one distinctive feminist methodology, one of the distinguishing features of feminist inquiry is the use of women's experiences as resources for social analysis (Harding, 1987).

In this chapter we take up the challenge of examining leadership from the perspective of the experiences of three women trustees who are both educators and chairpersons of school boards located in Ontario and Alberta. The focus of our inquiry into nontraditional pools of leadership in education grew out of the findings of previous research on the role of political leadership in educational policy change (Mawhinney, forthcoming). The impetus for this study grew out of the realization that despite the impact that these female political leaders (school trustees and provincial-level political advisors and policy makers) had on educational policy change, their unique experiences have not been the focus of extensive academic inquiry.

The selection of three trustee-educators for this study was, however, opportunitistic. The population of female educators who are chairpersons of school boards in Canada is not large, so the willingness of these three women to share their experiences provided us with an invaluable opportunity for inquiry into leadership. We recognized, however, that size of the population made the women visible in ways which might be problematic for them and for our study. We have, therefore, respected the confidentiality they requested. Although we have not named their school boards, we believe that we have conveyed through their narratives the critical aspects of their lives pertaining to the public and private dimensions of leadership.

Our study used both observation and dialogue as methods to generate personal stories or narratives of leadership (Ryan & Drake, 1992). During the period of inquiry from November, 1993 to January, 1994, we observed public meetings of the three school boards prior to meeting privately with each woman to discuss her leadership experiences as an educator, a school trustee, and a chairperson of her board. The purpose of the extended discussions, which each lasted from 2 to 4 hours, was to elicit narratives or stories of leadership experiences reflecting the constructs of discourse, subjectivity, power, and common sense in leadership (Capper, 1992). As a form of elite interviewing, the process encouraged the women to introduce notions of what was relevant from their own perspectives. Thus, although all three women were asked similar guiding questions, the foci of the discussions followed the developing narratives.

These interviews were tape recorded and transcribed. The narratives were then analyzed using constant comparative techniques of analysis to identify emerging themes and to develop a guide for a second round of interview/conversations on leadership (Marshall & Rossman, 1989). The intent was to involve the women in clarifying the developing themes and to elicit the meanings they used to construct their views of educational leadership. In the following sections of the chapter, we explore four of these themes and draw from them some implications for the study of gender issues in educational administration. We begin this exploration by first describing the views that Martha, Jane and Donna hold about their roles as trustees.

Three Women Trustee-Educators

Many of the dimensions of trustee roles described in the Canadian research on the school trustee are evident in the narratives of the three women trustees we studied (Awender & Hanke, 1984; Davis, 1991; Isherwood & Osgoode, 1986; Jakes, 1982; Levin, 1975; Robinson & Stacey, 1984). Martha, Jane and Donna fit the profile of the middle-aged, and middle-class trustees identified in that research (Awender & Hanke, 1984; Davis, 1991; Jakes, 1982). Martha has been a teacher for over twenty years, a trustee of a large and wealthy urban Ontario Public school board since 1985, and chairperson for two terms. Donna is an academic who began her career as a teacher, and who has been a trustee since 1985. She became a chairperson of the suburban Alberta Catholic school board in which she previously taught. Jane, who was trained as a teacher in the early 1970s, shares a similar middle class background with the other two women. She has been a trustee for her suburban Ontario Catholic school board since 1988, and chairperson for two terms.

Although none of the three women were acclaimed, a common phenomenon in many school board elections, their experiences in getting elected confirm the low profile accorded school board elections (except see Robinson

& Stacey, 1984). Donna recounts that during her first election campaign, although she felt compelled to campaign actively (she even hired a student to call electors), in the end she felt that the reason for her easy win was her previous involvement as a teacher with the board. Martha's initial experiences were similar, although she was not successful in her first informal bid at the trusteeship; after making more direct effort in the next election, she was easily elected. Jane's election was also a relatively simple affair. She had already been involved for some years in school board advisory committees and was well known in the church and school community through her voluntary work.

The narratives of all three women confirm the research suggesting that trustees are quite clear about separating their role as trustees from the role of administrators (Townsend, 1988). Donna's narrative describes this stance well. She states:

> I made a conscious effort right from the beginning, particularly when I became vice-chair, but even more as chair, . . . not to interfere in administration, to take their advice, to critique their advice, to even ask other questions that might make them even change their mind, but not to second-guess them.

All three women describe their school boards as exclusive clubs where conflicts are defused through routines and trustees share similar world views (Levin, 1975; Isherwood & Osgoode, 1986). Donna speaks of a sense of collegiality on her board:

> It not like we're all best friends. We're not. We fight like cats and dogs, particularly during committee meetings, but they stay there, we don't carry them on to the next meeting.

None of the three women portray themselves a leaders, although all three have been successful enough in navigating the quagmire of small "p" politics that characterizes school boards that their fellow trustees have elected them chairpersons. Martha describes how she worked towards becoming chairperson:

> I did my time on the board in that I'd already been a trustee for six years and I had chaired a number of different committees for the board. I have done my homework, so when I ran for chair, I [knew] my colleagues could see me in that role because they had seen me in other leadership roles at the board level and they thought I could handle the extra responsibility.

The experiences of these women confirm the constrained nature of the leadership exercised by chairpersons of school boards (Bacharach & Mitchell, 1981; Isherwood & Osgoode, 1986; Levin, 1975). At the same time, these narratives also suggest that trustees do have a special link between the public and private domains of social life. In some ways they are the bridges between these domains, and in this role they can take significant leadership in specific areas of board policy. In many cases these are policy areas that are driven by the particular ideological bent of the trustee. Martha, for example, describes one of her successes as promoting links between child care agencies and schools to meet the need to create a seamless web of services for children. Similarly,

Jane describes with some pride her leadership in instituting more open decision-making processes in her board. She comments: "I feel very good about opening up the communications lines with the various parent groups across the board."

Donna also expresses pride in the leadership which her board has shown in meeting the needs of its Catholic community. She observes: "We're known as not taking things lying down and I think that it's partly because we have some educators on the board, that we're a very knowledgeable board." Donna speaks to her own leadership for that community by noting that:

one of the things that I work on at this moment is the idea of religious education in this province. Working with [the Archbishop] and teachers and superintendents, I have been very active in that, [in promoting a university diploma program] in elementary and secondary, where we do all our religious education training. I could not have done that if I hadn't been a trustee.

Through these, and other actions, Martha, Jane and Donna demonstrate many of the characteristics of effective leadership outlined in current research. This research depicts leadership as effective when it is characterized by a focus on relational dimensions, and by a recognition of a distinction between managerial functions of system maintenance and functions of promoting adaptive change (Bolman & Deal, 1994). New research on the nature of educational leadership highlights symbolic and political dimensions, and underlines the importance of the qualities of ethical commitment, risk taking, self-knowledge, character, and courage (p. 78).

Given the roles that they have chosen, it is perhaps not surprising that all three women are relatively comfortable in negotiating political issues. Each has developed a unique orientation which demonstrates different aspects of this dimension of leadership. Donna is quite forthright in her delight in what she describes as the excitement of politics. To Donna it is a game of language:

it is not what people say, it's the hidden message underneath that fascinates me and I love it when I can see the play and the game, and I can watch where the ball is going . . . it is the whole idea that there is a bit of self-serving interest in it, the shakers and the movers and the decision makers, and I'm your head bee.

Martha describes her growing awareness of how to operate within the political dimensions of the school board. She comments on her first engagement in a political issue with the board:

I had to learn lobbying techniques very quickly [because of a conflictual situation]. We didn't win, but we came a long way. So we did a lot of learning in terms of dynamics and lobbying and pressure politics and how one works the room and how one watches the road and so on.

Central to learning how to operate politically is understanding how to handle conflict, and these women appear to be relatively comfortable working in the pervasive climate of conflict. Martha describes this dimension of leadership thus: "I am comfortable working in the trenches." Martha describes her response to the conflictual aspects of leadership in the following way:

sometimes you use a soft touch, sometimes you use a really hard push and it really depends upon the issue, it really depends upon the person, and I guess, some understanding or appreciation of human nature [is required], and some knowledge of the wisdom of what to do and to which person [is needed].

The capacity to communicate a vision, and to negotiate conflict are also described as important dimensions of leadership in current leadership literature. These were also evident in the narratives of the three women. Jane describes her capacity to communicate with others as central. She observes:

I think I have been quite successful in convincing people to listen to my views and in some cases, to do an about-face and agree with my views. I think that I articulate concepts very well. I don't think that I am politically astute . . . But I think that if you have the essence of truth, whatever truth may be, or the essence of a good idea behind your rationale, and if you're able to communicate it to people in a logical way, that they will accept it, even if it is something they don't find particularly palatable. If I have had success as a politician, I believe that's the reason.

Communication is central to Martha's style of leadership in situations of conflict as well. Martha describes a conflictual situation where she found herself

cut off from the community because they had no trust in me because I was new and they didn't know who I was; and the administration [also] cutting me off [from the information flow]. So I was working in a vacuum at some points in time.

Martha's response was to intitiate strategic communication with her community. In this effort she made certain that messages of symbolic importance to that community were conveyed.

The capacity to manage symbols, identified in current research as one of the key dimensions of effective leadership, is typically described as a kind of visionary leadership (Bolman & Deal, 1994, p. 84). Although each of the participants in our study identified particular projects and thrusts as important foci for their leadership, our analysis of their narratives leads us to conclude that the notion of visionary leadership becomes more complex in the politically charged arena of community and school board politics. One aspect of this complexity is evident in the narrative of the two Catholic trustees. Donna describes the effect of belonging "to the same club: we have a basic tenet of beliefs that are central to us." Moreover, being a member of a Catholic school board simplifies some issues for trustees. Donna comments:

we don't have to cater to a variety of basic clubs which in public school boards you probably do. Like Christmas is not an issue with us [but] public boards have to be very careful, because they have children of all denominations. We do too but when they come they agree that ours will hold sway.

We found evidence in the narratives of these women of the dimensions of political awareness, communication, and symbol management described in current research as characteristic of effective leadership. Indeed, the dimensions of leadership demonstrated by the women that we have described so far were largely drawn from the research on the role of trustees and the more recent specification of the characteristics of effective leadership. Our research suggests, however, that despite a typical nod to the issue, much of the literature on trustees and effective leadership does not look through the lens of gender. It typically does not consider the critiques by feminist scholars of the implicit gender patterning that has historically been associated with characterizations of leaders. We find that the understanding of leadership drawn from much of this literature is at best limited, and at worst flawed, because it fails to consider the implicit and deeply embedded gender relations that constrain and define women's experiences. In short, even though we have drawn from the experiences of school trustees as an alternative pool of leadership, we have not yet identified the themes that define the most relevant dimensions of leadership for women. We now turn to the issues that the chairpersons in our study confront as women.

Problematizing the Concept of Public/Private in Women's Leadership in Education

One of themes that has not been identified in current writings on educational leadership is the development of a career that includes the kind of public leadership exercised by Martha, Jane and Donna as trustees. Those who study gender divisions in education confirm the lingering influence of the public/private dichotomy in a pervasive ideology that continues to associate women with "marriage and children" and, thus, with problematic commitment to teaching as a career (Acker, 1989). Feminist scholars argue that this ideology continues to constrain the opportunities women have to take on leadership roles in education. At the same time, researchers find that the effects on women's careers of an ideology supporting a public/private dichotomy are complex. The traditional view of the development of a career which includes a leadership role in education perpetuates the notion of a separation of public and private spheres. In contrast, recent research on the careers of women educators suggests that alternative models of career are needed which fit more adequately with the integrated nature of the public and private lives of women educators (Grant, 1989). Studies of the influence of role expectations regarding marriage, pregnancy and child care on a woman's career development, and on her opportunities in male dominated positions of leadership have led to questions regarding the traditional conception of a career as linear, and predictable (Young, 1992).

Biklen (1986), for example, found that the career commitment of women elementary teachers in the United States did not preclude interruptions to deal with domestic responsibilities, nor was it dependent on ambition to move into traditional positions leadership in the educational hierarchy. Young's (1992, p. 157) study of the lives of four western Canadian women educators confirms the need for new models of career which emphasize individual growth and adaptability and takes into account the interrelations between the knowledge and experience acquired from formal paid roles such as teaching and from volunteer work or unpaid work in the home. Similarly, Grant (1989) concludes from her study of the career development of women "deputies" in New Zealand secondary schools that because female teachers' "career pathways are locked into, and shaped by, developments in their personal lives," (p. 35) it is likely that their ambitions will fluctuate.

Our analysis of the narratives of three female chairpersons uncovered a pattern of unplanned and evolutionary career development similar to that described in these studies. This theme is evident in the narrative of Martha who observes:

> I can honestly say I fell into this. It was not a conscious path that I chose. I fell into one thing after another and there was a snowball effect and the more I went down the hill, the more I said, 'oh well, I can live with this.'

Similarly, Jane expresses her surprise at the turn that her career has taken:

> I never in my wildest dreams would have seen myself in a public political role ... In many ways I am really at a loss to explain how I ended up as chair of the board where you're up front and centre all the time, other than the fact that I am comfortable speaking publicly, but it wouldn't be my preferred spot to be up front and center.

One of the themes implicit in the apparently unplanned and organic development of these women's careers in public life is the demand for balancing that Young (1992) identified as "competing urgencies" in the lives of the teachers she studied. Our analysis suggests that the theme of competing urgencies fits well with the unique career development of the three participants in our study. We find that capacity to manage the ambiguity that arises because of these competing urgencies emerges as a critical dimension of the leadership style of each of the women we studied. Jane, for example, analyzes her own capacity to handle the workload of the chairperson in this way:

> I am really blessed with a tremendous memory, it carries me through if I read over my back-up material once ... I am able to absorb the material very quickly ... The fact that I have a great memory has helped me to retain the necessary background to keep hold of the issues. I think the other characteristic I have is that I can really focus on what is essential for the moment and put other things in the background.

Both Jane and Martha speak of their ability to compartmentalize their lives as a coping mechanism to deal with the demands they face. Jane observes:

> There are days when it's very chaotic, I must say, but I really and truly compartmentalize very, very much. When I am teaching, I am teaching; when I am trusteeing, I am trusteeing. I don't allow myself to cross-think if possible.

At the same time that all three women have used compartmentalization as a coping strategy to deal with the demands upon their time, they have also all savored the challenges these demands have brought to them. In fact, both Martha and Jane describe their boredom as one of the impetuses for their involvement in public life. Martha links this specifically with her role as a teacher. She comments:

> I think [my involvement] came because I was bored . . . I worked for a very small school board and there are not a lot of opportunities for me for advancement. There just aren't because it has very few movement areas. Quite frankly I think if I had not had the challenge of being a trustee or something, I would have not enjoyed my teaching in the same way that has allowed me to do something at a different level and has allowed me to grow and develop. I am not the kind of person who could have taught 35 years in the same grade in the same room in the same school. That's just not me.

Donna describes her experiences on the school board as giving her a window on a more holistic view of education. She comments that

> one of the great things [about being a trustee] is seeing education through a rather unique perspective. There are very few of us after all that are trustees. Most of us see education through one lens: as a supervisor, as a superintendent, as a teacher, or as a researcher.

Trustees, in Donna's experience, see a much larger picture, because unlike the other roles, they are uniquely linked to the public. In fact, a central theme in the narratives of these women is the unique nature of the links between the public/private dimensions of the role of chairperson of a school board. One of the most problematic aspects of the role of school trustee for both Jane and Martha is the public scrutiny to which they are subjected, and the requirements that they intervene in the private lives of others. Martha is the most forceful in her views on the problems of leadership that arise when the private becomes public. She indicates:

> Because I am a private person, and I believe everyone has a right to privacy, what I have not enjoyed about this job are times when I have to intervene in people's personal lives. That goes with the job too. I have not found that appealing and have not been comfortable doing so.

For Martha becoming a public figure has also been problematic:

> If I have any regrets it's that I can't go anywhere within the city without running into somebody I know . . . I really resent it that there really is no privacy. I have come to develop a deep appreciation for people who have much higher profile jobs than I have, what it really does to their private lives.

The experiences of these female trustees illustrates the complexities of the private/public link in political leadership in education. These women describe how the public becomes privatized for the trustee. Martha comments:

> We get calls at home, some of which have been pleasant, some of which have not been so pleasant. During the elementary/secondary teachers' strike I was logging 50, 60, 70 calls on my answering machine a day. . . most of which were very hostile. My kids would say to me: 'Mom you really don't need to answer all those ugly phone calls.' Those kinds of things creep into your life.

The notion of the "private" contained in these observations is linked with home, and with the nurturing and support that home has traditionally provided. Feminist theorists recognize the significance of the separation of social life into public and private spheres for understanding the gender dynamics in educational and other organizations, particularly as they relate to assumptions about characteristics of effective leadership and administration (Blackmore & Kenway, 1993; Reiger, 1993). They claim that historically, educational administration and leadership has been associated with a construction of "masculinity" as the "rational, unemotional, logical and authoritative aspects of human behavior" carried on the public sphere (Blackmore & Kenway, 1993, p. 34). Conversely, teaching has been seen as a "feminine" activity undertaken by female members of the helping professions who were extending into schools the "mothering" they did in the family (p. 36). Thus, that which occurs in the public sphere has been characterized as "rational, instrumental, productive and effective – and activities in the private sphere of the family and home have been defined as irrational, expressive, consuming and ineffective" (p. 35). Feminist theorists observe that women have traditionally been linked with home and with caring and nurturing. They argue that this dichotomization has denied women equal access to public positions, including those of leadership in education.

Our study suggests more subtle effects of this dichotomy. Martha and Jane's experiences illustrate the complexity of the public/private link. Both women describe a key element to their success being the support they receive from their families. Jane says: "my husband has been extremely supportive . . . picking up the slack." At the same time, the private and public are intimately linked in the motivations and actions of all three women trustee-educators. Each one speaks of her route to public life through her immediate concern for her children and the community. Martha's involvement in the school board evolved from her concern for the specific needs of her own two children. She describes the impetus to become a trustee thus:

> I got to be a trustee because I was president of my children's day care centre. The eldest was just school age and we needed to arrange transportation between the school where he was going to attend kindergarten and the daycare which was in a different school. This seemed [to me] to be a very straightforward matter, but it proved not to be an easy task to achieve, and after doing a fair bit of lobbying at the school board . . . I thought 'I can do a better job than those people.' So I ran for the board at the last moment in 1982 . . . and didn't win, but certainly made a point about daycare and the need for children's advocacy. A number of people remembered me and in the 1985 election said 'why don't you consider running again, and do it really seriously this time?' I ended up doing it and that's how I became a trustee.

The impetus for Martha's decision to become a trustee came from her community activism and what she describes as her "vested interest" in the needs of her own children. The same kind of vested interest gave Jane impetus to enter the public political arena. Jane said that her route to the trustee role

> all started at a PTA meeting. When my eldest child entered four-year old kindergarten, I joined the PTA and before I knew it I was on the Executive . . . I just started with a general interest in education at my own child's school and got involved with a larger issue of representation through attending various

board meetings, and I thought that I could do as well if not better than some of those people.

We suggest that the link of private and public domains in the role of the trustee evident in these narratives cannot be isolated from the gender patterning that has traditionally constructed social relations. This patterning suggests a framework for understanding the assumptions made by Jane and Martha that their responsibilities lay in extending their nurturing role in the family into their roles in the school board. We conclude that the issue of gender dynamics in school boards must be examined in greater depth. The following discussion begins this examination. Much more must be done to give depth to our understanding of this dimension of organizational dynamics.

On Being a Female Trustee

Being female in the role of the trustee has particular meaning for the three women we studied. None describes herself as feminist; however, each gives a voice to that dimension of their involvement as trustees. At the time of her election, Martha recalls, "I brought a lot of novelty to the board because I was young, I was a parent of young children and I was a teacher." These character-istics made her an anomaly among the predominantly male businessmen who had traditionally acted as school trustees in her board. She observes:

> Because I was young and because I was a female, it was very difficult to establish any kind of credibility with a majority of my colleagues who had no children and were men. And I worked very hard to gain an image of being someone who was actually going to make an impact, who was going to bring a new dimension to the school board and be taken seriously.

Martha worked very systematically to gain the credibility she felt was required to be treated with respect by her male colleagues. She struggled to overcome the limitations of being viewed as simply a teacher who lacked understanding of "the real issues in the economy and in budgets." Martha recalls focusing on budget items in her preparations so that she could speak very knowledgeably during school board meetings. Despite being elected to chair a budget committee on the basis of this work, Martha points out that

> the superintendent of business and finance went into shock when the board actually elected me to be chair of management . . . He didn't speak with me for about three weeks after being elected. I realized that eventually he would have to work with me because it was a dual relationship. We had to work together on preparing things for the board to consider, the budget and management meetings . . . When he retired, he said: 'it wasn't so bad working with you after all.'

The conditions supporting Martha's experience are similar to the "chilly" climate that feminist scholars see as systematically marginalizing women by defining masculinist behavior as characteristic of leadership. Donna experi-enced similar responses from her superintendents and fellow board members.

She observes that her emotive responses were sometimes viewed unfavorably by fellow trustees. She comments:

> I know that at times I became quite emotional about something . . . [for example] my way of showing anger unfortunately is through tears, and men's ways of showing anger are very different and I had to learn that, and then had to become very cold . . . [You] learned it quickly because otherwise you undermine your whole authority, your whole credibility.

The powerful forces at work in these narratives confirm the pervasive construction of certain types of behavior as appropriate for rational leaders to display, and the censure of feminine types of behavior as being unsuitable for leaders.

The effects of gender patterning are also more direct. Donna illustrates the effect of this patterning on the trusteeship of the Catholic school boards in her province. She is concerned that few women have served as trustees, and very few have taken on the role of chairpersons and argues: "We definitely need a women's balance." She describes an experience which increased her frustration with the embedded biases which systematically exclude females from leadership roles in her board:

> We had new jobs advertised last spring, [but] I had to be away when the interviews were held. When I came back somebody said 'how are you going to tell Donna, she's going to be very upset because there wasn't a woman selected.' I don't believe women should be selected just because they're women . . . but I do want to know if there was a woman on the hiring committee.

Although Donna's anger is evident, it is clear that she feels constrained in making any changes to the culture of exclusion which marginalizes women in her school board.

Another issue noted by the three women concerns the relative powerlessness of a chairperson of a school board. Flowing along with the themes of the difficulties of negotiating conflicts in the narratives of these women is a theme of loneliness; of sitting "where the buck stops." Martha describes her role as chairperson as being very difficult.

> The role of being chair of the board is very different. I have at times made decisions quickly, and there have been serious ramifications. I have had to live with my board members afterwards if they decide they don't like the decision that I made on their behalf . . . There have been times when the board has not supported me in my decisions . . . they have been less than amorous with me and my decisions. I have to say: 'I am sorry, that was my decision, that is what has happened and that's it.' And you're always left with the flak or the wrath or the support, whatever the case may be.

Martha identifies a strike by teachers as presenting the most difficult time for her as chairperson, partly because she believes that her own role as teacher, although in another school jurisdiction, places her in some conflict of interest in collective-agreement related matters. Donna demonstrates similar discomfort in her description of a teacher's strike. The experience was formative for

Donna, who was the chair of the negotiating group that brought the system out on strike. She believes that because of the event, she lost the teacher constituency which had originally encouraged her to run for the school board. Donna describes her innocence in assuming that if she simply placed the board's bottom line on the table, the teachers would respond "reasonably." Donna recalls:

> I said [to fellow negotiators] 'let's go in and let's tell them what money we have.' Of course my colleagues said 'Donna, it won't work.' But I said 'Look it will work. [The teachers] know me, they trust me.' So I went in and I said 'how shall we divvy it up? Benefits, salary, increments, what?' And [the teachers] said yes, but we want more than that. So I was devastated because I had shown them the total books and . . . I didn't think that the game was more important than honesty, and it was a game, and not even a local one, it was a provincial game because we pit one [school district bargaining unit] with another. That left me with a very bitter taste for quite awhile. And I left them with a bitter taste because I was the one who signed the strike papers, I was the chair.

These narratives underline the loneliness of exercising leadership in difficult and conflictual situations. The narratives illustrate the potential for conflict of interest when trustee-educators are involved in negotiations that ultimately influence their own economic concerns. The narratives also illustrate the difficulty of compartmentalizing the roles of educator and trustee. Both Donna and Martha see conflicts between the roles and demands of the teachers and their own responsibilities as chairpersons. Embedded in their concerns are contradictions between the culture of caring so closely associated with the teaching role and the instrumental power which they felt compelled to exercise for the greater good of a community. Some of the implications of these contradictions for our understanding of gender issues in educational administration and leadership are explored in the following, and concluding, discussion.

Conclusion: A Call to Explore the Ecology of Public and Private Domains of Women's Experiences of Leadership

In this chapter we have attempted to broaden contemporary understanding of leadership in education by drawing insights from a group that has previously been invisible in the literature: female trustees. Research on school trustees has typically been descriptive and atheoretical. With the exception of Townsend's (1988) analysis of the discourse of Canadian trustees, there has been little theoretical examination of this group, and virtually no attempt to draw out the narratives of women educators who have chosen the trusteeship as an alternative means of taking a leadership role in education. Our intention has been to meet the need for an expanded focus on alternative pools of female educational leadership from the perspective of feminist critiques of educational administration as a "masculinist" enterprise, and feminist conceptualizations of teacher's careers and career development (Acker, 1989; Blackmore & Kenway, 1993; Reiger, 1993; Young, 1992).

We share the view of feminist scholars that understanding the practice of leadership will be made more comprehensive by considering women's experiences and their careers more carefully. However, our analysis of the narratives of three female chairpersons contradicts the essentialist arguments of some feminist theorizing. Martha, Jane and Donna's narratives problematize the notion of essential feminine characteristics. Our analysis suggests that these women act like trustees, display the kind of generic leadership characteristics described as effective, but that their experiences are also deeply influenced by the gender patterning in the social relations of the worlds in which they live. An implication of our study is that accepting and celebrating women's ways of being in the world as caring and nurturing has "the danger of accepting as real the dichotomous and essentialist view of men and women that marks common-sense discourse . . . and of obscuring the possibility that those of us who are women can understand our world and act within it in a wide variety of ways" (Weiler, 1994, p. 30).

The narratives we studied do not support the proposition that women's ways are solely those of caring and nurturing and that the exercise of power is an imposed masculinist construct. We believe that a central concern of this problematic is understanding "how power is exercised" by women (Weedon, 1987). Feminist scholarship has contributed to more relational conceptions of power (Wright & Hersom, 1992). Feminist poststructural theories, for example, refer to the "interactions and contradictions among language, subjectivity, power, and underlying assumptions (i.e., common sense) that are used to examine how power is exercised" (Capper, 1992, p. 103). Consistent with this problematic, we cannot ignore the theme of power in our analysis because of the place it occupies in the lives of the three women in our study. All three were uncomfortable discussing power and did not raise the issue of how they used it directly until well into our interviews. Their feelings were highly ambivalent. Although they happily described what they had done to bring about a decision or a change they considered desirable – clearly an exercise of power – they did not frame their activities in terms of power.

All of the women disclosed their enjoyment of political life – sometimes much to their own surprise. Donna expresses her particular delight in watching the games of power: "It's a wonderful game. It's like alcoholism or cigarette smoking; it's addictive." Donna's choice of metaphors in this description is a telling one – it articulates the unease with which the women expressed their interest in politics. For example, despite her evident political acumen Jane comments: "I am not really politically astute. . . . I don't have any interest in politics." Both Donna and Martha are more forthright in discussing their interest in being involved in larger political arenas. Donna observes: "a big regret in my life is that I didn't run for a provincial election."

At the same time that these women acknowledge their enjoyment of politics, they also express fear at being seduced and corrupted by power. They are afraid of becoming more concerned with position, status and prestige than with those things that brought them to their trustee role initially. Donna expresses these contradictions by observing that:

> power is interesting because it's addictive. [As a chairperson] you're the one who makes the decisions, you're the one people look to for answers. It's very rewarding. I mean, no matter how old or tired or abused you feel from the day's work when you go to a [school board function] and somebody says 'Now [Donna] will bring you greetings from the board,' and everyone looks. This is wonderful. I could read the yellow pages and they would listen.... I think that's the bad side of it, and I learned to take the hat off very quickly once I left the situation . . . [because] it's all reaffirming of the hierarchy, that bowing and scraping, and I don't think that's good.

Donna expresses one of the implicit sentiments held by all three women when she describes the appeal of power as "warming to those who have it." At the same time, contained in the narratives of all three women are powerful thrusts towards using the authority and even the power that their roles as trustees carry, to achieve some good for the whole community. Martha notes, for example, that she is a community trustee, and like the other women she sees herself as an "advocate for children" first, and foremost. These women are also very aware of the constraints imposed on their capacity to exercise power unilaterally. Martha describes the need to build consensus around an issue among trustees, and the cost to the chairperson for not doing so. Power, for these women, therefore, seems to reside not so much in their position as an individual chairperson as it rests with the collaborative endeavors of their boards.

These contradictory currents underline that not only must we continue to expand the pool from which we study leadership in education, we must also draw from theoretical frames which create new lenses for inquiry. We have shown that much more must be done to analyze and account for the discrepancies and contradictions implicit in feminist critiques of leadership which adopt essentialist postures. The narratives of Martha, Jane and Donna in this chapter show some contradictions. We have shown that feminist theorizing on women's' lives offers valuable insights into the private/public dimensions of leadership. Our study suggests that the links between these dimensions create particularly complex effects for women. It is important to continue to examine the gender patterning of the private and public dimensions of leadership. We conclude, however, that further research on educational leadership must begin from more holistic conceptions of the ecology of public and private domains in women's lives. We advocate new research that takes into account both the convergences and the fractures in women's experiences as mothers, educators, trustees, chairpersons and leaders.

References

Acker, S. (1989). *Teachers, gender & careers.* London: Falmer Press.

Awender, M.A., & Hanke, M. (1984). The board member's role. *Orbit 70, 15*(2).

Bacharach, S.B., & Mitchell, S.M. (1981). Critical variables in the formation and maintenance of consensus in school districts. *Educational Administration Quarterly, 17*(4), 74-97.

Biklen, S.K. (1986). "*I have always worked,*" Elementary school-teaching as a career. *Phi Delta Kappan, 67*, 504-508.

Blackmore, J., & Kenway, J. (1993). 'In the shadow of men': The historical construction of educational administration as a 'masculinist' enterprise. In J. Blackmore & J. Kenway (Eds.), *Gender matters in educational administration and policy* (pp. 27-48). London: Falmer.

Bolman, L.G., & Deal, T.E. (1994). Looking for leadership: Another search party's report, *Educational Administration Quarterly, 30*(1), 77-96.

Capper, C.A. (1992). A feminist poststructural analysis of nontraditional approaches in educational administration. *Educational Administration Quarterly, 28*(1), 103-124.

Davis, J. (1991, June). *The changing role of the Ontario school trustee.* Paper presented at the annual meeting of CSSE, Queen's University. Kingston, ON.

Grant, R. (1989). Women teachers' career pathways: Towards an alternative model of 'career'. In S. Acker (Ed.), *Teachers, gender & careers* (pp. 35-50). New York: Falmer Press.

Harding, S. (1987). *Feminism and methodology.* Bloomington: Indiana University Press.

Immegart, G.L. (1988). Leadership and leader behavior. In N. J. Boyan (Ed.), *Handbook of Research on Educational Administration* (pp. 259-277). New York: Longman.

Isherwood, G.B., & Osgoode, N. (1986). What makes boards tick? *Education Canada, 26*(1), 4-11.

Jakes, H. (1982). Profile of elected school board trustees in Ontario. *Ontario Education, 14*(4).

Lather, P. (1991). *Getting smart: Feminist research and pedagogy with/in the postmodern.* New York: Routledge.

Le Compte, M.D., & Preissle, J. (1993). *Ethnography and qualitative design in educational research,* 2nd ed. San Diego: Academic Press.

Levin, B. (1975). Reflections on past disillusion. *Interchange, 6*(2), 23-31.

Marshall, C., & Rossman, G.B. (1989). *Designing qualitative research.* Newbury Park: Sage.

Mawhinney, H.B. (upcoming). Persistent dilemmas in exercising political leadership in educational policy change. In S. Jacobson, (Ed.), *Persistent dilemmas in administrative preparation and practice.* SUNY Press.

Reiger, K. (1993). The gender dynamics of organizations: A historical account. In J. Blackmore & J. Kenway (Eds.), *Gender matters in educational administration and policy* (pp. 17-26). London: Falmer Press.

Robinson, N., & Stacey, C. (1984). Serving on the school board: A political apprenticeship for higher office. *The Alberta Journal of Educational Research, XXX*(2), 115-125.

Ryan, J., & Drake, S.M. (1992). Narrative and knowledge: Teaching educational administration in a postmodern world. *Journal of Educational Administration and Foundations, 7*(2), 13-26.

Smyth, J. (1989). *Critical perspectives on educational leadership.* London: Falmer Press.

Townsend, R.G. (1988). *They politick for schools.* Toronto: OISE Press.

Weedon, C. (1987). *Feminist practice and poststructural theory.* New York: Blackwell.

Weiler, K. (1994). The lives of teachers: Feminism and life history narratives. *Educational Researcher, 23*(4), 30-33.

Wright, R., & Hersom, N. (1992). *A novel perspective on power in organizations.* Paper presented at the Annual Meeting of the Canadian Society for Studies in Education, Charlottetown, PEI: University of Prince Edward Island.

Young, B. (1992). On careers: Themes from the lives of four western Canadian women educators. *Canadian Journal of Education, 17*(2), 148-161.

Postscript

Where Do We Go from Here?

Beth Young

Many issues relating to women and leadership in Canadian education have been identified by the contributors to this collection. Some of those issues are being presented and discussed in thoughtfully nuanced ways here and elsewhere, as we explore various complexities and diversities among women's experiences of educational leadership. Other issues have so far received less attention or more simplistic treatment in our Canadian work, where they are identified only in passing allusions or they exist only as subtexts of our discourse.

My purpose in this chapter is to turn our attention to some of those over-looked or over-simplified issues. I note what I see as some promising avenues for continued exploration with respect to women and leadership in education and I name some of the seemingly inherent tensions and contradictions of that exploration. Throughout the chapter, I also raise questions that might fruitfully be given more consideration in the next few years by those of us who continue to work for gender equity in education.

Good Intentions

In my experience, trying to do feminist work related to women and leadership in education is plagued by a persistent tension. That tension arises from attempting to celebrate the particular achievements of a relatively small number of women educators who are already recognized by one means or another as "leaders," without ignoring or devaluing both the contributions to and the queries about "leadership" proffered by many other women and men in education. The emphasis on a few women begins, ironically, with a more general concern for social justice – in this case, women's rights to equitable participation in administrative and policy-making roles in education organizations. Just recently, that concern has been expanded to explicitly acknowledge women's rights to their own diversity as a significant dimension of equitable participation, although that diversity remains little represented or reflected in many formal administrative and policy-making roles. Even the (early) attempts at greater inclusiveness, however, do not necessarily result in critique of existing hierarchical structures and practices. And as Cecilia Reynolds points out in the first chapter of this collection, deconstructing is one challenge but reconstructing a discourse of administration and leadership is a yet more difficult and nebulous endeavor.

Scholars in education administration have typically associated the term "education" with "schools" and the term "leader" with those few individuals who hold formal administrative (and, sometimes, policy-making) roles in hierarchically organized education institutions that have traditionally been dominated by men. Often, researchers concerned with women and leadership in education have accepted that framework. Therefore, we have generally been documenting the experiences, perspectives, and actions of women who have learned how to "succeed" according to rules that they had no part in making and that they likely have little power – and perhaps little desire – to reinterpret.

By selection if not by definition, then, most such women are not engaged in querying the nature of the rules themselves or the assumptions that underlie them. For them to do so would be risky business. For us to ask that of them or be critical of them – for not being critical – is to place such women in a kind of double jeopardy. Many of us have "resolved" this issue when reporting our research by emphasizing the positive aspects of such women's achievements and perspectives, or by creating spaces in which the women speak for themselves. There is little commentary from us about the ways that our study participants are, relatively speaking, organizational insiders – a circumstance that many of us share or have shared with them because of our own formal roles or aspirations in education organizations. At a minimum, we should acknowledge the ambivalencies of our circumstances and the lacunae in our research that have resulted from conducting inquiry that is situated within a traditional framework.

The suggestions and questions which follow are intended to "open up" our inquiries. The ideas are combined from many sources. Several were articulated by the contributors to this book, in their own chapters or in response to our invitation that they comment on possible future directions for this on-going field of inquiry. Some thoughts have arisen from my own five-year project of collecting and synthesizing quite a bit of the pertinent Canadian educational administration research and working with graduate students who pursue studies related to women and leadership. And, of course, I have also been influenced by the excellent work of feminist scholars in education here in Canada and in Australia, the United States, and Britain. My emphasis in this chapter is on research and reflection about various expressions of leadership that might inform or re-form existing administrative, organizational, and policy practices in Canadian education.

Learning More from the Research That Has Been Done

Publishing this collection at this time provides some examples of recent work placed in the context of earlier Canadian work, so that we can undertake future inquiries better informed about what has been learned already. In these times of dwindling support for gender equity concerns, we need to make good use of our resources by moving beyond, expanding on, or revisiting in critically reflective ways what has been done rather than repeatedly asking similar questions of similarly situated women.

Over the past decade or so, there has been a substantial increase in research related to women and leadership in Canadian education. Much of this work has been undertaken by recently appointed faculty members in departments with Educational Administration programs and by graduate students in those programs, or it has been sponsored by the Canadian Education Association, the Canadian Teachers' Federation, or various provincial teachers' associations. Some demographic information is made available by Statistics Canada, provincial departments of education, and individual school jurisdictions.

Too often, however, the studies have been undertaken without much reference to one another, as I have recently pointed out in my own review and synthesis of some of that research (Young, 1994). For example, assumptions that have been given thorough and critical examination by some writers continue to be taken for granted uncritically by others. While I am not arguing for a false or forced consensus, there is a need for continuing comparison or synthesis of existing work, and dialogue among interested persons. Tracing and collecting that work is a major undertaking in itself. A start can be made by grouping similar studies and doing more systematic meta-analysis of them. Being able to situate the experiences of individual women within the context of a collection of studies might also help to alleviate some of the ethical problems regarding the identifiability of study participants within the particularly "small worlds" of administration and leadership in Canadian education. As well, comparative analyses of our own situation(s) and those of other countries could be very fruitful, given the quality of the scholarship regarding women and leadership issues in Australia, Britain, and and the United States, for example.

Who, What, When, Where?

For several reasons, it is as difficult as it is important to obtain and maintain the sort of statistical data analyzed by sex that would provide an accurate record of participation over time in various aspects of work in the field of education (Gaskell & McLaren, 1991, p. 396). The annual Statistics Canada reports on education are invaluable as a source of such information, but they are of necessity very general. As well, they do not address complexities such as differences between "categories" of women (related to factors such as ethnicity or color), nor differences between organizations regarding the titles used to designate various kinds of work, nor the breakdown by gender of part-time and full-time appointments to administrative jobs. For more detailed statistical information we are reliant on the data made available by individual education organizations themselves and by provincial governments, whose commitments vary considerably when it comes to providing accessible, systematic information pertinent to gender equity issues. It is also difficult to gain any overview of education activities in Canada, given provincial jurisdiction and traditional reporting patterns that separate information about the various sectors and levels of public and private education and training.

We need to monitor women's and men's patterns of participation in all official administrative and leadership roles and with respect to a much more wide-ranging array of education endeavors. These would include both appointed positions in various public and private education or training organizations and elected positions as trustees and as association leaders. Even with much more comprehensive longitudinal tracking of men's and women's participation, we would still not be addressing differential participation by men and women in less formal leadership capacities. Without more systematic, on-going and reliable statistical information, it is impossible to assess the nature and extent of any changes that are taking place with respect to women's and men's patterns of participation in education administration and leadership.

While there are some indicators of some women's increased participation in certain administrative roles and contexts, the data that are readily available to us at this time leave many questions unanswered. Unhappily, even the tentative indications of change that we have seem to be feeding backlash impressions such as the complaint that all administrative appointments now go to women. Assertions of that kind – usually based on something like the appointments list for one school system in one year – are difficult to counter or set in larger socio-historical contexts without adequate data. On the other hand, no one is volunteering information about whether financial cutbacks and organizational restructuring (in Alberta, for example) are having differential effects on men's and women's careers within existing education organizations. As resources decrease in the public sector, who holds the remaining discretionary power and under what titles? Finding ways to probe these sensitive issues will require, in itself, careful strategic planning.

Why and How?

Women school administrators' stories of their own career experiences are our most abundant source of knowledge related to women and leadership in Canadian education, and the sound of these women's voices was long overdue.

The stories are usually treated in a very straightforward manner, without exploring the complexities of narrative inquiry (Clandinin & Connolly, 1994) or the quandaries associated with feminist analysis of other women's stories (see, for example, Weiler, 1994). As I have pointed out elsewhere (Young, 1994), a great many of the existing accounts have documented the experiences of white middle-class women who are school-site administrators in elementary schools, and the accounts have numerous similarities. There are many other perspectives to solicit if the diversity among women educators is to be acknowledged and similarities and differences in the attitudes and opportunities of differently situated women are to be better understood.

Researchers would do well to seek out the perspectives of women from and in a wider variety of circumstances, demographically and professionally. We have not heard much from women who are union leaders, trustees and governors, or administrators in private/alternative schools, or who work in bureaucratic settings such as school district central offices or government departments. Whether it is within the world of schools or other types of public and private education organizations, we have paid very little attention to the careers of women who can be identified as teacher-leaders (including perhaps school department or program heads) and those who do administrative work but do not have titles as administrators. What might we learn about constructing careers from those women who want but are not offered formal administrative or leadership roles, or who decide against what many view as "advancement" in the hierarchy? What alternative options for leadership or administrative work do they create or exercise, and why? There is evidence to suggest that many women work in different roles in a variety of education settings over their careers. What careers do women (and men) construct and what are the constraints and possibilities of their contexts, if they choose or are forced to move outside institutionalized public education? The study of those careers may particularly help us as we anticipate the probable restructuring of employment opportunities in education. Could we study and honor a wider range of career commitments and achievements that involve administration or leadership, rather than ignoring or diminishing important aspects of many women's priorities, experiences, and circumstances as educators?

Career-related narrative accounts that are explicitly situated in their socio-historical contexts are a welcome expansion of our literature. More career stories of or from our pioneer women administrators and educational leaders would provide a needed historical dimension to our picture of women's involvement in school administration and leadership in Canada. In the contemporary context, we might ask what effects the implementation of employment equity, as an official or an unofficial policy, is having on both the perceived and actual structures of opportunity (Kanter, 1977) available to women and men in various contexts? How are the work lives and effectiveness of those promoted through employment equity or affirmative action initiatives affected? In a discourse that too often dichotomizes the notions of "employment equity" and "merit," how do people charged with making administrative appointments implement each of these two concepts? And how do they rationalize their decisions to their fragmented constituencies? In what circumstances are groups of women still finding it valuable to turn to one another as sources of support, or to develop collective strategies for changing their situations?

Another issue that might be more fully explored is the conventional attitudes toward the nature of administrative work and careers. Why is it that the language used by study participants and researchers alike implies that a career "progression" involves leaving the classroom? The language rarely makes problematic terms that describe administrative work as a "promotion" or as "career advancement" to a "position of added responsibility." Such language undervalues both women's honorable history as classroom teachers and the challenges and complexities of classroom work.

Existing constructions of the demands of administrative roles also tend to be taken for granted. The findings are replete with inferences that women are accommodating to the demands of administrative roles which were shaped by men whose wives' full-time job was to provide the requisite supports for their husbands' career pursuits. There are allusions to, but little discussion about, the ironies of women's coping strategies when they include the delegation of domestic work to other (lower paid) women, or, less often, to partners/spouses who do not work outside the home. It would be interesting to hear multiple perspectives on the ways that personal and professional responsibilities are being combined these days, by women and by men. Are there education organizations which support the integration of the professional and the personal in non-traditional ways, such as through job-sharing? What are the risks or costs associated with attempting that, and for whom?

Talk about leadership

Many of the "women in leadership" studies that have been done in the past decade are reminiscent of traditional educational administration research on leadership, except that the study participants are women rather than men. Given the academic backgrounds of many of the researchers, who have graduate school education from traditional Canadian educational admininstration programs, the similarities are perhaps not surprising. Those research initiatives that have broken away from traditional "Ed. Admin." approaches and questions are a welcome enrichment of our literature. Their contributions reinforce the need for us to expand the range and depth of our enquiries regarding women leaders and their leadership in education. The comments I have made in earlier sections of this chapter about the types of questions we might ask, and of whom, have application here as well. It is time to learn to recognize and explore women's various ways of enacting leadership in education, whatever the context.

I am increasingly uncomfortable with the univocal sound of those claims about women's administrative and leadership practice that have an essentialist ring to them. Since I have recently outlined the concerns about such claims elsewhere (1994), I will not reiterate the arguments here. However, it bears noting that female/male, feminine/masculine dichotomies have been criticized as ideological constructions (Blackmore, 1993; Gaskell & McLaren, 1991, p. 8) and modified in significant ways by many feminist scholars (for example, Brown & Gilligan, 1992; Weintraub, 1990). The challenge, then, is to document and discuss respectfully the diverse ways that women go into the world as education administrators and leaders rather than to accept or promote one (right) way for them to do so (Weiler, 1994).

In our talk about leadership, it is also important that we distinguish between what we are learning about how our women administrators and leaders view their own practice wherever it is situated and what we are learning about these women's administrative and leadership behavior in those situations (Shakeshaft, 1989). Research that relies on the self-reporting of administrative and leadership styles has often been criticized as an inadequate indicator of practice, especially as that practice is experienced by those with less power in the organization. Indeed, women have often been the least powerful – and consequently silenced – members in supposedly democratic school organizations. It therefore seems particularly inappropriate to gloss over the distinction between claims about enlightened, democratic practice and how that practice is being experienced, simply because the administrators now making the claims are women rather than men.

There is not nearly enough discussion in our literature about access to and use of formal and informal power by women leaders. Perhaps that is because of their reluctance, or ours, to acknowledge the power relations in education organizations. For example, what do our women administrators and leaders – and those whom they work with – have to say about the late Thom Greenfield's (1984) image of administrative leadership as "the violence of authority" in the lives of students? How would they react to Shirley Grundy's remark that educational leadership and emancipatory praxis are contradictory (1993, p. 176)?

Contextualizing Leadership

It would be worthwhile to gain a more detailed understanding of the values and convictions that various women educators do enact in their leadership and administrative work in various settings. We need more specific case examples, observations, and stories that illustrate what our study participants mean by those well-worn phrases such as a "student centred" orientation or "in the best interests of the student." Which student(s)? For example, what do these women have to say about gender differences or gender relations among their students or among their colleagues on staff? Do they support and encourage anti-sexist or anti-racist teaching and organizational policies? If so, how do they deal with the controversy and resistance that they must encounter from various sources (e.g., Briskin & Coulter, 1992; Kenway & Modra, 1992). Likewise, we lack detailed description and analysis to help us understand how and when women administrators' educational "vision"(s) for their organizations differ from traditional administrative control. Or does it? Should it? How do our women leaders and administrators avoid coopting collaboration as a management tool, a new tyranny? Or is that an issue for them?

In a professional field that is known for its vulnerability to trend-of-the-year and bandwagon approaches on the one hand and extreme conservatism on the other, it seems very important to learn how and why our women leaders and administrators ground – and revise – their own priorities. If female administrative leaders, for example, are agents for improving professional practice, as is often claimed, does that mean that they are, in effect, changing organizational structures? A promising approach may be to examine with them and others, over time, the innovations they introduce in particular contexts and how those innovations relate to their philosophies of learning and education.

Although Canadian schools and school systems (and many other public sector education organizations) are surprisingly similar in organization and appearance across the country (Levin & Young, 1993), there are contextual aspects that vary significantly and very likely influence significantly the leadership/administrative possibilities. The macro and micro policy environments – federal, provincial, local, organizational – may be significant in various ways. The mandate of the organization or sub-unit is often important, including for example the age range and socio-economic and cultural mix of the students served, the types of programs and services traditionally offered. So is the culture and the "ethos" (Coleman & LaRocque, 1990) of the organization, the nature of an organization's "community" (however that may be defined in each case), and the geographic setting. How women administrators are experiencing and interacting wtih those aspects of their contexts has not been sufficiently, or critically, explored.

There are many questions unanswered and, apparently, unasked. For example, how do the policies and regulations of a particular school system interact with administrative work in a specific school? What provincial or system parameters of policy and practice would our women administrators change, or do they subvert, and how? What about parent/community relations, particularly where women administrators, for example, still encounter negative, gender-stereotyped reactions from those sources? What about the interplay of race and gender in various settings, or the intersection of gender and class? What are the stresses that some of those women in some of those situations may be experiencing from subtle forms of discrimination? And how are the politics of fiscal restraint changing Canadian contexts for administration and leadership in education? At a time when more women appear to be moving into some areas of education administration, the resources available, for public-sector education at least, are shrinking. How are our women administrators and leaders addressing the challenges of doing more with less? What options are available to them?

Taking care to contextualize women's leadership/administrative beliefs, experiences, and actions increases our understanding of the leadership opportunities and constraints of a given situation (Gaskell & McLaren, 1991, p. 397; Levin, 1994). It is good to celebrate our women leaders' legitimate accomplishments and to honor their beliefs, but we should take care not to over-simplify or sentimentalize their realities and practices.

Related Questions?

Thus far in my own discussion, and in this collection, the focus has been on women administrators and leaders, and my emphasis has been on the contextualization and critical exploration of those women's perspectives and activities, in all their diversity. More fully acknowledging differences between women – and between men – means accepting that gender is an institutionalized but mutable social construction. In our Canadian work there is potential for more exploration of gender relations as they pertain to the leadership, administration and politics of organizational life in education.

A suggestion that gender relations be given more explicit attention is not intended to diminish the importance of continuing work with and for women, but to acknowledge that many women and men live out their lives in various forms of cross-gender relations. Attention to gender relations provides an additional way of exploring the systemic inequities of our worlds, including shifts and changes if and where they are occurring. Where are the gender-sensitive policy impact and organization culture studies that would provide additional insights regarding gendered relations in education? How do various women and men experience the gender politics of particular organizations at or over a given period of time? Just how do those politics affect the climate of an organization? What are the perspectives of men who dispute, resist, or are excluded for various reasons from the benefits of "hegemonic masculinity" in fields such as school administration? Is it not time to seek out and weave together the common threads of concern for the congruence of empowering substance and process in educational leadership that have appeared in the writings of many scholars over time (Kenway & Modra, 1992)?

In this chapter, I have been oriented to inquiry, the asking of questions. I have not separated out implications or recommendations "for practice" because I believe that inquiry is itself a significant form of practice, with all of the associated political, social, symbolic, ethical, and technical facets. Moreover, the contributions in this collection surely demonstrate to us that practice is contextualized. Therefore, I leave it to you, the reader, to draw out of this collection, and my commentary, the implications and recommendations that speak to your realities. It is a truism about inquiry that the questions we ask have a major influence on the knowledge we construct and, of course, on what we ignore altogether. In our work for gender equity with respect to the leadership and administration of Canadian education, we cannot expect or accept simple resolutions to complicated issues. Let us make it part of our practice to question our questions.

References

Blackmore, J. (1993). 'In the shadow of men': The historical construction of administration as a masculinist enterprise. In J. Blackmore & J. Kenway (Eds.), *Gender matters in educational administration and policy* (pp. 27-48). London: Falmer.

Briskin, L. & Coulter, R.P. (1992). Introduction to feminist pedagogy: Challenging the normative. *Canadian Journal of Education/Revue canadienne de l'education, 17*(3), 247-263.

Brown, L.M., & Gilligan, C. (1992). *Meeting at the crossroads: Women's psychology and girls' development.* Cambridge, MA: Harvard University Press.

Clandinin, D.J., & Connelly, F.M. (1994). Personal experience methods. In N. K. Denzin and Y.S. Lincoln (Eds.), *Handbook of qualitative research* (pp. 413-427). Thousand Oaks, CA: Sage Publications.

Coleman, P., & LaRocque, L. (1990). *Struggling to be good enough.* London: Falmer Press.

Gaskell, J., & McLaren, A. (1991). *Women and education* (2nd Ed.). Calgary, AB: Detselig.

Greenfield, T. (1984). Leaders and schools: Wilfulness and nonnatural order in organizations. In J.J. Sergiovanni and J.E. Corbally (Eds.), *Leadership and organizational culture* (pp. 142-169). Urbana, IL: University of Illinois Press.

Grundy, S. (1993). Educational leadership as emancipatory praxis. In J. Blackmore and J. Kenway (Eds.), *Gender matters in educational administration and policy* (pp. 165-177). London: Falmer.

Kanter, R.M. (1977). *Men and women of the corporation.* New York: Basic Books.

Kenway, J., & Modra, H. (1992). Feminist pedagogy and emancipatory possibilities. In C. Luke & J. Gore (Eds.), *Feminisms and critical pedagogy* (pp. 138-165). New York, NY: Routledge.

Levin, B. (1994, April). Schools coping with a changing world. Paper presented at the annual meeting of the American Educational Research Association, New Orleans, LA.

Levin, B, & Young, J. (1993). *Understanding Canadian schools: An introduction to educational administration.* Toronto: Harcourt Brace.

Shakeshaft, C. (1989). The gender gap in research in educational administration. *Educational Administration Quarterly, 25*(4), 324-337.

Weiler, K. (1994). The lives of teachers: feminism and life history narratives [Book Review]. *Educational Researcher, 23*(4), 30-33.

Weintraub, L.S. (1990). Equitable conceptions and resistance to delivery: Employment equity in the education sector. In F. Forman, M. O'Brien, J. Haddad, D. Hallman, & P. Masters (Eds.), *Feminism and education* (pp. 67-124). Toronto: OISE Press.

Young, B. (1994). An other perspective on the knowledge base in Canadian educational administration. *Canadian Journal of Education/Revue canadienne de l'education, 19*(4), 351-367.